HISTORIOGRAPHY, RELIGION AND STATE IN MEDIEVAL INDIA

BY THE SAME AUTHOR

Social Change and Development in Medieval Indian History

Medieval India: From Sultanat to the Mughals—Delhi Sultaat (1206-1526) — Part One

Medieval India: From Sultanat to the Mughals—Mughal Empire (1526-1748) — Part Two

Parties and Politics at the Mughal Court 1707-1740

Historiography, Religion and State *in* MEDIEVAL INDIA

Satish Chandra

HAR-ANAND
PUBLICATIONS PVT LTD

HAR-ANAND PUBLICATIONS PVT LTD
E-49/3, Okhla Industrial Area, Phase-II, New Delhi-110020
Tel.: 41603491
E-mail: info@haranandbooks.com/haranand@rediffmail.com
Shop online at: www.haranandbooks.com

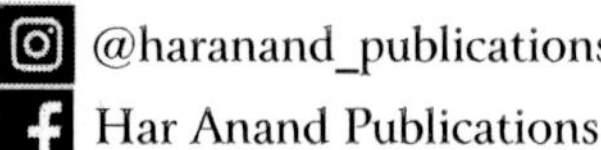

Reprint, 2026

Published by Ashok Gosain and Ashish Gosain for
Har-Anand Publications Pvt Ltd

Printed in India at Megha Enterprises

To

Professor S. Nurul Hasan
(1921-93)
who was
not only a friend, but a scholar
of vision
who gave inspiration and was
always prepared to share his ideas
with others

PREFACE

Little excuse is needed to bring forward another collection of articles. Some of these articles were published in Journals or collections, in India and abroad, which are difficult to have access to. Some papers represent new thinking on my part, or an effort to assimilate much that has gone on. This includes the article on "Society, Culture and the State in Medieval India" which was read in a preliminary form some years ago, and has been drastically revised. The sections on historiography and culture reflect changes in historical thinking which began in the country after India attained independence, and was faced with the problems of forging a unified polity on the basis of a multi-cultural, multi-religious, multi-lingual society. It was also influenced by new thinking on approaches to history in the West following World War II, and the process of decolonization which signalled an end to the Euro-centric view of history.

I am grateful to the Nehru Memorial Museum & Library; to Dr. A.P. Srivastava, Director of Libraries, University of Delhi; and the Librarian, Indian Council of Historical Research for helping me with procuring books for study and to check references. I am grateful to Shri J.K. Gosain from the Society for Indian Ocean Studies, who has typed out all the papers which needed revision and updating.

Lastly, I am grateful to Shri Narendra Kumar, Chairman Har-Anand Publications, at whose friendly instance I agreed to undertake this work. I hope the readers will find some use in this work in their on-going study of Indian history not in a narrow, or narrowly Indian, but in an Asian, or world context.

Satish Chandra

ACKNOWLEDGEMENTS

1. *Diogenes,* Paris, No. 72, 1972, pp. 92-109.
2. *Spirit of India,* Vol. II, Asia, pp. 75-82.
3. *South Asian Studies,* Jaipur Vol. 2, No.1, 1967, pp. 17-28.
4. Prepared for Indian National Communication for Co-operation with UNESCO, 1972.
5. Paper presented at Heras Institute Diamond Jubilee Symposium, Bombay, 1986.
6. Written for the 100th Birth Anniversary of Jawaharlal Nehru, Printed in 'The Hindustan Times', New Delhi, 14 Nov. 1989.
7. Presented at the Seminar on "The Indian Revolution in Perspective," Leningrad, 1987.
8. Savitri Chandra, *Social Life and Concepts ill Medieval Hindi Bhakti Poetry.* Delhi: 1983, pp. 1-19.
9. *Cultural Interaction in South Asia,* ed., S.A., Tirmizi, Delhi, 1993, pp. 100-115.
10. *Seminar,* Mythifying History, No. 364, 1989, pp. 35-38.
11. Originally Written for Encyclopaedia India, 1990.
12. Printed in part in "Central Asia: Movement of People and Ideas from Times Prehistoric to Modern", ed. A. Guha, Delhi, 1970, pp 167-73.

13. Based on Inaugural address to Indo-French Bi-National Seminar on "Transition from Feudalism to Capitalism", Delhi, 1979.

14. Revised version of paper presented as Nihar Rajan Ray Memorial Lecture, under the auspices of the Indian Institute of Advanced Study, Delhi, 1991.

Contents

1. HISTORIOGRAPHY

2. RELIGION & POLITICS

3. STATE

1

DECENTRING OF HISTORY

It is possible to assert that the present crisis in history on which there has been so much discussion is more specifically a problem affecting the historical sciences in the West rather than in the Afro-Asian countries. In the Afro-Asian countries, particularly those which have either become independent recently or have been able to assert their independence recently, history is considered important in forming a national self-image, help in the processes of national unity, and in the processes of modernization or social change within the nation. The role of history in providing an ideological-cultural framework for national unity and growth is important, for in many of these countries the concept of a nation has not grown out of a long historical process by which people belonging to different race, religion and regions have become emotionally welded together. Rather, nationalism in these countries is a means for bringing about such a unity. The interpretation of the past therefore becomes a matter of wider public concern. In this context, history can hardly be regarded by anyone as irrelevant: it remains a prestigious subject in most universities (not only because it offers a better opportunity for entering into a civil service career), and national historians command a measure of public esteem which is becoming rare elsewhere. On the other hand, history has been displaced from its preeminent position in the West. The profession no longer enjoys the prestige which it enjoyed among nineteenth-century intellectuals: many social scientists consider that "the destruction of the conventional historian's conception of history is a necessary stage in the construction of a true science of society"; "a significant number of philosophers seem to have decided that history is either a third-order form of science, related to the social sciences as natural history was once related to the physical sciences, or that it is a second-order form of art, the epistemological value of which is questionable, the aesthetic worth of which is uncertain."[1]

However, it would be superficial to conclude from these outward appearances that the crisis which has overtaken history in the West need not be faced by the historian in the Afro-Asian countries. In fact, any attempt to divide the historic processes on any such regional basis would be harmful. The problems regarding the nature of the discipline of history, the nature of the historical fact and of historical knowledge; the problems of methodology, causation and objectivity are of world-wide significance and have to be treated as such. There cannot be two separate methodologies in history, one applicable to the Western countries, and the other to the "Orient" or to "Africa" or to the other under-developed parts of the world. Yet, such has been the assumption and approach of many western historians in the past. The concepts "Oriental despotism," "Oriental barbarism," "the unchanging East" etc. are all too familiar.[2]

[1]Hayden A. White, "The Burden of History," *"History and Theory,* V (1966) pp. 111-134. There is a vast literature on the subject. Most of the significant works are listed *seriatim* in *History and Theory.*

[2]The literature on this theme is too vast to be even listed here. Some of the recent works on the subject are A.J. Toynbee, *"A Study of History" (1933-61); Civilization on Trial* (New York, 1948); *The World and the West* (New York, 1953); Grace E. Cairns, *Philosophies of History, Meeting of East & West in Circle Pattern Theories of History* (New York, 1962); H.P.R. Finberg, (ed.), *Approaches to History* (Toronto, 1962); Philip P. Weiner, and Aaron Noland, *Ideas in Cultural Perspective* (New York, 1962); H. McNeill, *The Rise of the West* (Chicago, 1963). For an Asian view, see D.P. Mukerjee, *On Indian History;* K.M. Panikkar, *Asia and the Rise of Western Dominance;* S. Radhakrishnan, *Philosophies of East and West.*

While these are not used so often now, they still colour the thinking of many historians. It would be easy to continue the old attitudes under the garb that different peoples must have their own approaches to history.

* * *

The assumption among historians during the 19th and early 20th centuries that the political and economic domination of large segments of the world by some powers, in a word, the system of western colonialism, was something ordained by history is no longer tenable; seemingly, it has been abandoned. However, the moral and intellectual bases of the belief in Western superiority have continued. In part, they rest on certain assumed superior values in Western civilization, such as rationalism, individualism, a deep seated spirit of adventure and experiment etc. which are not to be found in civilizations outside Europe and its cultural extension (the U.S.A., Australia, etc.). There can be many variations on this theme. Like Toynbee, it could be traced back to the superior ability of the Christian mind to respond to external or internal stimuli; or like Dr. William S. Haas, the difference between the civilizations of Asia and Europe could be explained in terms of two divergent thought processes—one subjectifying and centripetal, the other, the Western, objectifying and consequently centrifugal.[3] The idea of the superiority of the West may perhaps be traced back to the Christian idea that all those who were not received in the bosom of the Church were to be eternally damned.[4] The

[3]William S. Haas, *The Destiny of the Mind: East and West* (London) 1956.

[4]The effects of this thinking on the western interpretation of non-European civilizations have been deeper than have been generally accepted. For a view on the western interpretations of Islam, see Albert Hourani. "Islam and the Philosophies of History," *Middle Eastern Studies*, III (1967), pp. 206-268. It is true that every civilization has produced its own myth of being the chosen people. But no previous civilization has been as successful in imposing this belief on the rest of the world as the Western civilization. This lends a sense of sharpness to the reaction against it.

Renaissance thinkers only secularized this belief by postulating a special link between modern Europe and the civilizations of Greece and Rome which, in course of time, became the classical civilizations from which all modern concepts of progress, liberty, law, etc. were traceable. With a better understanding of the role of the Medieval phase and of the Arabs in the formation of modern Europe, these views have been considerably modified. However, they continue to colour the entire European *ethos,* and are reflected in historical writing. For example, it is still possible for a history of the world written in the West to devote only a preliminary chapter or two to the role of the classical civilizations of the Middle East and to India and China. The Greco-Roman civilization, far from being a Western achievement, was an integral part of the civilization of the old world which included the countries bordering the Mediterranean, and had ramifications extending beyond it to India and China. The early processes of what is regarded as the glory of Greek science were, in fact, developed in this area; these views are rarely projected in the standard history books written in the West. The tremendous achievements of the Achaemenian and the Sassanid empire in Iran, of the Mauryas in India, of the Ch'in-Han in China, each of which comprised territories which in size were as extensive as the Roman Empire in Europe, affected a larger segment of humanity, and provided stable conditions for the growth of economic and cultural life for a comparable period, are either overlooked, or mentioned cursorily. The fact that until as late as the 16th or the 17th century, the East rather than the West was the centre of the then civilized world is still not accepted. The peculiar concatenation of circumstances which placed tremendous power at the disposal of the Western countries, and allowed them an opportunity to dominate almost the entire world, is already passing. With the shifting of the balance of power to countries outside the traditional boundaries of the West, a more balanced historical appraisal should be possible of the Age of European Domination. With its passing, the comfortable belief that somehow all earlier history was working for the emergence of Europe as a world power, and that Western civilization constituted the mainstream of human civilization has to go. It has to be replaced by a concept of multi-focal growth of human civilization, with history as the discipline of the study of their processes and interactions.

* * *

Perhaps the most important basis of the persistence of the belief in the superiority of Western civilization is the myth of "scienticism" or the chauvinism generated by the leading role of Europe in the growth of science and technology from the 15th century onwards (more particularly from the "scientific revolution" in the 17th century) till the present. At a time when the level of the growth of science and technology in a particular country more or less fixes its position in the hierarchy of nations, this attitude is understandable. However, the idea that the growth of science and technology is a specifically European achievement has not been accepted by the best minds in Europe. George Sarton, Professor J. Needham, to name only two among the distinguished scholars who gave spent long years in studying the development of science, as well as the best scientists of the time, have regarded science as being truly international.

Two questions are at issue here: *a)* the early origins of Western science and technology, and *b)* the socio-cultural processes of the sustained growth of science and technology in Europe after the 15th century. As far as the first is concerned, it has been fully proved that "the origins of Western sciences (not only of religion and art) are Oriental—Egyptian, Mesopotamian, Iranian..."[5] What is not clear is the role of India and China in the process. The monumental work of Professor J. Needham on science and civilization in

[5]G. Sartori, *Introduction to the History of Science* (Baltimore, 1947) vol. 3. part I, reprinted *Sarton on the History of Science,* ed, Dorothy Stimson, (Cambridge, Mass, 1962), p. 17.

China has made it clear that neither India nor China were isolated from the West during antiquity, and that their links have been much closer than have been generally imagined. The Indian origin of the atomist theory, and the contributions of the Indians in the field of mathematics and medicine are now widely accepted. Needham has established the transmission to Europe of such Chinese inventions as paper, gunpowder, the magnetic compass, the wheelbarrow, the collar-harness, and possibly of a host of other processes such as deep drilling, iron foundry, iron suspension bridges etc.[6] A satisfactory study of the growth of science and technology in India and Iran has yet to be carried out. We do not know enough about the processes through which other inventions such as the watermill, the spinning wheel, the windmill etc. reached Europe. Only a careful study of the state of the sciences in the countries of the region, the channels of communications, the attitudes of different strata, the intellectual and religious climate affecting science and technology will enable us to elucidate these problems. The cooperation of scientists, historians, linguists, etc. belonging to different countries and cultures from Europe to China will be necessary to elucidate these processes. In order to do so, the upgrading of the study of the history of science in universities, in the West as well as in Asian countries, will be necessary, regarding it as something more than peripheral to the main study of history. In this context, one may recall Sarton's dictum that "the acquisition and systematization of positive knowledge is the only human activity which is truly cumulative and progressive," and that "the history of science in this broad sense becomes the keystone of all historical investigation."[7] The invention of the zero by the Mayas, of the wheel by the Aztecs

[6]J. Needham, *Clerks and Craftsmen* in *China and the West,* (Cambridge, *1970); idem., The Grand Titration; Science and Society* in *East and West,* (Cambridge, 1969). For fuller details, reference must, of course, be made to the author's larger work, *Science and Civilization* in *China.*

[7]G. Sarton, *Encyclopedia Americana,* vol. 24, (1956). p. 413.

independently shows that human ingenuity was not confined to anyone area. A fuller study will undoubtedly show that the Africans were not lacking in scientific ingenuity either.

As regards the stages and processes of the growth of science and technology in Europe since the 15th century, how deeply indebted Europe is to the Arabs, who acted as carriers of East Asian technology, and themselves contributed greatly to the growth of European science in the early stage has now been accepted. That does not, however, help us in answering the question: what specific socio-cultural features in the European situation have been responsible for the sustained growth of science over the past three centuries? No satisfactory answer to this query is available so far. Tawney's attempt to link the rise of science and technology, specifically the growth of capitalism, with the Protestant ethic has been discarded by the historians, as also the idea that the Industrial Revolution in Britain was the product of individual scientific men of genius. The historian of the Industrial Revolution in Britain, with rather more material available to him than for any comparable processes during the earlier period, has been compelled to fall back upon the concept of effective demand (which is traceable, in part, to the natural growth of population). Methods of quantitative analysis may be able to resolve some of the problems (though , historians are aware of the inherent limitations of such methods in interpreting broad human movements and motivations). Recent experience shows that science and technology can grow under vastly different socio-cultural circumstances. The earlier assumptions about the specificity of European socio-cultural circumstances for the growth of science and technology can, therefore, no longer be accepted without modification. With the passing of the lead in space exploration to the U.S.S.R. and the U.S.A., and the rapid advance in the field of science by other nations far removed from European culture, such as the Japanese and the Chinese, science is becoming truly international once again. The historian will continue to search for the specific features—for the determining factors, if you like, for the self-generating growth of science in Europe after the 15th century. These, however, will be comparable to processes which have taken place in the world in the subsequent period, or in a more limited manner, anterior to it in other parts of the world.

* * *

From the above it may be concluded that while the conditions and the intellectual premises on which the notions of Europe's supremacy were based are rapidly disappearing, Eurocentrism or Western ethnocentrism is still a marked feature in history writing, and has a definite effect on the types of subjects chosen for research. An example of this is the manner in which the history of African and Asian countries is studied (or not studied) in most Western universities. In trying to assess the impact of foreign rule on Afro-Asian countries, primary emphasis still tends to be placed on the policies, programmes, and processes of Imperialist rule, rather than on the study and understanding of the pre-colonial patterns and relationships in these societies, and the manner and the extent to which they were modified by foreign rule.[8]

* * *

The growth of and persistence of an ethnocentric view of history have had other effects as well on history writing in the West. The belief that rationalism, individualism, respect for law and liberty, a detached scientific spirit etc. were the prerogatives of the West led to the notion of the East being mystic, contemplative, a slave to religion, otherworldly, indolent, negligent of material incentives, etc. This notion of

[8] A number of universities have, in recent years, sponsored programmes dealings with the pre-British period in South Asia. Such programmes existed already for the Middle East, whereas there has been a tradition of Sino logy in a number of Ll.S. universities. The U.S.s.R. has also an old .tradition of Oriental studies, and has published a number of monographs on the ancient and medieval periods in India. The above remarks have, therefore, more relevance to the state of area studies in Britain and Europe.

the dichotomous nature of the East and West precluded any attempt at developing or applying any common historical categories or regularities applicable to both. This, in effect, meant an abandonment of the attempt to develop any concepts encompassing the history of the entire world. This was all the more remarkable as it coincided with the maximum expansion of European domination and control over the rest of the world during the second half of the 19th century. During the period, instead of the canvas of history being broadened with the experience of other areas of the world being brought into focus, it was steadily narrowed down. Thus, the history of Europe remained the main discipline of history, "orientalists" and others who studied history of peripheral areas being virtually treated as outsiders. Thus, the conditions were created for the wholesale acceptance of German historicism. It is neither necessary nor possible to go into the causes for the retreat into historicism. Under the influence of German historians, the historians certainly improved their techniques, but narrowed their vision. Implicit in the entire development was the rejection of the Marxist historical method, and Marx's postulate of certain necessary stages of historical development called slavery, and feudalism, before the attainment of a rapidly growing (and rapidly decaying) society characterised as capitalist. Marx was not certain in his mind whether these broad categories could be made applicable to societies outside Europe as well. His concept of an "Oriental society," by-passing the stages of slavery and feudalism, has led to a considerable debate among Marxist historians. Without attempting to go into this debate here, it may be noted that the dominant trend of thinking among Marxist historians in China and India[9] is to deny its validity, either to their own

[9]For the views of Indian historians such as KM, Ashraf, D.D. Kausambi, D.R Chananna, RS, Sharma etc., see note on "Main Trends in Historical Sciences in India, 1900-1970" prepared for UNESCO by a committee of Indian historians, (Ch. 4 below), Reference may also be made to Daniel Thorner, Marx on India and the Asiatic mode of production," *Contributions* IX, pp. 36-66.

countries or as a useful general concept. But there is no general consensus on this point so far.

However, rejecting the Marxist categories and deeply influenced by scientific nominalism, the bulk of the Western historians turned to the concept of "uniqueness." The concept of every civilization and country, nay every historical event, being unique did, to a certain extent, promote a meticulous study of historical events, ideally without importing any preconceived notions. The results of this approach, and its growing stultification, need not be gone into here, except to note that the reverse side of the coin was the growth of "exceptionalism" in the field of oriental studies. Thus, in India and in many of the Islamic countries, in some circles, science, which was associated with the West, was considered the enemy of religion, ascribing to it all the evils of European society, and extolling the idea of a return to primitive simplicity, based on religious revivalism. These views had a definite effect on political processes in these countries, as well as on history writing.

***

While Western historians accepted the concepts of slavery, feudalism and capitalism as stages in the development of Western society, by treating the rest of humanity as outside the scope of these processes, they automatically denied the validity of universal concepts in history. If the bulk of humanity living in the Orient was an exception to the law of development, the concept of development or progress as a basic category in history could not be maintained. The theory of "uniqueness" was hardly capable of solving this dilemma, and only papered over the cracks. The inability to put forward any general concepts applicable to history must be regarded as one of the fundamental causes of the present crisis in history, flowing in turn from the essentially ethnocentric view of history developed in the West.

***

In his essay on Comparative History of European Societies,

Marc Bloch had long ago brought out the dangers as well as the possibilities of the comparative method in history. Following him, and the school of history set up by him in France, comparative studies in the history of European society has made progress. Marc Bloch had favoured the method of choosing "from one or several social situations, two or more phenomena which appear at first sight to offer certain analogies between them," and warned against "grouping together under the expression 'the comparative method' two widely different intellectual processes."[10] Intra-regional studies spanning the oceans, encompassing the effect of the sea on countries bordering on it, have been attempted with some success. However, it would not be wrong to say that historians are still chary of adopting the comparative method. Comparative studies in the processes of growth, spanning countries having widely different social and cultural backgrounds, have made more progress among economists and social scientists as a whole. The only recent study of social processes between countries widely separated in time and space. has been the study on feudalism in history organised in the U.S.A by Joseph R. Strayer and Rushton Coulbom, Explaining his approach to the problem, Coulbom remarked:[11]

"The larger aim ... is not to produce a new definition of feudalism, but to see if the study of feudalism will throw light on the question of uniformities in history. That question, in its simplest terms, is this: historians, for many generations, have insisted that every historical event, every historical personage, is unique and will never be duplicated or repeated. At the same time, in their writings, and the thinking that lies behind that writing, they use words and concepts of general

[10]Marc Bloch, "A Contribution towards a comparative history of European Societies," (reprinted in *Land and Work in Medieval Europe)* London, 1967, (English trans. of selections from his *Melanges historiques,* Paris, S.E.V.P.E.N., 1963), p. 45.

[11]*Feudalism in History,* ed. Rushton Coulborn (Princeton, 1956), Introduction, p. 4.

rather than specific meaning: they assume that every new situation has something in common with certain other situations which have preceded it..."

Starting with these premises, the results of the study must be disappointing, inasmuch as they showed that feudalism as defined in the study did not extend outside Europe; with the possible exception of Japan. This brings us back to the starting point—is it possible to talk of uniformities in history, and if they can be found, can they be made applicable only to Europe, with the rest of the world (the major portion of humanity) treated as an exception? Perhaps the study could hardly have led to any other conclusion than the one arrived at since it took the European pattern as the normative pattern, and insisted that "Feudalism is primarily a method of government, not an economic or social system."

* * *

If history is to be regarded as the study of the processes of the development of human society, the processes of development in the 'Orient,' i.e. in the areas of Asia and Africa where the largest mass of humanity resided and still resides, must be regarded central to the study of history, instead of being considered as an expansion or an additional dimension to the study of history, as it is at present. This, in turn, would imply that history should be studied not so much from the viewpoint of power equations existing in the world at the time, as was the case in the 19th century and has, with some exceptions, continued to be the case till now, but from the viewpoint of humanity as a whole. In this case, greater attention would have to be given not only to historic processes in the most populous areas of the world, but to the processes of the communication of ideas, inventions, products between various sections of humanity, and the contribution of various sections and areas to the development of human civilization as a whole.

Such a shift in the focus of history can only be regarded as a long process. It would require an intensive effort for making available to the historian the type of historical information needed for these studies: literary sources, manuscripts and documents (many of them still buried in remote libraries), the study of folk traditions, physical objects, field studies, etc. It would also require the development of the necessary academic infrastructure in the countries concerned, for experience has shown that where the study of societies with living cultural traditions is concerned, the perception of its *ethos* and inter-connection requires a very long period of training for persons not born and reared within it. Even the development of "area studies" in many of the Western countries can play only a limited role in this process. For one, many of the area studies programmes in these countries have a heavy presentist bias, being dependent for their finances upon government and/or private foundations, and geared to fulfill certain political or business purposes. Secondly, within these countries, area studies are often considered peripheral to the study of history by the university departments. In consequence, they sometimes fail to attract the right type of student or researcher, thereby further strengthening the ethnocentric bias in history. To an extent area studies programmes have tended to perpetuate the notion that Afro-Asian countries are "patients" in the field of history, and that the history written by the historians of the area are somehow inferior, being tainted by the "nationalist" bias, whereas it is presumed that the writings of historians from metropolitan countries, i.e. the former colonising powers would be free from the "Imperialist" bias. This tendency to attempt to, continue the colonial situation in, the field of history in the name of the centre and the periphery is bound to have harmful repercussions.

* * *

The specific problems of history writing and research in Asian countries have to be viewed in the context of the observations above. It is clear that one of the major tasks facing the historians of the area is to rise above purely "national" history, and to study the history of their countries in a wider, "Asian" or world perspective. It is being slowly realised that the Old World, from the Mediterranean to India and across Central Asia to China, was much more closely knit together than has been generally accepted. The upper reaches of the coastal areas in East Africa, as well as south-east Asia, had been brought into close relation with these areas with the growth of sea trade. The transmission of Buddhist and Hindu ideas, and the growth of cultural and economic relations between South India and the countries of south-east Asia, between the 5th and 12th centuries A.D., which in terms of human enterprise, the size of the area and the numbers involved parallels the expansion of Christianity in Medieval Europe, and must be regarded as a major development in the expansion of the frontiers of the Old World. Yet it hardly merits more than a paragraph in any standard history of the world written in the West. It is obvious that this expansion could not have been taken place without a considerable expansion in the growth of the knowledge of sea-faring, geography and of ship-building, and without considerable daring in exploring the seas. However, Western historiography is still not prepared to look much beyond Prince Henry the Navigator.

That India, both north and south, had commercial and cultural relations with Mesopotamia as well as with Egypt since the 3rd millenium B.C., and that many Assyrian legends (such as that of the great flood, Gilgamesh etc.) have found their way into Indian mythology is well known to historians. Recent studies have shown a close link between Assyrian science, particularly astronomy and mathematics, and growth of science in ancient India. The nature of these processes, the manner of the transmission of ideas and of the extent of mutual borrowing are still largely unknown. Nor do we know much about the manner in which, at a later period, Buddhist and Hindu ideas travelled to the Mediterranean world, their traces being found not only in Greek neo-Platonism but in Christian monasticism and Islamic mysticism.[12] The role of the Central Asian empires, particularly those which controlled the Central Asian trade routes—the Sassanids, the Scythians and Huns, the Arabs, Mongols etc. (not excluding the Tibetans), in the exchange of ideas and goods not only between India and China, but between these and the Mediterranean world, is crucial, not only for understanding the processes in individual countries in this region but of the processes of the entire ancient and medieval world. Such a study is only possible with the close cooperation of the historians of this area, and by giving up the deeply rooted ethnocentric view of history which tends to limit and inhibit such approaches.

* * *

The question of the impact of Islam on the unity of the classical world has been a subject of debate for long. Recent scholarship does not accept the earlier proposition that the rise of Islam, or of the growth of the power of the Ottoman Turks, disrupted the trade relations between the West and East, and hastened the onset of the medieval age in Europe. Nor does it consider that the Portuguese discovery of the new route to India resulted in a diversion of Asian trade from the Mediterranean to Atlantic ports, i.e. to a net decline in overland trade, and the revenues it secured to the countries of

[12]Professor Needham has observed that "the science of Asia has a dividing line running north and south through Bactria and the opening of the Persian Gulf." Professor Needham calls this a barrier or filter across which East Asian science did not filter through to the Franks or Latins. He goes on to say: "The science of Arab culture ... was focal; it gathered in East Asian science, pure and applied, just as it built upon the work of Mediterranean antiquity. But ... while on one hand East Asian applied science penetrated to Europe in a continuous flow for the first fourteen centuries of the Christian era, East Asian pure science was filtered out; it came into Arabic culture but no further west. Obviously this is a historical phenomenon of much interest and importance." (J. Needham, UNESCO Month Lecture, Beirut, 1948, reprinted in *Clerks and Craftsmen in China and the West*, (Cambridge, 1970), pp. 14-29.)

the region.[13] There is growing evidence that the rise of Islam in West Asia did not result in a sundering of the cultural relations between East Asia and the Mediterranean areas. The Arabs strengthened rather than weakened the movement of ideas and goods across the region, with a sharp understanding of the importance of both. Why, in this context, Western science and technology did not filter to the countries of this region and to East and South Asia from the 15th century onwards is a question of careful consideration. Was it due primarily to the socio-cultural atmosphere in the countries of the region (as al-Biruni suggests in the case of India), or was it the effect of the socio-cultural impact of Islam as modified by the Turks? In this context the wider question of the bearing of religion or religious value systems on social stagnation or resistance to innovation needs to be examined more fully.

* * *

A powerful ideological superstructure had been built up by historians to explain the absence of change in Oriental societies, and their resistance to Western science and technology. While this was mainly the work of Western historians, many Asian historians subscribed to this view also, in the name of continuity. Amongst the views that have been put forward to explain the absence of change in Oriental societies, the most widespread as well as the most persistent have been: the retarding influence of religion and/or caste/tribe (Max Weber); selfishness and self-indulgence of the ruling classes (W.H. Moreland); absence of private property in land, resulting in the absence of a landed aristocracy which could limit royal despotism (Bernier, Wittfogel); a social structure based on an unvarying distribution of labour, and village self-sufficiency (Sir Henry

[13]J.H. Parry, "Transport and Trade Routes" in *The Cambridge Economic History of Europe*, ed. E.E. Rich and C.H. Wilson (Cambridge, 1967), IV: *The Economy of Expanding Europe in the Sixteenth and Seventeenth Centuries*, pp. 155-200.

Maine, Marx) etc. Even the old idea of climate as a factor either on character or communications has been recently revived. Experience of planning in many countries of the region has compelled the historians to review many of these concepts. Thus, the experience of India has shown that in many areas peasants have been remarkably responsive to new cropping techniques or seeds or new imputs if they give them assured opportunities of making more money. It has also been shown that caste has not been as rigid or the pattern of distribution of labour in villages been as unvarying as had been believed. It has, however shown considerable variation from region to region, calling for detailed studies aimed at arriving at a better understanding of the social structure and its processes taking as its unit a village, or a group of villages or a definable region. However, to be meaningful such descriptive studies have to be co-related to a conceptual framework within which the processes of change and conservation operate in traditional societies.

***

A careful study of religion, its social structure and value-system, the manner of its filteration of external ideas, the phases of its development, etc., have to be carefully analysed in order to understand the leadership pattern, communication structure, authority system and processes of change and conservation in traditional societies. The study of the function and role of religion in traditional societies has suffered from pre-conceived notions based on the value-attitudes of Western/Christian societies; or has been based on pure ethnocentric interest; or on the assumption of stability, harmony, etc. Careful training in the tools of social analysis, as well as deep familiarity with the history, languages, and literary forms and traditions in which religious thought and movements have expressed themselves, as well as familiarity with folk traditions, is needed for a purposeful understanding of these societies, so that the historian and sociologist can play a useful role in their present processes. The extent to which this can be done by outsiders, not born and bred in the traditions of the country, will depend upon the stage of development in each country.

* * *

As has been emphasised earlier, the problems of national identity, national unity and national growth are bound to interest the historians of Asian and African countries which are just emerging on the world scene as independent entities. In this context, the concept of region or tribe has become important for many of these countries. Tribal conflicts have threatened the unity of a number of African countries. But Africa has also had the tradition of large tribal empires, sometimes consisting of a number of tribes linked together by various ties. The complete isolation of tribes is an. ethnologists' myth which does not exist, or existed only in remote areas. The manner of the linking together of tribes, and of the manner of the breakup of tribes into territorial communities is of more than antiquarian interest to African historians. In India, both region and tribe have come increasingly to the forefront. Although the region has generally been conceived in terms of language, it is not certain that language is the most important element in regionalism (any more than that religion is the most important element in it). The recent demands for breaking up some of the bigger linguistic regions (such as the present Andhra, or Maharashtra, or U.P.) is indicative of this. This has led to a need to reassess the nature of the regions, and their relationship to what might be called the Indian *ethos*. It should be made clear here that the need to reassess the nature of religion or regionalism in India does not necessarily lead to a rejection or questioning of the concept of the basic unity of India.[14]

[14]This is not the place to expatiate on the basis of Indian unity, this being a favourite theme for long for Indian historians, literateures, politicians. Difference of approach on this issue continues to be a cause for sharp differences of opinion between Indian and Western scholars. For an approach to Indian sociology, making the unity of India functionally vital to the study, see Louis Dumont, *Religion,* Politics *and History* in *India* (Paris-The Hague, 1970), pp. 4-6.

The problem of tribe and tribalism has of late received greater attention from historians (as distinct from anthropologists) in Asia and India. The pattern of tribal settlements, of transformation of tribal society into peasants, the role of tribal settlements in the formation of linguistic units and regions are questions which are of deep interest to historians. The manner of assimilation of tribes into Hinduism, which is proceeding apace, is of considerable interest to the historians for interpolating historic processes on a retrodictive basis. It is being realised that the tribes are not on the margin of society, and as such of academic interest to a select band of anthropologists only, but are closely involved with social processes. A clearer understanding of the nature of the region and tribe is important for understanding historical evolution, as well for development strategy and political processes, for India as well as for a number of other Asian and African countries.

* * *

It has been argued in this essay that continued Western ethnocentricism limits and distorts the processes of historical development, in the West as in the rest of the world, by establishing an unreal dichotomy between the two. This does not imply that we should subscribe to a unilinear view of history, but that we should abandon the concept of centre and periphery, with the West as the centre. Despite the tremendous contribution of the West in the sustained growth of science and technology which is transforming the face of the world, there can be no centre and periphery in world history for any length of time. In the long run, history has to come back to the fundamental unity of mankind: despite differences in social organisation, mores, cultural traditions etc., similarity of the human thought processes and responses are revealed in them. Apart from studying the differences between different countries, areas and civilizations, history must study their interactions, and the role played by them at varying times in the growth of human civilization. Not ethnocentrism, but multi-polarity should be a key-note of history.

2

CULTURAL INTEGRATION AND INDIAN HISTORY

The manner in which a country views its past is directly related to what a country is and what it aspires to be. While India was in slavery, the views of the British administrative historians dominated the field. Though nationalist historians attempted to break away from the British point of view, it can be demonstrated that many of their intellectual categories were based on British thinking. Thus they generally accepted the British view that the Indians were essentially spiritual and other-worldly, looking upon the created world as illusory and, hence, less interested in it than in *moksha* or liberation from the cycle of birth and rebirth; that religion was the warp and woof of Indian life; and that Indian culture, political life, etc., all turned largely on religion. It is not that these aspects did not contain an element of truth. But to overemphasize them to the neglect of others, such as the rich Indian tradition of the development of science and technology, the growth of material culture in India, etc., means distorting the whole picture. It was this view of history which portrayed the Hindus and Muslims as being divided into two warring camps with little in common between them, thus paving the way for the emergence of the two-nation theory.

Though Jawaharlal Nehru in his book, *The Discovery of India,* was at pains to refute the view that the common people of India were more concerned with their spiritual than their material welfare.[1] the earlier British view of India as a land of spiritualism was picked up uncritically both by the nationalists and the communalists and continues to influence historical thinking in the country.

An important element in the distortion of Indian history was the emphasis on racialism. Thus, the word 'Arya' began to be equated with a race of people who had come into India a long time back and who, allegedly, were mainly responsible for the growth of the religion and culture in ancient India. It was forgotten, owing to the influence of German racial theories repeated by some British historians, that in the Sanskrit tradition, the word 'Arya' was applied most of the time to a culture, and that in the evolution of this culture various sections in India, belonging to different regions and races had contributed.

The distortion of Indian history has not only provided a rationale and intellectual sustenance to communalism in our country, it is also the backdrop to the recent Aryan-Dravadian controversy. One of the major issues in the understanding of Indian history is the manner of cultural development and assimilation of various sections in the cultural stream. The second is the nature of the state in India during various historical phases. As far as the first is concerned, two ideal prototypes have been put forward—first, the alleged assimilation of the Dravadians into Aryan culture, and second, the assimilation of the Scythians, Hunas, etc., in the Hindu fold later on. These are contrasted to the situation following the arrival of the Muslims in India in the twelfth century. Dr. RC. Majumdar, representing this point of view, deplores that the Muslims "did not merge themselves into this pattern and form with the Hindus a single type of homogeneous culture". His picture of medieval India is one which remained "permanently divided into two powerful

[1]Jawaharlal Nehru, *The Discovery of India*, (Asia, 1969) pp. 506-14.

units, which did not prove amenable to a fusion or even any close permanent co-ordination".[2]

It may be noticed that in this approach, cultural development or synthesis is equated with merging, or loss of identity in something given, rather than with the evolution of new forms. Whether this was the manner in which the Aryan and Dravadian or pre-Aryan cultural synthesis took place is in fact questionable. We know now from archaeological data, as well as from analysis of languages, that the Aryan tribes who came into India did not bring with them a higher civilization and culture. Mohen-jo-daro, Harappa, Kalibangan and Lothal represented a civilization which was decidedly more developed than anything the Aryans could boast of. Even in the cultural field, many of the later ideas seem to be of non-Aryan origin. Recent excavations show that an advanced urban civilization—known to archaeologists as the Red and Black ware—existed even in the Ganga valley. What is now considered the Aryan civilization was thus a synthesis, i.e., development of new forms based on these civilizations and the culture the Aryans brought with them.

There is every reason to believe that the attempt to absorb the Scythians and the Hunas led once more to profound changes in society, and even in the field of values. Historians subsume many of these changes under the broad head of growth of feudal elements in Indian society.[3]

There is no doubt that the arrival of the Turks, Afghans and Mughals in India from the twelfth to the sixteenth centuries led to profound changes once again in social structure, religious ideas and beliefs, and culture in the country. In the process, not only Indians, but the Turks, Afghans and Mughals underwent many changes. One of the

[2]Ed. R.C. Majumdar and others, *The Delhi Sultanate,* 1960, p. XXVIII (Vidya Bhavan Series, Vol. VI).

[3]See R.S. Sharma, *Feudalism* in *India,* 109; D.D. Kosambi, *Introduction to the History of India.*

important tasks of Indian scholarship is to assess the exact nature of these changes. The strongly held belief that Hindu and Muslim societies remained permanently divided and that the Muslims developed a type of culture which was unassimilated and unassimilable has tended to interfere with this work.

A closer look at the manner of cultural development in India shows that it has proceeded not on one level but at multiple levels, with the pattern varying from region to region, as the Aryan-Dravidian pattern varied between north and south India, and between the west and the east. As we know, the structure of caste itself varies from area to area. Any study of the pattern of cultural assimilation in India, whether in the ancient period or in the medieval period, has to take into account the two basic ingredients of region and caste.

How far is it historically correct to regard Hindu or Muslim cultures as being single entities, impervious to mutual assimilation? It is argued that Hinduism would have assimilated the Turks, Afghans and Mughals, too, if the latter had not been so determined to maintain their separate identity and/or, had not held political power in their hands. With the events of 1947 in the background, this argument appears to be an appealing one, and puts the responsibility for failure of cultural assimilation between Hindus and Muslims squarely on Muslim political and religious leaders and thinkers. It is, of course, fashionable in some historical quarters in Pakistan to argue that the *leit-motif* of Muslim movements in medieval times was to assert the uniqueness of Islam. Simultaneously, they blame the Hindus for their casteist narrowness.[4] That caste prejudices played a considerable role in keeping Hindu and Muslim societies

[4]See I.H. Qurehi, *The Muslim Community in the Indo-Pakistan Subcontinent,* 1962, pp. 78-82; I.H. Ikram, *History of Muslim Civilization in India and Pakistan,* Lahore 1961, pp. 209-10.

separate is undeniable. But this presumes that the Muslims would have been willing to be assimilated in a common culture in such a manner as to lose completely their separate identity but for the caste system. Unity in diversity has always been regarded as a basic feature of Indian culture which, even before the arrival of the Muslims, contained within itself different sects and religions, such as Buddhism, Jainism, Brahmanism, etc., as well as sub-cultures based on region. The Muslim community, too, revealed wide differences. An Arab or an Ottoman lurk professing the Muslim faith was culturally far different from an Indian Muslim. Even Iranians and Turanians who had lived in India for a couple of generations were considered to be different.[5] The Muslims in India were powerfully influenced not only by the Indian environment, but also by the regional sub-cultures. Scant attention also so far been paid by the Indian historians to the growth of these sub-cultures. As we study the growth of Bengali, Maharashtrian, Gujarati, or Punjabi sub-cultures, the Hindu-Muslim differences on an all-Indian plane appear in a different perspective. Both Hindus and Muslims contributed to the growth of Punjabi and Bengali languages and literatures. Which part of them can be called Hindu, and which Muslim? Similarly, the outlook of a Muslim Bohra merchant and a Gujarati Bania were hardly distinguishable. In Awadh (Eastern UP.), the manner, appearance, language and outlook of the Hindus and Muslims in both towns and villages were hardly distinguishable in the nineteenth century.

In the field of architecture, painting, and music, while the Turks destroyed a great deal, particularly in the early phase, they also built a great deal. The magnificent buildings which the Khalji, Tughlaq, Afghan and Mughal rulers constructed in north India were equalled, if not surpassed, by

[5]See Satish Chandra, *Parties and Politics at the Mughal Court, 1707-40*, 2nd ed. 1971, Intro. XXXII.

the rulers of Gujarat, Malwa, and the Deccan. These buildings, which assimilated both Indian and West Asian architectural traditions, gradually led to the evolution of a national style under the Mughals. This style continued to have vitality till the early twentieth century. Sir Edwin Lutyens incorporated this style in his design of New Delhi. In recent years, a few persons have started asserting that some of the medieval buildings are really Hindu or Rajput buildings. These arguments fly in the face of historical evidence, and are against the entire development of architectural style in medieval India. In any case, what does it prove? Did the Muslims not put up magnificent buildings outside India? Hence the attempt to deny the cultural contribution of the Muslims only shows a remarkable insularity, or a deep-rooted sense of inferiority.

It is not possible here to try to trace the growth of painting and music during the period. The classical music we know today in north India was really the product of this period. Many new *ragas* and modes as well as instruments were introduced and incorporated during this period. In fact, classical music is the best example of the fusion of Hindu and Muslim traditions. The impact of Mughal painting (itself a fusion of Persian and Indian traditions) on Rajput and Pahari painting is too well known to be repeated here.

It may be argued that the real problem of medieval India was not cultural assimilation but the distribution of political and economic power between the Hindus and the Muslims, and the allied problem of the relationship between state and religion. Communal writings in Indian history distort the notion of the state. The state in ancient India is presented as a vehicle of *dharma* or righteousness by some writers. If the state in ancient India is to be based on the Dharmashastras, it would be difficult to deny that this implied the oppression of the shudras indirectly by saddling upon the ruler the responsibility of maintaining the four-fold caste system, and of being responsible for enforcing the extreme injunctions prescribed by Manu, such as cutting out the tongue of a shudra if he recited the Vedas.[6] But the reality was different. As a tenth century writer, Medhatithi, explains, the king's duty was derived both from the Dharmashastra and the Arthashastra, i.e., both from canon law and politics. His *rajadharma* or public duty is based substantially on the latter. This means that religion and politics are separate, and the king is guided mainly by politics, though he does have a preceptor to advise him, and would not commit an open breach of canon law if avoidable. Thus, in a real sense, the State in ancient India was essentially secular.

The situation in medieval India under the Sultans was not fundamentally different. Alauddin Khalji bluntly told Qazi Mughisuddin that he did not know what was lawful and unlawful, but whatever was the need of the situation or the good of the state, that he decreed. The result of this approach was that even an orthodox man like Ziauddin Barani, the historian, concluded that a *truly Islamic State could not exist in India.* It could only be a state which had the outer trappings of Islam. A Muslim king was supposed to see that there was no open breach of the laws of Islam, that honest God-fearing Muslims should be appointed as qazis (judges), etc., that no honour should be shown to the Hindus, and that in general the ruler should continually wage war *(jehad)* against the unbeliever. The private conduct of the citizens did not concern the king; nor did the private life of the king concern the public. A state policy of this type he called *jahan-dari* as distinguished from the policy of

[6]U.N. Choshal, *The Age of Imperial Kanauj* (Vidya Bhavan Series, Vol. IV, Chapter X), pp. 232-33.

Medhatithi, the tenth century commentator on Dharmashastras, brings out clearly the dominance of the King's public functions: 'Rajadharma, while equivalent to the whole duty of the King, comprises, chiefly his public acts, or to put it more generally, is synonymous with politics'. Rajadharma, then, has a twofold source, namely, the Vedic and the non-Vedic *(Arthashiistra).*

din-dati which visualized the strict enforcement of all the laws of *shariat.*[7] A second effect was the growth of secular laws called *Zawabit,* in contradistinction from Holy law or shariat. It is significant that one of the most important compendiums of such laws, the *Zawabit-i-Alamgiri,* was compiled in the reign of the most orthodox Muslim ruler, Aurangzeb. It is thus clear that the state in India was never truly Islamic, and in course of time, as the Hindus were admitted to the highest offices owing to the force of circumstances, it became even less religious and more secular in outlook.

Recent studies have shown conclusively that during the sixteenth and seventeenth centuries as well as during the earlier period, economic power and political authority, particularly at the local and regional level, almost everywhere rested in the hands of a class of people designated zamindars by the writers of the period. Unlike the zamindars of the British period, these zarnindars were generally not outsiders, or money-grabbers. They enjoyed great prestige in the rural areas, being closely linked with the castes and communities settled on the land. Normally they did not interfere with the traditional rights of the peasants. They also had considerable military forces at their disposal. During Akbar's time, the forces at the disposal of zamindars amounted to 3,84,558 cavalry, 43,77,057 infantry, 1,863 elephants, 4,260 guns and 4,500 boats.[8] No wonder the Turkish and Mughal rulers tried to establish friendly relations with the zamindars. For all practical purposes, the village affairs thus continued largely to be managed by persons familiar to the villagers. In the time of Akbar, many of these zamindars were admitted to the nobility and thus given authority over a wider region. During the second half of the

[7]Ziauddin Barani. *Fatawa-i-Jahandari,* English tr. by M. Habib and A. Jahan, *"Political Theory of the Delhi Sultanate",* Advice, IX.

[8]*Ain-i-Akbari,* quoted by I. Habib, *Agrarian System of Mughal India,* p.164.

seventeenth century, the proportion of Hindus in the nobility at various levels, from the highest to the lowest, rose to about 33 per cent.[9]

The communal interpretation of medieval Indian history, which considers conflict between Muslims and Hindus as the major theme, over-simplifies a complex reality and slurs over social problems. The relations of the Turkish and Mughal rulers with the zamindars, who were predominantly Hindu, was not primarily a communal but a social problem. The zamindars posed a serious administrative problem because they engaged in mutual warfare, sometimes acted as petty tyrants to the peasants, and resisted and opposed centralized political authority and administration. At the same time, they were indispensable by virtue of their influence and knowledge of local affairs. This was a dilemma which the medieval state and society were unable to resolve. It had important implications for the subsequent period.

Muhammad Tughlaq in the fourteenth century was the first Turkish ruler who systematically tried to enroll Hindus into the central ruling elite, the nobility, in order to develop a homogeneous ruling class. Points of contact between the Hindu and Muslim ruling classes increased after the disintegration of the Delhi Sultanate. In Bengal as in Gujarat, in Kashmir as in the Bahmani Kingdom.[10] Hindus were appointed ministers and they continued to man the lower rungs of the administration. Matrimonial alliances between the two was an index of the convergence of their interests and greater social intercourse. Thus, Firuz Shah Bahman married the daughter of the Vijayanagar ruler, Deva Raya, in 1403. The Gujarat rulers married Rajput princesses. And the favourite queens of Zain-ul-Abedin, the famous Kashmiri ruler, were Hindus. The Sufi and the Bhakti movements developed in this atmosphere of liberalism.

[9]Athar Ali, *Mughal Nobility under Aurangzeb, 31.*

[10]*The Delhi Sultanate,* ed. M. Habib and K.A. Nizami, pp. 754-58, 861, 981-82, *ct. seq.*

The deliberate effort made by Akbar to integrate the Hindu and Muslim ruling classes by granting high offices *(mansabs)* to the Rajputs, and by forming personal relations with them was a logical culmination of this process. Matrimonial relations were formed by him and members of his immediate family with many saintly families, and with the families of leading zamindars, both Hindu and Muslim. In Akbar's time matrimonial relations became a means of forging political and personal bonds with these sections. Even before the fall of Chittor and the siege of Ranthambhor, Akbar had clearly indicated to the Hadas that the sending of *dola* was not a precondition for good relations.[11] The struggle between Akbar and Rana Pratap was not, therefore, concerned with the question of marriages but with political issues. The marriages, though they were essentially political in nature, did help to bring the Mughals and the Rajputs together in more ways than one. It is significant that during the nineteenth century, reputed Hindu historians such as Banki Das, Kaviraj Shyamal Das, etc., did not condemn these marriages, or consider them an outrage on Hindu honour.

In the end, it may be said that despite assimilation and understanding at different levels in various regions, Hindu and Muslim cultures contained many separate elements. The reasons for this may have been two. In the first place, a unified culture presupposes a unified society, at least at the higher level. The extent to which either Hindu or Muslim societies at the higher level were unified is questionable. Hindu society was always riven by claims of superiority between the two higher castes—Brahmans and Kshatriyas. To this may be added regional and linguistic disparities. Muslim society too was riven by racial and sectarian differences. Secondly, in the field of religion and thought also, many new ideas were broached. But the basis on which a measure of agreement was arrived at between Hindus and Muslims was mysticism. Although the medieval mystical

[11]Satish Chandra, *Medieval India*, Ch. X.

movement in India has many remarkable achievements to its credit, its essential approach was emotional and non-rational. This was an insecure basis for unity and could be subverted at any time by both rational and non-rational arguments. How weak this basis was made manifest towards the end of the nineteenth century when the interests of the upper classes in the two communities began to diverge.

An objective interpretation of Indian history does not imply denying cultural and social differences between Hindus and Muslims. But it means that an aspects, not merely religious differences, should be studied. Not only points of difference, but points of contact and understanding should also be brought out. Secondly, in order to understand the medieval reality, we should study not only the attitudes of a few rulers but the entire relationship between the different communities including, above all, the masses. The communal interpretation of history overlooks, the role of the people. It concerns itself more with heroes and villains than with the structure of society, the distribution of political and economic power within it, and the cultural patterns between different sections, communities, and regions.

Enough has been said to show that without carefully analysing the role of different castes, classes, and regions, we cannot understand the processes of cultural integration in India. The terms Hindu and Muslim tend to obscure these divisions. The refusal of many historians, both Hindu and Muslim, to look beneath the surface has led to the misuse of history and the distortion of the medieval reality. Recent events on the subcontinent, particularly the emergence of Bangladesh, hold out the hope that many historians who had been virtually mesmerized by the terms Hindu and Muslim will be enabled to embark upon a more realistic appraisal of the complex process of cultural integration in India.

3

HISTORY WRITING IN PAKISTAN AND THE TWO-NATION THEORY

Although the demand for Pakistan was based avowedly on the two-nation theory, the theory failed to make any deep impression on historical writing in India till the formation of Pakistan in 1947. Muslim historians, such as I.H. Qureshi[1], A.B.M. Habibullah[2] and even Aziz Ahmad[3] (Lahore) did not emphasise the idea that Muslim culture was a distinctive and separate entity, and the Muslim community in India a unified body, alien in character and essentially separate from the non-Muslims in the country. In fact, the idea of Pakistan as an Islamic state based on Muslim culture and the Muslim community had so little crystallized by 1947 that M.A. Jinnah was aggrieved at the partition of traditional linguistic and cultural units such as the Punjab and Bengal, and the exclusion from Pakistan of the predominantly non-Muslim areas in these units, and protested against the achievement of a "truncated" Pakistan. Thus, the particular manner of the creation of Pakistan and the accompanying holocaust on the two sides of the new frontier itself became a major factor in the rise of the two-nation theory.

[1] *Administrative System of the Delhi Sultanate,* (Delhi, 1942).

[2] *Foundations of Muslim Rule in India,* (Lahore, 1945).

[3] *Political and Administrative Institutions of the Early Turkish Rule in India,* (Lahore, 1949).

We are here not concerned with the impact of these events—the agitation for Pakistan and partitioning of the country—on historical writing in India. We shall confine our attention to the elaboration of the two-nation theory by the historians of Pakistan since 1947.

An exposition of the two-nation theory should, one might expect, be preceded by a clear understanding of what is implied by the term 'Nation'. Pakistan historians do not define their concept of the nation as such, but they generally reject the definition of the term as commonly understood in the West. The nationalist movement in Europe in the nineteenth and early twentieth centuries was essentially territorial and largely based on language and culture, rejecting religion as a basis, since religion was considered a divisive rather than a unifying factor. The adoption of religion as a basis for nationalism in Pakistan leads logically to Pan-Islamism. Yet, in the present international context and the context of Pakistan, this idea has to be reconciled to territorial nationalism, thereby posing a dilemma which neither the historians nor the politicians of Pakistan have as yet succeeded in resolving. It might be emphasized at the outset that the problem faced by Pakistan in this respect is entirely different from that faced by any Islamic country in the Middle-East. The United Arab Republic and Iraq can be both Islamic and Arab, Iran can be both Islamic and Persian, since none of these countries contain any substantial number of non-Arab and non-Persian non-Muslims in their population. Pakistan as an Islamic state has to cope with the largest number of non-Muslims in its population as compared to any other avowedly Muslim country.[4] For a

[4]For a further discussion of this point see W.C. Smith, *Islam in the Modern World,* (New York, 1949); also Harry W. Hazard, *Atlas of Islamic History,* (Princeton, 1954); Louis Massignon, ed. *Annuaire du monde musulman statistique, historique, sociale et economique,* (Paris, 1955).

The non-Muslim population of Pakistan, residing mainly in East Pakistan, is estimated at about 9 million.

similar, though by no means parallel situation, we have to go to South East Asian countries, such as Malaysia or Indonesia.

From a close analysis of recent historical writings in Pakistan, including the officially sponsored *History of the Freedom Movement* (6 volumes published) prepared under the chairmanship of Mahmud Husain, and the works of leading historians such as I.H. Qureshi, S.M. Ikram, Moinul Haq etc. the arguments in favour of the two-nation theory and the cultural distinctiveness of Pakistan may be summarised as follows:

(i) That West Pakistan has existed as a distinct cultural entity since the time of Mohen-jo-daro, the civilization of which was essentially similar to the ancient Babylonian and Sumerian civilizations.[5] In the case of East Pakistan, an attempt has of late been made to claim a separate tradition on the basis of the persistence of Buddhism there till the 13th century followed by Muslim conquest and conversion.

(ii) That the medieval "Indo-Muslim" or "Hindustani" culture was essentially Islamic in spirit and content and that Pakistan is the natural heir to this tradition which has been repudiated by India as a result of Hindu revivalism reflected in such things as the rejection of Urdu.

(iii) That the Muslims of India (or "Indo-Pakistan") are a distinct and unified community based on the teachings of Islam, and while not alien ethnically, they have always been an essentially foreign element in Indian society.

(iv) That the loss of political power by the Muslims after the fall of the Mughal Empire and particularly after the conquest of India by the British who adopted a pro-Hindu policy created a situation in which Islam itself

[5]This point was first put forward in R.E.M. Wheeler, *Five Thousand Years of Pakistan*, (London, 1950).

> was in danger. A series of religious reformers from Shaikh Ahmad Sarhindi and Shah Waliullah to Sayyid Ahmad Barelvi saved Indian Islam from utter demoralisation and absorption into Hinduism by purging from it the alien Hindu practices and beliefs and revivifying the community. The work was completed by Sir Syed Ahmad and M.A. Jinnah, Pakistan being the logical culmination of the process.

The emphasis laid by different writers on the different points above and their interpretation of various aspects naturally vary. We shall, however, examine the argument as a whole. The attempt to co-relate Pakistani culture to the Mohen-jo-daro civilization on the one hand, and to Tantric Buddhism on the other, has not been seriously undertaken by Pakistani historians so. far. Recent excavations establishing the extension of the Mohen-jo-daro civilization into Gujarat, Rajputana and the upper reaches of the Indo-Gangetic valley have considerably reduced the force of this argument. A positive gain, however, has been a marked growth of interest in Pakistani academic circles in ancient archaeology and pre-Islamic culture of the areas comprising Pakistan. The most notable contribution in this respect has been that of A.H. Dani of the Dacca University .

Regarding the character of medieval Indo-Muslim culture, I.H. Qureshi argues that by assimilating many aspects of Indian culture in the field of fine arts (architecture, painting and music), social manner and customs and even religious practices and beliefs, the Muslim immigrants into India created a new culture which established their separate identity from other Muslim peoples, such as Arabs, Persians, etc. However, he simultaneously maintains that this 'new' culture. remained essentially Islamic in spirit and foreign in character. He says: "Whatever the degree of toleration developed between the communities, the Indo-Muslim culture remained mostly Islamic and Central Asian in spirit ... at all times the Muslims of the sub-continent were resolute in refusing to be assimilated to the local population and made conscious efforts to maintain their distinctive character. In view of the great assimilative qualities of Hinduism, which has absorbed within its bosom many a foreign community, this needed constant vigilance and effort. The continuity of such an effort is in itself a great cementing force"[6] Qureshi conveniently slurs over the contribution of poets and scholars like Al Biruni, Amir Khusru, Zia Nakshabi, Abul Fazl, Dara and a whole host of mystics and sufis who found in the doctrine of pantheism (Wahdat-ul-Wajud) a meeting point between Islam and Hinduism. Though forced to admit that the majority of the Indian Muslims are of "native blood", Qureshi tried to buttress the argument for the "foreign" character of the Indo-Muslim culture by maintaining that "Many a distinguished family of administrators, soldiers and scholars during the Mughal rule hailed from Central Asia and Iran... Because of their links with traditional Islamic culture the influence of these elements in giving a shape to the culture of the Muslim community of the subcontinent was far greater than their numbers would have justified."[7]

The contention that medieval Indo-Muslim culture was essentially foreign, and that the Muslim community in India could save itself from absorption into Hinduism only by maintaining its distinctive (i.e. separate) character, leads Qureshi to the conclusion that Islam in the Indian context could survive only by maintaining the political domination of the Muslims over the Hindus. Any sharing of political power with the Hindus was dangerous and a first step towards the political abdication of the Muslims since "surrender does not succeed unless it is complete." By the same logic, all movements which emphasized the common features of Hinduism and Islam, or regarded them as roads leading to the same God, were dangerous heresies since they

[6]*The Muslim Community of the Indo-Pakistan Sub-continent*, (Herderstra, 1962), pp. 78-82.

[7]*Ibid.*, pp. 78-82.

weakened the feeling of the uniqueness of Islam. Qureshi, therefore, draws the faultless conclusion that it was Akbar who was primarily responsible for the downfall of the Mughal empire. He says, "Akbar tipped the balance just sufficiently to make it certain that the equilibrium could be maintained in future only through making concessions that would make Muslim domination more and more difficult."[8] "It was a crime to lull the Muslims into believing that the maintenance of the Empire was not their primary responsibility. Even more disastrous was the encouragement of the feeling that toleration implied the belief that all religions were merely different goals, all equally good, of reaching the same God."[9] The final conclusion of Qureshi is that in an Islamic state, power must be retained firmly in the hands of the Muslims, though the economic interests of the non-Muslims should be looked after, and the unity of the Muslim community should be maintained by a rigid adherence to the orthodox creed.

It should be obvious from the foregoing analysis that not only is Qureshi's view of history coloured by the kind of state he would like Pakistan to be, but that the entire history of the Muslims in India is viewed as merely a prelude to the establishment of Pakistan. This is "determinism" with a vengeance.

Neither Qureshi's vision of Pakistan as a state in which the *mullas* act as the conscience keepers of the nation and keep everyone in line, nor his interpretation of medieval history is found acceptable by all the historians in Pakistan. For example, S.M. Ikram argues that the medieval Muslim state in India was essentially secular and that beginning from the time of Iltutmish, the Muslim rulers refused to let their policies be determined by the orthodox *ulama.* Although Firuz Tughlaq tried to reverse the process to some extent, it had become too well established by the time. The movement

[8]*Ibid.*, p. 168.

[9]*History of Freedom Movement*, (Karachi, 1961), Vol 1. p. 34.

of cultural assimilation between the Hindus and Muslims went on apace from the time of Amir Khusrau and was furthered by Akbar whose policy of "religious toleration and giving adequate share in administration to all class of people" stood the test of time, and became "a part of the Mughal political code."[10]

Ikram maintains that the relationship between the Hindus and the Muslims remained tenuous due largely to the caste system: "The Hindus maintained no social intercourse with the Muslims by way of interdining or inter-marriage; they regarded the touch of the Muslims or even the scent of their food as pollution... In such an atmosphere a real rapproachment between the Hindus and Muslims was impossible."[11] Nevertheless, he maintains that the essential atmosphere under the Mughals was one of cultural assimilation; "the warp and woof of the Muslim civilization in the sub-continent was made of four different strands: the indigenous (which will include not only the Indian but also the Afghan-element); the Islamic (or Arabic); the Turkish and the Persian. Recently there has been a tendency to overlook the indigenous component but its influence is deep-rooted and all pervading. It has been powerful, not only on account of the predominantly non-Muslim environment in which Indo-Muslim culture developed or because of the heritage of an ancient civilization, but because of the Indian origin of the vast majority of the Muslims of this sub-continent. Indian element is in their very blood and shows itself not only in numerous usages and practices carried over from their ancestral Hindu society, but even in unconscious reactions and the basic material make up. Influence of Islam has been equally comprehensive."[12]

While pleading for a further study and understanding of Aurangzeb's policies and motives, Ikram does not defend his

[10]S.M. Ikram, *History of Muslim Civilisation in India and Pakistan*, (Lahore, 1961), p. 246.

[11]*Ibid.*, pp. 209-210.

[12]*Ibid.*, p. 501.

policy of temple destruction and religious bigotry, regarding these as "a departure not only from the political philosophy generally governing Mughal government, but also from the policy followed hitherto by most rulers in the sub-continent."[13]

Thus, Ikram and historians who follow his line of thinking do not regard Pakistan as being rooted essentially in the medieval political tradition or following inevitably from the cultural distinctiveness of the Muslims. They find both cooperation arid antipathy, assimilation and divergence in the cultural relationship of the two communities. While thinkers like Ahmad Sirhindi and Shah Waliullah helped to rally the Muslims under the banner of *shariat,* the movement for Pakistan is essentially related by them to developments since the "Mutiny", and "the Hindu repudiation" of the medieval Indo-Muslim cultural heritage.

From the foregoing, it may be concluded that the validity of the two-nation theory during the medieval period is by no means accepted by all sections of historians in Pakistan. Which trend of thinking will ultimately dominate remains to be seen. But it is unfortunate that in some recent British and American publications there is a tendency to lay a one-sided emphasis on the divisive factors between the Hindus and the Muslims, while largely ignoring the traditions shared by both. Thus P. Hardy, tracing the Indian traditions during the medieval period, remarks, "... neither educated Muslims nor Hindus accepted cultural co-existence as a natural prelude to cultural assimilation. Thus long before British rule and long before modem political notions of Muslim nation-hood, the consensus of the Muslim community in India had rejected the eclecticism of Akbar and Dara Shikoh for the purified Islamic teaching of Shaikh Ahmad of Sirhind and Shah Waliullah. Cultural apartheid was the dominant ideal in medieval Muslim India, in default of cultural victory."[14]

[13]*Ibid.*, p.316,

[14]W.M. Theodore du Bary and others (ed.) *Sources of Indian Tradition,* (New York, 1958), p, 370.

The danger of such an outlook becomes all the greater when it is borne in mind that considerable numbers of young Indian, and particularly Pakistani scholars still go abroad for advanced degrees and research. British and American publications still dominate the field of historical research, though, once again, India is in a comparatively stronger position than Pakistan. The absence of research and library facilities, the lure of scholarships and the unfortunate premium on a foreign degree placed by government and even by heads of educational institutions in the two countries help to perpetuate this situation.

II

On the whole, Pakistani historical writing covering the period from the establishment of British rule upto the "Mutiny" of 1857 is free from any heavy sectarian bias. The factors emphasised are:

(i) The political humiliation and economic ruination of the country, affecting Hindu and Muslim alike, due to the growing estrangement of the British ruling class from all sections of Indians; the unconcealed contempt with which they regarded their subjects and their culture (the spirit of Mills and Macaulay soon triumphed over that of Orientalists such as William Jones, Colebrooke etc.); faulty administrative methods, and British institutions and policies which adversely affected both the agriculturists and the artisans.

(ii) A systematic British policy of divide and rule, by discriminating against the Muslims, denying them their legitimate share of employment and maligning their history and culture. "The Hindu was to be frightened to an extent that he would consider British rule the only safeguard against Muslim tyranny and as such the greatest boon of the Gods."[15]

[15] I.H: Qureshi, *History of the Freedom Movement,* (Karachi, 1961), Vol. II Part II, (Karachi, 1960) p. 233.

These and other humiliations attendant upon British rule which led to mass resentment are rightly considered the basic causes of the "Mutiny" of 1857. All sections of those who revolted, without any distinction of religion, forgetting the struggles between the Marathas and the Muslims, acknowledged as the head and symbol of their supreme effort to free their home-land from the shame of foreign rule the aged Mughal Emperor ... this was a national uprising, the effort of a people to free itself from foreign rule, in short, a war of independence."[16]

Thus, the early period of British rule emerges as a period when Hindu-Muslim relations were the most free from sectarian bitterness or political passions, and the "Mutiny" as a symbol of Hindu-Muslim cooperation for a common Purpose.

When and why the situation changed the role of Syed Ahmed Khan and the Hindu revivalist movements, the British policies, and the social and economic background-all these are yet to be seriously studied by scholars in India and Pakistan. In a recent work, the early 1870s are designated as marking an important change in British public opinion towards the Indian Muslims. "From the Mutiny till 1870 it is hard to find anyone in Britain who did not blame the Muslims for insurrection ... by about 1875 British public opinion had generally come to believe in Muslim loyalty."[17] Modern Pakistani historians try to refute the charge of "loyalism" against the Muslim leaders and the Muslim League movement. Thus, Aziz says, "One myth created and sustained by the conservative alone (though at times accepted by others) was that of the 'loyal Musalman'... He must be supported, encouraged, even honoured. He was the basis of British rule in India or at least of its continuance." He further declares, "In India the myth was strengthened by Syed Ahmad Khan, who declared that the Muslim future in India was closely tied

[16] *Ibid*, pp. 259-60.

[17] K.K. Aziz, *"Britain & Muslim India"*, (Lahore 1963).

up with the sustenance of British rule and called upon his co-religionists to support the British regime lest they be "devoured by the increasing tempo of Hindu agitation."[18]

It is argued that the "loyalist" policies of Syed Ahmad were abandoned by the Muslims by the turn of the century. "There is not a shred of evidence to show he (Lord Minto) conspired with the Muslims to lead a delegation to him (for separate electorates)", and finally that the "creation of Pakistan during the last years, was opposed by even the Right which had always been friendly to Muslim aspirations."[19]

These arguments are hardly convincing, particularly when it is admitted that L6rd Minto, and presumably other British Viceroys, were actuated in their Muslim policy by a motive "clear, precise and, from his point of view, praiseworthy to help the continuance of British Rule in India."[20] The same author goes further and lables the charge against the British that they pursued a policy of divide and rule "a myth put up by the Left." Likewise, the slogans of self-determination for India and the unity of India, are also called "myths". Apparently, we are asked to believe that Britain pursued a policy of divide and rule as long as she discriminated against the Muslims, but stopped doing so as soon as she started discriminating in their favour!

The rise of the "Moslem nation" is dated by many Pakistani historians from the agitation against the Partition of Bengal. It is argued that the partition was actuated by motives of administrative convenience and efficiency, but that the Hindus gave proof of their bias against the Muslims by agitating against it because it would have created a Muslim majority province.[21] It might be mentioned that the Curzon Private

[18] *Ibid.* p. 17.

[19] *Ibid*, pp. 20-66.

[20] *Ibid.*, pp. 17-19.

[21] I.H. Qureshi, *History of the Freedom Movement*, (Karachi, 1961), Vol. III Part I, pp. 8-28. In a speech at Dacca, Lord Curzon declared that the proposal for a partition would make Dacca the centre, and possibly the capital, of a new and self-sufficient administration and this would give the Muslims of Eastern Bengal "a unity which they have not enjoyed since the days of the old Mussalman Viceroys and Kings". (*Parliamentary Papers*, 1905, ed. 1946, p. 222).

Papers in the Commonwealth Relations Library, London, which the present writer has had occasion to examine, contain enough material to substantiate the nationalist charge that British policy was actuated by a desire to divide and rule. According to the Pakistan historians, the Muslim League was born as a result of the mass Muslim disillusionment with the Congress and Hindus. They virtually condone the British government's role in the exacerbation of the communal situation in India, and fasten all the responsibility for that on the Congress and the Hindu leaders. At the same time, they forebear from examining the nature of the Muslim League Movement, the character of its leadership and the question why the Muslim League Movement failed to develop a positive social programme, unlike the National Congress.

Pakistan's appraisal of the later period of the national movement and of British policies can well be deduced from the foregoing analysis. Recent developments have tended to encourage the growth of a more critical attitude towards the West in Pakistan. One result of this mood of disillusionment might be the eventual growth of a more independent and objective appraisal of British rule and policies. Better contacts between Indian and Pakistani scholars in various ways, including the exchange of publications and facilities for research by scholars of one country in the other, however, chimerical they might seem at present, should also not be lost sight of.

III

As the present writer has stated elsewhere, 'Basically, the problem before both India and Pakistan is the same. Both seek to attain internal stability by drawing to themselves, the emotional loyalty of all sections dwelling within their territory."[22] Apart from differences of race, religion and language, Pakistan has to cope with the stupendous problems posed by the physical separation of its two wings by 1000

[22] *Seminar*, No. 48 (September 1963) p. 17.

miles of Indian territory. It may be doubted if the two-nation theory helps in the process of consolidation in either country. Islam alone cannot be a sufficient bond of unity between the two wings of Pakistan. The same process which made the Indian Muslims a nation separate from the Muslims of Arabia and Iran can make the Muslims of East Pakistan a new nation separate from West Pakistan. The fear of such a development haunts the present rulers. of Pakistan. But whereas India has sought to solve the problems of 'sub-cultures' or 'sub-nationalities' by frankly recognising their existence and giving them a large measure of. autonomy, Pakistan, in the name of the unity of the Muslim community, has sought to suppress them and has imposed a unitary form of government. The two-nation theory also implies for the non-Muslims of Pakistan the denial of their just rights and their assignment to a status of permanent inferiority. It makes the Kashmir problem practically insolvable, except by a complete surrender of the Valley by India. It also vitiates generally Indo-Pakistani relations. While the problem of good neighbourly relations between India and Pakistan is part of a bigger, more complicated process, the renunciation of the two-nation theory by Pakistani politicians and academicians on the lines once suggested by Shahid Suhrawardy, namely that the two-nation theory no longer has any validity after the creation of Pakistan, will certainly help to ease the situation and hasten the process of the growth of territorial nationalism in the two countries, embracing both the Hindu and the Muslim residing in their respective territories.

In the long run, the abandonment of the two-nation theory by Pakistan is, a test of its maturity. A nation that is self-confident of itself does not need artificial props. Whatever may have been the circumstances leading to the creation of Pakistan, no responsible person or considerable section of opinion in India today has any desire to undo it. Unlike the Middle-Eastern countries, and like most South and South-East Asian countries, both India and Pakistan are faced by the problem of creating a stable state on a multi-racial, multilinguistic and multi-religious basis. Though forms may vary, a secular and democratic order based on social justice and regional autonomy seems to be the most suited to such conditions. A clear realisation of this is bound to have far reaching effects on history writing in Pakistan.

4

MAIN TRENDS IN HISTORICAL SCIENCES IN INDIA: 1900-70

Although the modern tradition of historiography in India is often traced back to the establishment of British rule in India, it is important to realise that India had its own indigenous traditions of historiography, sometimes called the *itihas-purana* tradition. This tradition not only included the geneological tables of kings, and definite historical data, but contained a philosophy of history. The 12th century Sanskrit history of Kashmir, *Rajtarangini* by Kalhana, shows a clarity and maturity in historical analysis which suggests the development of a long tradition of historiography in India, the early phases of which are lost to us. This historical tradition was strengthened and diversified during the medieval period with the introduction into India of the Persio-Arab tradition of historiography—one of the most advanced and productive school of history writing in the world for several centuries. The tradition of bardic writing, represented by the *khyat, vat,* etc., also flourished during the period. These various traditions of history writing continued though in an attenuated form, throughout the 19th century, and in some of the Indian states even till their merger in the Indian Union in 1947-48. Tales, legends and songs about heroes. past or present, continued to be written. All these have played a definite role in shaping the popular view of history and to that extent, have consciously or unconsciously, influenced Indian historical writing as well.

The growth of the modem tradition of historiography in India can be divided into three broad phases: the early stage extending upto the end of the 19th century; the second phase (sometimes called the 'Nationalist' phase) extending roughly upto the end of the Second World War and the attainment of Indian independence; and the present phase starting thereafter. No water-tight demarcation can be made between these, of course, for the trends and tendencies of one phase often continued in the subsequent phase, and the seeds of the subsequent phase were present in the earlier phase. We shall touch upon the first phase only in passing in order to underline some of the features which have influenced the subsequent phases directly or indirectly.

Many of the early British historians took for granted the superiority not only of Western science and technology, but of Western civilisation as well. This was extended back in time to cover Greek and Roman history which became the classical age, and the apogee of human attainment in antiquity. To these British historians, Indian history appeared to be a dull chronicle of the rise and fall of individual rulers and dynasties and wars, thus turning history into 'a mere record of butchery of men by their fellowmen'. It lacked the interest of any orderly growth of institutions as in Rome (or in Great Britain). Some of them, particularly the Indologists, did study Indian languages, literature, religious ideas and beliefs, castes and communities, laws and customs of the Hindu and Muslims, etc. But so strong was the belief in the unchanging character of Indian society—a belief to which Marx unwittingly lent his support, that no attempt was made to relate the various facets of Indian life to particular periods, or to trace their historical evolution. The tradition of history writing and Oriental studies or Indology have not always coincided—so much so that even today there exist separate professional organisations, the Indian History Congress, and the All-India Orientalists' Congress. However, many distinguished Orientalists, including linguists, philosophers etc., made a considerable contribution in the growth of historical studies in India.

A great deal of the historians' time and attention during this period was, of necessity, taken up with establishing broad facts and chronology with the help of genealogical tables, coins, inscriptions, Buddhist and Jain canons etc. The painstaking reconstruction of the chronology of the early political history of India was a major achievement, and a prelude to many other studies on the period. R.G. Bhandarkar's *A Peep into the Early History of India (1900),* and Vincent Smith's *Early History of India* (1904) were land marks in this development.

Most British historians who wrote on the 'Muslim period', generally followed faithfully the Persian chronicles written during the period. These chronicles devoted their attention almost exclusively on the rulers and their courts, only occasionally straying into the field of administration and social history. The most prestigious, at the same time the most typical work in this field was Elliot and Dowson's eight Volume *History of India as told by its own Historians (1867-77).* The selections concentrated on political history, while underlining the harsh treatment meted out by the Muslim rulers to the Hindus, and how much better off the latter were under British rule. The innervation, lack of administrative ability, and military incompetence of the Indians in the face of foreign invaders was also emphasised.[1]

The Second Phase

The growth of the nationalist movement in the last quarter of the 19th century gave a definite fillip to the writing of Indian history by Indian historians. These historians reacted against many of the implicit attitudes of the British historians, and tried to create a sense of pride in India by

[1]See for instance S.A. Rashid's Introduction to S.M. Ikrams *History of Muslim Civilization in India and Pakistan* (Lahore), (n.d.).

dwelling upon the uniqueness and antiquity of Indian culture, and its independent identity (not based on Greek or Persian culture). The remarkable continuity of India's culture was also emphasized. The view put forward earlier by some western scholars, such as Max Muller, that Indian culture was essentially spiritual in nature, also found wide acceptance. This view inspired many modem Indian scholars to undertake a closer study of Indian philosophy and religion. However, it resulted in the adoption of a narrow attitude in tracing India's social and cultural development. All foreign influence tended to be viewed with suspicion. Interest grew in the extension of Indian culture to countries in the south-east, Far east and central Asia. However, hardly any attempt was made to study the processes of cultural growth in the specific social context of these countries which were sometimes dubbed India's 'colonies'.

The influence of German historiography on Indian historical writing appears more openly after the First World War. Indian historians who went to London or Oxford for their training came back deeply impressed with German historiography. Thus, inaugurating the First Modem Indian History Congress in 1935, the President elect, Sir Shafaat Ahmed Khan, expressed the hope that "it would be the authoritative organ of historical scholarship, imbued with the principles which have made history in the West almost an exact science". Indian historians were asked to prepare their accounts on the solid sub-stratum of 'facts', duly attested and verified on the basis of the critical methods developed by German historiography. One effect of this was to put the historical chronicles on a pedestal as undisputable 'authority'. The production of critical texts and monographs became a main concern of the historian during the period. The monographs dealt in the main with prominent rulers such as Chandra Gupta Maurya, or Asoka, or Harsha or Akbar or Aurangzeb, Shivaji etc., or with the rise and fall of dynasties which had ruled over large parts of India. Monographs were also written on local rulers such as Haider

Ali, Tipu, Ranjit Singh, etc., who had built their own regional states, and resisted the British inroads.[2]

These texts and monographs certainly added to the available historical information, and trained historians in the critical utilisation of contemporary source material. From the point of view of methodology, the major weakness of most of these monographs was that political history, social and economic life, administration, culture, etc., were all treated as entirely separate entities, with hardly any attempt to establish an organic relationship between them.[3] An integral part of this methodology was the emphasis on narrative history.[4] The production of this type of monographs has continued to be the main stay of Ph.D. dissertations in many Universities both in India and in the West. The major rulers and dynasties having been dealt with, some scholars have felt

[2]The list of these historians and their works is very large. For works written in the earlier period, special reference may be made to H.C. Ray Chaudhri's The *Political History of Ancient India* (1924); R.C. Majumdar, *Corporate Life in Ancient India* (1922); D.B. Bhandarkar, *Asoka (1923);* K.P. Jayaswal, *Hindu Polity* (1924); R.K. Mookerjee, *Harsh* (1926); *Asoka* (1928); Beni Prasad, *The State in Ancient India* (1928); N.N. Law, *Aspects of Ancient Indian Polity* (1921) etc. For the later period, see Jadunath Sarkar, *History of Aurangzeb* (1912-28), *Shivaji* (1919); Qanungo, K.N., *Sher Shah* (1921); *Dara Shikoh;* Beni Prasad, *Jahangir* (1922); Habib, *Mahmud Ghazni* (1922); Ishwari Prasad, *Medieval India* (1925); Banarsi Prasad, *Shah Jahan* (1932); N.K. Sinha, *Haider Ali, Ranjit Singh;* Mohibbul Hasan, *Tipu Sultan* (1951), etc. British scholars also produced many books during the period, some of them being rather critical towards these Indian heroes. See for instance, V.A. Smith, *Akbar the Great Moghul* (1917), *Ashoka the Buddhist Emperor of India* (1920). The most representative work of British scholarship during the period was the six volume *Cambridge History of India.*

[3]The best example of this may be considered the volumes entitled *The History and Culture of the Indian People,* ed. by R.C. Majumdar etc: (1951 onwards). These volumes bring together the wide range of Indian scholarship and Indic studies upto the time of their composition.

[4]For a critical evaluation of the 'nationalist' school of history writing, See R. Thapar, *Interpretations of Ancient Indian History, History and Theory,* Vol. III, 1968.

compelled to embark upon the study of the political history of minor rulers and dynasties. After 1947, the British Governor-Generals and Viceroys have also been taken up for a treatment on the lines of the earlier Indian rulers. However, a new trend of writing critical evaluative monographs has .started recently. Examples of this are S. Gopal's *The Viceroyalty of Lord Ripon (1953).*

While narrative political history, with its emphasis on the date of birth and accession of a ruler, his caste or personal status (free or slave), his wars of conquest etc., continued to occupy the energies of a large number of historians, the study of institutions received increasing attention. In these writings, we may discern two separate traditions at work. German historiography considered the state to be the decisive agency in the growth of human civilisation, everything else including culture being subordinated to it. The influence of German historiography led a number of Indian scholars to investigate the nature of the state in India. The discovery of Kautilya's *Arthashastra* strengthened the view that in India also the state had played a decisive role in modulating social and economic life. Some historians attempted to prove that all the western political institutions and ideas (such as constitutional monarchy, the Cabinet system of Government, etc.) were to be found in ancient and to some extent in medieval India as well. The further point as to why these ideas and institutions could not germinate in the Indian soil was, however, hardly taken up. The second trend may be called the indigenous tradition which considered the moral law *(dharma),* and the social order *(varna* or caste) as the decisive factors in social evolution. P.V. Kane's monumental study, *History of the Dharmasastra* (Poona 1930-46) helped in focussing attention on the *Dharmasastras* as a source for Indian social evolution. Similarly, many writers tried to trace the fundamental basis of state and society in medieval India to *sharia.*

While these two traditions acted and reacted on each other, another question which the historians of the period had to cope with was the nature of India's unity, and its reflection in history. The British view that India was never a nation with any deep sense of unity, but a conglomeration of races, religions, castes, etc., led to the emergence of two sharply opposed trends of thinking. One trend postulated the view that a culture was more or less unique, and could only make a marginal adjustment with another, except at the cost of extinction or losing its uniqueness. Hindu and Muslim cultures were two such distinct cultures, based on distinctive communities, their own religious and legal books, ethics, value-systems, etc. This view postulated a permanent dichotomy between the two. To this view of thinking, the partition of India in 1947, was a natural corollary.

The second trend of thinking emphasized that India's cultural development continued apace during Turkish and Mughal rule, that the Hindus continued to play an important part in administration and political life, and that in a large measure a composite culture had been evolved by the time the Mughal empire disintegrated.

These controversies of the time, raised a whole host of problems relating to the nature of the state in India, the relationship between state and religion, the character and motives of the administration, etc.[5] It quickly became obvious that in order to assess these and other aspects i.e. the nature of the Hindu and Muslim communities, their relationship with each other and with the state would require a fresh evaluation of the nature of the information provided by the medieval chronicles and also uncovering fresh evidence by

[5]For the medieval period reference may be made to W. Irvine, *The Army of the Indian Mughals* (1903); J.N. Sarkar, *Mughal Administration* (1925); W.H. Moreland, *Agrarian System of Moslem India* (1929); Ibn Hasan, *The Central Structure of the Mughal Empire* (1933, published 1936); P. Saran, *The Provincial Government of the Mughals* (1941); I.H. Qureshi, *The Administration of the Sultanats of Delhi* (1942). For the British period, where there was no dearth of source material, the problems were of a different kind. In general they presented a eulogistic picture of progress from strength to strength.

tapping different sources. While a large number of scholars from various Universities etc., were drawn into this direction, a notable contribution was made by the Allahabad School of History.[6]

A number of books were written during this period on fine arts, such as architecture, painting, sculpture etc. However, most of them adopted the narrative method. Hardly any attempt was made to co-relate them with the social reality.

Interest in regional history also developed during this period. Studies of the political system, and social and economic life in South India helped in counteracting excessive emphasis on the Gangetic valley, and making generalisations for the entire country on that basis. Interest in regional history also resulted in greater attention being paid to the regional languages, and some of the works, such as N.R. Ray's classic on Bengal, *Banglir Itihas,* G.H. Ojha's *History of Rajputana,* were written in the languages of the region.[7]

While a number of books were written on social and economic conditions in India,[8] the ambit of social life was largely confined to dress, food, ornaments, condition of

[6]Among works of this trend, special mention may be made of Tara Chand, *Influence of Islam on Indian Culture;* M. Habib, *Mahmud of Ghazni* (1927); R.P. Tripathi, *Some Aspects of Muslim Administration* (1926); *Rise and Fall of the Mughal Empire* (1956).

[7]Particular reference may be made to books dealing with the Deccan; P.T.S. Aiyangar, *History of the Tamils* to *600 A.D.* (1929); K.N. Shivraja Pillai, *Chronology of the Early Tamils* (1932); K.A.N. Shastri's *The Cholas* (1935). Others include A.S. Altekar, *The Rashtrakutas and their Times (1925);* D.G. Ganguly, *The Paramaras* (1934); R.C. Majumdar, *History of Bengal* (1943).

[8]Some of the earliest works of this type are Subba Rao N.S., *Economic and Political Conditions in Ancient India,* (1911, Mysore); B.K. Sarkar, *The Positive Background of Hindu Sociology,* (Allahabad, 1914); Pran Nath, *A Study in the Economic Conditions of Ancient India* (1924); S.K. Das, *Economic History of Ancient India,* (Calcutta 1925)); U.N. Ghosal, *The Agrarian System in Ancient India* (Calcutta 1930); K.M. Ashraf, *Life and Condition of the People of Hindustan* (1935), etc.

women, etc. The narrative method remained, therefore, the main method in these studies as well. It was in the field of modern and medieval history, however, that some fresh ground was broken. R.C. Dutt, in his classic works, *Early British Rule* (1901), *Economic History of India in the Victorian Age* (1903), underlined the growing impoverishment and economic stagnation of India. He related both these to the policies of the British government, and to the structure of Indian society which again, had developed in a lop-sided manner due to British policies in India. R.C. Dutt was followed by a number of others who analysed the structural defects in Indian society, co-relating most of them to the British rule. The most notable among these are Shelvankar, K.T. Shah, R.K. Mookerjee, Rajni Palme Dutt, etc.[9]

A number of nationalist writers during the period had pictured the ancient and medieval periods of Indian society as idyllic periods where there was general prosperity and contentment. Partly as a reaction to this approach, W.H. Moreland in his book *India at the Death of Akbar* (1920) and *From Akbar to Aurangzeb* (1923), adopted a more critical attitude by appraising the economic position of the ruling classes (or what he called the consuming classes) and the masses separately. While Moreland's conclusions—that the Indian peasant remained at the subsistence level despite the external glitter of the Mughal empire, and that his lot has improved under British rule, were challenged, he undoubtedly broke fresh ground in his methodological approach to the study of economic life, such as production, distribution, internal and foreign trade, population etc. He also demonstrated how chronicles, administrative manuals, and the papers of the various European trading companies could be utilized for the purpose.

Archaeology also developed considerably during the

[9]K.S. Shelvankar, *The Problems of India* (London, 1940); K.T. Shah, *Wealth and Taxable Capacity of India* (Bombay 1924); R.K. Mookerji, *Land Problems of India* (London, 1935); R.P. Dutt, *India To-day* (1942).

period. The excavation of Mohen-jo-daro and Harappa dating back to the third millenion B.C. fed nationalist pride by demonstrating the antiquity and independent character of Indian culture. But due to the paucity of funds for archaeology which remained under tight official control, not much work was done in order to establish the sequence of cultural growth in the pre-historic and proto-historic periods.

The Present Phase

The attainment of independence by India and Pakistan in 1947 was followed by the establishment of a large number of departments of history in the new Universities which were set up in different parts of the country. As in the twenties of the century, the establishment of new University departments of history provided a fillip to the growth of historical studies. The newly independent Government of India, conscious of the need of providing a new historical image to its own people and to the world, supported the Universities with funds and other facilities. However, it was sometime before the stream of historical publications by Indian scholars began to swell. That is why, the new phase may be dated more appropriately from about the middle of the fifties. Interest in Indic studies also developed in a number of countries, notably the U.S.A., Japan, Australia etc., while the old traditions of Indological studies were strengthened in countries such as the U.S.S.R., Czechoslovakia, etc. Germany (both east and west), and France maintained their old interest. In Great Britain interest in Indic studies declined markedly, but shows some signs of revival. The geographical expansion of Indian studies, and the growing impact of sociology on social sciences in the West was bound to have an impact on the scope and methodology of historical studies in India. However, this impact has been limited due to two factors. First, most of the countries concentrated their attention mainly on recent developments in India, viz. the nationalist phase and the period which served as a background to it. Secondly, it was not adequately realised in a number of these countries that Indian scholars had both a definite tradition of their own, and their own view of Indian history. These countries either ignored the Indian tradition of history writing or what was worse, uncritically adopted the British view that India was only a conglomeration of hostile regions and communities. Recently, some countries, including the U.S.A. and others such as the U.S.S.R. which have had a tradition of Oriental Studies, have established deeper programmes for the study of Indian history. Their impact on Indian historical studies will be assessed in the course of evaluating different trends in Indian historical writing.

A marked shift of interest from narrative political history to problem oriented studies, and to other fields, especially social and economic history, had taken place in Indian studies during the last 10 to 15 years. It is hardly possible in the limited scope of this paper to evaluate in detail the different trends that have emerged. It would thus be more appropriate to pin-point the methods and the approaches that have been adopted and some of the main centres of study that have emerged.

Archaeology

The rapid growth of archaeology during the past 20-25 years and the development of new methods of dating (Carbon 14) have helped in establishing a definite cultural sequence, both in North and South India. Apart from the central and regional Archaeological Departments of the Government of India, the Universities of Allahabad, Banaras, Aligarh, Patna, Poona, Calcutta, Baroda, etc., have played a notable, part in the growth of archaeology. Archaeological evidence has compelled historians to re-examine the pattern of Aryan settlements in India, and the stages of the growth of Aryan society. The discovery of neolithic and chalcholithic cultures in the Ganga Valley, East India, the Narbada valley and South India has thrown light on the pre-Aryan cultures in these areas.[10] The impact of these cultural developments during the subsequent periods has yet to be studied adequately. With the definite dating of the use of iron in North India to the 11th century B.C., attempts have been made to co-relate the clearing of forests in the Gangetic Valley with the help of the iron tipped plough, to the rise of urban centres and large territorial empires in East India. The rise of Buddhism and other heterodox movements is being studied against this background, greater attention being laid on the role of caste-class and cultural tensions in the growth of these movements.[11]

It should, however, be noted that much of the recent archaeological evidence, particularly that relating to the period after 1500 B.C., is not fully acceptable to those historians who base themselves more on literary texts and tradition, or who consider that archaeological evidence cannot override these sources.

Archaeology has influenced history writing in two other directions as well. First, the archaeological method is sought to be extended in time to the later period, extending upto the 17th or 18th century, to provide more information about the pattern of life, tools and techniques etc., in different parts of India. Second, more attention is being made to excavations in West or Central Asia in order to determine the

[10]Among recent books which have thrown some light on the subject, reference may be made to B. Subba Rao, *The Personality of India* (Baroda 1959); H.E.M. Wheeler, *Early India and Pakistan* (London 1958); S. Piggott, *Pre-historic India* (1962); H.D. Sankalia, *Indian Archaeology To-day* (Asia *1962); The pre-history and Proto-history of India and Pakistan* (Bombay 1963). The journals *Ancient India and Indian Archaeology, a Review,* published by the Archaeological Survey of India, contain up-to-date information on excavations. The Deccan College, Poona has also published a number of monographs. Also G.R. Sharma, *Kausambi* (Allahabad 1960); A. Ghosh, *Rajgriha.* See also Allchin, *The Birth of Indian Civilization* (Penguin 1968).

[11]See in particular, Banerji, *Iron Age in India;* N.G. Wagle, *India at the time of the Buddha* (1968). See also R. Thapar, *Asoka and the Decline of the Mauryan Empire* (Oxford 1963). See also, *Buddhism, the Marxist Approach* by R. Sanskrityayan and others (PPH, Delhi, 1970).

process of economic relations and cultural inter-change between India and these areas. Excavations conducted jointly between Indian scholars and scholars of the area have been started and may yield good dividends. To this end, the strengthening of West and Central Asian Studies and archaeology (including Egyptology and Sumerology) in Indian Universities may be expected.

Ethnographic and field studies, particularly anthropology may be. seen in relation to the above. These studies have led to a better realisation of the importance of the tribes and the tribal forms in the evolution of such institutions as the caste.[12] The spread of different crops to different parts of the country, tools and techniques, land use etc., as factors in social development have also received greater attention from historians. However, unlike both archaeology and sociology, the Indian historian has been comparatively slow to assimilate the techniques of social anthropology and adapt them for his purposes. One reason for this is the absence of departments of Anthropology in most Indian Universities.

Social and Economic History

Not only has interest in social and economic history grown rapidly during the last fifteen years, the entire concept of social history has changed. The focus has shifted from descriptions of dress, food, manners and customs, etc., to the structure of society, inter-relations, and the process of growth. While the new sociological orientation of history in the west has had a definite impact, an equally if not more important factor has been the developments in India since it became an independent country. The setting up of a

[12]The works of J.H. Hutton, *Caste* in *India* (Cambridge 1946), and I. Karve, *Hindu Society, an Interpretation* (Poona 1961), have replaced the earlier compilations such as N.K. Dutta's *Origin and Growth of Caste* in *India.* M.N. Srinivas's *Caste* in *Modern India and other Essays* have also created an interest in the subject.

Planning Commission in order to plan the economic development of India involved economists, social scientists and many others in studying the problems and processes of change in India. It led to a more sustained study of social forms, attitudes, motivations etc., with a view to the 'modernization' of Indian society. Experience of planning in India showed that the peasant was neither as hide-bound or other worldly, nor resistant to change and innovation as some sociologists, such as Max Weber, arid social philosophers and thinkers, Indian and foreign, had been led to believe. Simultaneously, a number of Indian scholars influenced by the Marxist historical methodology, tried to establish the different phases in the growth of Indian society, and the concrete institutions of Indian society, such as caste, the village economy, etc. All these developments have tended to concentrate the attention of a large number of Indian scholars on the concrete problems of Indian society and its growth. Little attempt has been made during this period to seek to draw parallels between developments in Indian society and the west, which was the fashion during the 19th century, and had, to some extent continued in the next phase as well.

Amongst the earliest attempts of Indian scholars to apply the Marxist categories to the study of Indian history were B.N. Dutt's books, *Dialectics of Land Ownership in India* and *Caste and Class in Ancient India.* However, these pioneer studies failed to evoke much response. Nor was there much of a favourable response to S.A. Dange's book in which he postulated the emergence of a slave society in India following the breakdown of the primitive commune of the Aryans. He, thus, argued by implications that India passed through the same phases of development, viz., slavery and feudalism, as in the West. Ashraf,[13] on the other hand, adhered to the view that India had not had any social revolution 'since the first dawn of Indian history' (p.v.). But he did postulate

[13]S.A. Dange, *India from Primitive Communism* to *Slavery* (Bombay, 1949); K.M. Ashraf, *Life and Conditions of the People of Hindustan* (1936).

certain stages within this unchanging society due to the incursion of the Huns and Scythians, and later of the Turks. Although Ashraf did not use the word 'Oriental Society', it was obviously at the back of his mind.

The debate whether India and other Asian countries did or did not pass through the phases of slavery and feudalism has continued to engage the attention of Marxist scholars, both in India and abroad. There has been renewed discussion about Marx's concept of the Asian Mode of Production, especially his concept that the combination of agriculture and rural handicrafts was the chief feature of this mode of production. The concept of an Asian mode of production has not found much favour with Indian Marxist historians, largely because it has been associated with an unchanging pattern of society, from the breakdown of primitive communism to the rise of a capitalist society. Recent studies have tended to show that the village economy was neither as unchanging, or as uniform over different parts of India[14] as 19th century British observers, on whom Marx based his conclusions believed it to be. Amongst Indian Marxist historians, D.D. Kosambi has undoubtedly been preeminent, and has powerfully influenced the thinking of many younger historians. Kosambi's two books, *An Introduction to the Study of Indian History* (1956) and *Culture and Civilization of Ancient India* (1964) are a landmark. Kosambi has argued that there were slaves but no slave society in the early period in India, the non-Aryan *dasa* helots being collectively exploited by the Aryan tribes. Later, with the break up of the Aryan tribal system, (which Kosambi associates with the introduction of the plough and the iron-axe and the establishment of the four-fold system of caste) the

[14]See *The Journal of the Anthropological Society, Man in India*, ed. N.K. Bose See also, Satish Chandra, Some Aspects of the Growth of a Money Economy in India during the 17th Century in *Studies in Asian History* (Asia 1969); Irfan Habib, *Potentialities of Capitalist Development in the Economy of Mughal India*, I.E.H. 29(i), 1969.

dasa helots and Aryan peasants were collectively exploited by the tribal chiefs: "There was neither enough surplus nor enough commodity production to make slavery profitable", he asserts. While Kosambi's conclusions will be, and are a subject of controversy among historians, his greatest contribution to ancient Indian history may be considered his methodology. Kosambi's combination of the Marxist methodology with a concrete study of the Indian reality with the help of archaeology, physical objects, field surveys of ancient trade routes, ethnography, mathematics etc., promises to be one of the most fruitful and productive trends of history writing in India. The works of R.S. Sharma, D.R. Channan, Romila Thapar, L. Gopal, B.N.S. Yadav, etc., may be mentioned in this context.[15]

One of the important problems which has engaged the attention of many historians is the problem of the decline of the classical age in India and the subsequent establishment of Turkish rule in the country. The social background to this has been examined of late by a number of scholars, including Kosambi, R.S. Sharma etc. These scholars speak of the rise of 'feudalism' in India which implied, among other things, the emergence of a powerful class of territorial magnates who disposed of the rural surplus, and became the socially dominant class in India. While the use of the word 'feudalism' continues to arouse controversy, a number of useful studies have been made on this rural aristocracy (called Thakurs, and later zamindars), their character, role in society and rural production etc. A large number of scholars have contributed in his. However, special mention may be made of the works of S. Nurul Hasan,

[15]R.S. Sharma, *Shudras in Ancient India* (1958); *Indian Feudalism* (1965); D.K. Channan, *Slavery in Ancient India* (1960); C. Drekuier, *Kingship and Community in Ancient India* (1968); R. Thapar, *A History of India* (1966); L. Gopal, *The Economic Life of N. India, c. 700-1200* (1965); B.N.S. Yadav in *Land System and Feudalism in Ancient India,* ed. D.C. Sircar (Calcutta 1966), *idem, The Kushanas.*

Irfan Habib, B.R. Grover etc.[16] These studies show that the role of the *zamindars* was crucial in many social, political and cultural developments during the period. Some attempts also have been made to study other aspects such as the position of the official nobility (called *amirs* during Turkish and Mughal rule), the peasantry and its associates (the rural artisans, called *balutedars* in Maharashtra) the merchantile community, trade and banking etc.[17]

These studies have tended to disprove the belief that there was no social change in India from the time of the break-down of the primitive commune till the establishment of British rule in India. The problem of the periodisation of Indian history on the basis of social forms rather than the accidents of the race and religion of the ruling class has, therefore, engaged the attention of Indian scholars. Interest has shifted from the processes of political rule to the impact of empire, such as the Mughal empire, on Indian society and on the processes of growth. Attempts have been made to show that the centralising process in the Mughal empire did lead to the growth of the Indian economy, the development of a money economy and of large towns which became centres of trade and manufacture, the emergence of a national market in many commodities, the weakening of

[16]S.N. Hasan, *The Position of the Zamindars in Mughal India, IESHR,* 1964, also in ed. R.H. Frykenburg, *Land Distribution and Social Structure in India,* (Wisconsin, Univ. 1968); S. Chandra, Introduction to, *Parties and Politics at the Mughal Court* (1959); I. Habib, *Agrarian System of the Mughal Empire* (Asia 1962); B.R. Grover, Nature of Land Rights in Mughal India, *IESHR,* I. No. 12, 1963; N.A. Siddiqui, *Mughal Revenue System* (Aligarh . 1970). In some of these works, the word 'feudal' is avoided, though social relations are analysed on a class basis. Among the early writers to use it in the Indian context was W.C. Smith, Lower Class Rising in the Mughal Empire, *Islamic Culture* (1946).

[17]M. Athar Ali, *The Mughal Nobility under Aurangzeb,* (Asia 1966); S.B.P. Nigam, *Nobility during the Sultanat Period* (1968); A.R. Kulkarni, *Land Rights in Maharashtra.* For recent Soviet writings on the subject, see L.B. Alayev, Soviet historians on Indian Feudalism, *Proceedings Seminar on Problems of Social and Economic History,* Aligarh, 1968 (mimeo).

village self-sufficiency, etc. These studies are necessarily tentative. Some attempt has been made to use the statistical method in studying economic trends, particularly in the field of foreign trade. The work of Balkrishna earlier, and of Tapan Raychaudhuri and K.N. Chaudhuri in this field are some notable examples of this approach.[18] But it is generally conceded that a great deal of work will have to be done, using the tools of modem economic analysis such as statistical study or quantification, proceeding on a regional and local basis, before any definite ctmc1usions can be drawn.

The attempt to study social processes and institutions, and their internal relationship has drawn the historian to the intensive examination of land grants, inscriptions, revenue, administrative and judicial documents; coins etc. Many of these were known earlier but were hardly utilised by social historians, being used largely for political and chronological history. From the 16th century an enormous addition has been made to the historical sources by tapping the records in the various archival offices, such as Allahabad, Hyderabad, Rajasthan, etc., or collecting family papers, as in Maharashtra.

The growing interaction between historians and the social scientists has resulted in attempts by the former to adopt and adapt the tools and techniques of the latter. For example, some historians have tried to form 'models' in order to examine the economic processes of earlier societies. It cannot be said that studies of this type have been conspicuously successful. Few historians have had the necessary experience of model building, nor the detailed statistical information needed for it. (Economists, on the other hand, tend to be both ignorant of, and impatient of the historical method). Similar problems have arisen in the field of sociology, anthropology etc. The chief attempt, therefore, has been to study a limited segment amenable to statistical study. A fair number of monograph have been written on

[18]Balakrishna, *The East India Co.* T. Raychaudhuri, *Jan Company in Coromondal* (1962); K.N. Chaudhuri, The Foreign Trade of India in the 17th Century *(IESHR).*

agriculture, trade (both foreign and internal), industry and labour, handicrafts, communications, money, banking and prices, population, national income etc.[19] These confine themselves to the last 100 or 150 years.

It was generally held till recently that in the absence of documents and reliable statistical information, studies of this type could hardly be extended to the earlier period, (with the partial exception of foreign trade for which the records of the various European trading companies could be drawn upon). This assumption has had to be modified partially with the discovery of detailed records on agricultural production, prices etc., from the last quarter of the 17th century available in the Rajasthan State Archives. Records of a similar nature are found in Hyderabad, as well as in Maharashtra, Allahabad, Patna etc. The historian has also become aware of such data as family records, accounts of business houses etc., for the study of social and economic trends. The use of these documents entail a new methodology in as much as they represent broken time-series for which the normal methodology of economics is insufficient. Something beyond 'the well known economic tools' are needed, and that perhaps can only be historical training and imagination. This is important even for the 19th century for which a good deal of continuous statistical data is available, for the unreliability of much of the data is well known to historians.

Study of Broad Movements

The growth of the social and economic studies outlined above have a wide-ranging effect on history writing in such diverse fields as political and cultural history. Thus, some of the problems in the political field, which are being investigated are as follows:

[19]The list of these works is very large. For an excellent bibliography, reference may be made to note prepared by the Dharma Kumar, *Recent Research* in *Indian Economic History.*

(i) Did Indian society (and/or the Mughal empire) have the potential for, or was it on the verge of a capitalist revolution which was aborted by the British?
(ii) Did the British rulers try deliberately to thwart India's economic development, and ruin its handicrafts? At any rate, did India develop economically under British rule, or did it stagnate or even suffer a decline? (Alternatively, can we determine different phases of these developments?)
(iii) Did the Indian national movement represent a struggle between elites, foreign and indigenous, or did it involve the interests of the broad masses?
(iv) Was the partition of India the result of conscious British policy or was it rooted in Indian society and culture? etc.

It is obvious that questions like these cannot be answered with the type of documentary material i.e., official notes, memoranda, etc., which has been the main stay of the historians so far. While there is no dearth of source material, and the ease with which it can be availed of (not to mention the number of scholarships available on the subject), only a few scholars ventured in the area of field studies, or tried to tap indigenous local material. A number of books have appeared which have either helped in opening up the field for fresh studies, or which has sought to apply new sociological, ethnological or statistical methods to old themes. Thus Tapan Raychaudhuri studied society in Bengal in the 15th and 16th centuries.[20] S.C. Mishra of Baroda has studied the nature of the Muslim community in Gujarat during the medieval times, the manner of its growth, and its relations with other sections of society.[21] Satish Chandra and a

[20]T. Raychaudhuri, *Bengal under Akbar and Jahangir* (2nd revised edn., 1969). Also on this topic, see A. Karim, *Social History of the Muslims* in *Bengal (down to 1538)* (Dacca 1959); A. Chatterji, *Bengal in the Reign of Aurangzeb* (Calcutta 1967). See also L. Sunder, *Caste Instability* in *Moghal India* (Seoul, Korea, n.d.)

[21]S.C. Misra, *The Muslim Community* in *Gujarat.*

number of others at the Aligarh University raised the question of the. social factors in the disintegration of the Mughal empire. Moving away from personalities and from the theme of discord between Hindus and Muslims, some of them tried to co-relate the political and administrative crisis to the contradictions within the ruling class (zamindars and nobility), the contradictions in the working of specific institutions as the system of land assignment (the jagirdaii system), and the clash of interests between the ruling classes and the peasantry[22]. The further problem whether the social and political structure of the times was a barrier to growth has resulted in a number of studies. Some of these have tried to draw upon statistical data for the 17th and 18th centuries in regional archives such as the Rajasthan State Archives.[23]

Work on the British impact on India seems to have been centred more in London than in India so far. The University Department of History, Delhi University, had started a project on this, but nothing on this subject has been published-so far. A number of studies have appeared on the growth of education, administration, foreign policy etc. In some recent studies, an attempt has been made to investigate the impact of British revenue policies on different segments of Indian society. S. Gopal's *The Permanent Settlement of Bengal,* Ranjit Guha's *Rule of Property in Bengal,* are examples of this approach. A more descriptive approach has, however, been

[22]This topic is scattered in a number of books. See Satish Chandra, *Parties and Politics at the Mughal Court* (Aligarh, 1959); I. Habib, *Agrarian System of Mughal India* (Asia 1962); *idem.* Agrarian Causes of the Fall of the Mughal Empire, *Enquiry,* Nos. 2, 3 (1959, 1960) etc.

[23]See, B.N. Ganguly, ed. *Contributions to Economic History* (Delhi 1964); Satish Chandra and S.P. Gupta, The Jaipur Pargana Records, *IESHR,* III, 3, 1960; S.N. Hasan, etc., "The pattern of Agricultural production in the territories of Amber" *Proceedings I.H.C* XXVIII 1066; S.N. Hasan etc., "Prices of Food Grains in the Territories of Amber (1650-1750), *Proceedings of I.H.C.* XXIX, etc. Work on these revenue records is being carried on at the Universities of Aligarh and Rajasthan.

adopted by B.B. Misra in his book, *The Indian Middle Class* (London, 1961). Gadgil's *Origin of Modern Indian Business Class* (1959) is also a descriptive but useful study. Some attention has been paid recently to the impact of British policies on the economic growth of rural India. Reference may be made on this score to Walter A. Neele's *Economic Changes in Rural India* (Yale University 1962); Dharma Kumar, *Land and Caste in South India* (1965). Binay Chaudhuri on Bengal; A.V. Raman Rao on Andhra Pradesh, R.D. Choksey and Ravindra Kumar on Western India have also touched upon this problem.[24] The intellectual background to British agrarian policies in India has been studied by Eric Stokes in his book *The English Utilitarians and India* (1959).

A great deal of attention has understandly been devoted to the social, intellectual and political processes of the rise of the national movement in India. The writings on the subject are too large to be surveyed been cursively in the present paper. Leaving aside the descriptive studies and broad surveys, two trends are discernible. Emphasis is placed in a number of studies to elitist conflicts in Indian society as a major factor in the growth of Indian nationalism. R.L. Park's *Leadership and Political Institutions in India* (Princeton 1959); J.N. Broomfield's *Elite Conflict in a Plural Society* (Oxford 1967); and Anil Seal's *The Emergence of Indian Nationalism* (Oxford 1970) may be regarded as good examples of this trend. The second trend of thinking emphasises the growing social and economic imbalance in Indian society due to British policies, and, as a result, a deepening conflict between the interests of the broad masses and British vested interests. This trend finds reflection in the writings of many Indian scholars, who are sometimes dubbed 'nationalist' by the representatives of the first trend. Recent books on the subject

[24]Apart from Dharma Kumar's bibliography referred to above, see J. Adams and Wallimade, Studies of Village Economies, a Bibliographical Essay *IESHER* VII, 1, 1970. See also the work of A. Guha on Assam.

Lavkovsky's *Capitalism in India* (Eng. ed. 1966) is a general survey of economic trends in India under British rule.

include A.B. Desai's *Social Background* to *the Rise of the Indian National Movement*, Tara Chand, *History of the Freedom Movement in India* (Delhi 1961, 1967), Bipin Chandra, *The Rise and Growth of Economic Nationalism in India* (Delhi 1966).

The growth of interest in the social processes of Indian society before the advent of the British has led to the study of social, political, religious and intellectual movements on an inter disciplinary basis. Much of the new thinking on these issues is confined to Seminars and learned journals. Buddhism and Jainism and the various heterodox movements, including the rise of the Bhakti and Sufi movements have provided one focus of study. The oppositional movements, such as those of the Jats, Sikhs, Marathas, Afghans, etc. have provided a second focus. Meanwhile, a large number of works have continued to be produced, in English and in various modern Indian languages, dealing with the doctrinal or philosophical aspects of important religious movements such as Buddhism, Jainism, the Bhakti movement, the Sufi movement, modern movements such as the Brahmo Samaj, Arya Samaj, Ramakrishna's movement, the Wahabi movement etc. While some of these do provide an insight, or help to unravel intellectual inter-connections, most of them follow the traditional descriptive method. An attempt to study religious movements on a sociological basis has been made in N.C. Wagle's *Society at the time of the Buddha* (1968). SK Day's *Vaishnavism*, a classic in its field, also touches on this aspect.

While a number of books have been written on the growth of mathematics, astronomy, medicine, chemistry and botany[25] in India, no attempt has so far been made to appraise and

[25]Apart from the work of Colebrooke on the *Algebra, Arithmetic and Mensuration of Brhmagupta and Bhaskara* (London 1817), and E. Cordiar's *Etude sur la Medicine Hindous* (Paris 1894), recent works on the subject are P.C. Ray, *History of Hindu Chemistry* (2 vols. Calcutta 1902, 1925); G.N. Mukhopadhyaya, *History of Indian Medicine* (3 vols. Calcutta 1923); Jean Filliozat *Medical Doctrines in India* (Paris 1949); Zimmer *Hindu Medicines* (1948) etc. For a fuller bibliography see, A. *Concise History of Science in India*, ed. S.N. Sen. (in press).

evaluate the growth of science as a whole, its intellectual inter-connections, and its relationship with society. The Indian History Congress had drawn attention to this long back. However, it was only in 1963 that the Ministry of Education and the National Institute of the Sciences of India set up a Commission consisting of scientists and historians to do the spade work in the matter. The Commission decided to prepare bibliographies of the books and manuscripts on the subject available in Indian libraries, to publish a brief monograph on science in India, and to print the more important texts. *A bibliography of Sanskrit works on Astronomy and Mathematics* by S.N. Sen (Calcutta 1965) has been published. The bibliography on Medieval Sciences in India is due to be published soon, and monographs on individual aspects have been planned.

A limited amount of work has been done during this period on historical geography. While D.C. Sircar's *Studies in the Geography of Ancient and Medieval India* (Delhi 1960) is based on literary and epigraphic information, S.N. Hasan and Moonis Raza at the Aligarh University prepared detailed maps of India under Akbar by combining literary sources such as the *Ain-i-Akbari* with the study of terrain, geographical regions etc. Further work on historical geography of the medieval period is being continued at the Aligarh Muslim University.

Some study has been made of the economic conditions obtaining in the seas around India, and the role of ocean routes, techniques of ship building etc. Apart from R.K. Mookerji's pioneer study on *Indian Shipping* (1912) which is now dated, the only recent work has been Hourani's *Arab Sea-fearing in the Indian Ocean in Ancient and Early Medieval Times* (Princeton, 1951).

Regional and Local History (Including Tribal History)

Interest in the study of regional history has grown along with the growth of nationalism which had stimulated a sense of pride in local history and culture. But in most cases, regional history had continued at a lower level the tale of the rise and fall of kings and dynasties. The study of the social and economic institutions and processes has led to a clearer realisation that in a country of India's size and complexity, there are bound to be considerable regional variations, and that a study of these regional variations is essential for making meaningful generalisations for the country as a whole. For instance, it is realised that the typical nuclear type of village economy did not exist in outlying areas, such as Assam or Kerala, or even in some parts of Rajasthan. Land rights differed from region to region and sometimes even within a region. Regional history has, therefore, come to imply a concentrated study of the social, economic and political forms in a limited area. For instance, studies for the Vidarbha region, or some parganas in the former states of Jaipur, Marwar etc., or the Mughal subah of Allahabad have been chosen by students as research theses in a number of Universities.

The various tribal forms and their interaction with Hindu caste society has hardly been studied so far. Anthropologists and geographers suggest a steady process of the retreat of the tribes into jungles and less fertile tracts and their assimilation into caste society. Many medieval zamindars, in fact, appear to be tribal in nature. The persistence of large tribal tracts, interplay of caste and tribe and its impact on political and administrative forms has recently begun to interest Indian historians. Some limited efforts have been made to study the history of aboriginal tribes, such as the Meenas of Rajasthan or the manner in which migratory tribes disintegrate and lead to the emergence of zamindaris.

In the absence of written records, different methods are being adopted for studying tribal history. The study of tribal folk lore and traditions, of geographical place names associated with particular tribes and castes (e.g. Gujar in North-West India), routes of internal migration etc., are some of the methods which have been adopted.

It will thus be seen from the foregoing survey that the period from 1950 or 1955 onwards has been a period of vigorous growth of historical sciences in India. Indian scholars have been able to assimilate and adapt many of the sophisticated techniques of analysis developed in the west during the period. The methods and constructs adopted by the Indian historians have relevance for a wider context than the Indian sub-continent alone. It is now recognised that the Asian and African countries had their own social forms, modes of conduct and inter-relationship, and their own processes of assimilation and change. The historical processes in India would be more meaningful for a comparative study of similar processes in these countries, since they have many features in common and had many points of contact with Indian in the past.

5

THE USE OF HISTORY

The purpose or use of historical writing has varied, from age to age and from region to region. The Greek historians glorified and upheld the institutions (including slavery) in the Greek city states, ascribing different virtues to them, e.g., stoicism as in Sparta, or love of democracy as in Athens etc. The ancient Indian concept, as gleaned from the great epics, the Ramayana and the Mahabharata, was predominantly moral—of the victory of good over evil, of the upholding of the path of righteousness *(dharma)*, and of the fulfilment of duty by all, unmindful of the consequences or hope of reward. Kings, warriors, men and women were, therefore, the instruments of a higher destiny. Simultaneously, there was the tradition of small states whose object was material gain, with power resting in the hands of a ruler who was guided not so much by the *Dharmashasims*, as by considerations of polity *(raj-niti)*. These two traditions ran side by side, and shaped both conduct and legend writing *(itihas)*.

Neither the Christian nor the Arab view of the purpose of history was strikingly different from the Hindu traditional view. However, the Church held pride of place in the Christian view of history since the Church alone was competent to guide the people in matters of morality or sin, or prepare men for entry into the Kingdom of Heaven. The Arab writing of history was aimed at glorifying Islam and those who laid gown their lives for its advancement. The spiritual and the secular conquests went hand in hand. This may explain the dual character of much of Arab and subsequent history writing; the glorification of Islam was meant to impress the common man and further firm up his belief, but the empire which was even more crucial depended on the ruling classes, the Sultan, his ministers, advisers, administrators, etc. The maintenance and further expansion of the Islamic empire thus became both a proof of the power of Islam *(ghalba-i-Islam),* and th e means of sustaining the faith. This also implied a firm putting down of all heterodox movements which might create a schism in the community, and hence weaken the empire.

History, therefore, had to be used to proclaim the glory of Islam, strengthen the empire or the states which succeeded, and sternly put down all heterodox movements. These are fully reflected in the writings of the 14th century Indian historian, Ziauddin Barani, Barani not only calls history the twin brother of the science of *hadis,* "it is also the province of history to relate the circumstances of the age of the Prophet and his Companions and to explain and analyse that which strengthens the heart and confidence of both ancient and modem members of the Muslim community." Since Barani says there is no written proof of historical tradition, readers could only trust the historian himself and that only if he was an orthodox Muslim. Of course, Barani considered that history taught by example and would benefit the Sultans, wazirs and nobles, but not "the evil, the base, the low-born", who had no use for history.

What about the more secular view which, as we have argued, was reflected in the *Arthashastra?* It would be wrong to think that such a view made its appearance only with the introduction of western historiography by the British in the 19th century. By. the time Abul Fazl wrote his books, the *Akbarnama* and the *Ain-i-Akbari,* the central problem no longer was to what precise extent Islamic laws, customs, traditions could or could not be followed in India, but the manner in which the prosperity of the realm could be increased, and its foundations strengthened. And the lesson Abul Fazl drew was that it implied the ruler making no distinction between votaries of different religions, and seeking the active support and co-operation of all sections, especially all sections of the ruling elites—Rajputs, Afghans and Mughals—in the task of administration.

That history writing no longer reflected or could be used by narrow orthodox or racial groups was reflected by two developments during the 17th century: first, the appearance of history books written by Hindus (lshwardas, Bhimsen, Mehta Nainsi's *Khyat* and *Vigat,* etc.) and the discontinuation of official history writing by Aurangzeb. The latter step was perhaps more than a measure of economy. It reflected Aurangzeb's inability to mould history (as also poetry) writing for his own orthodox purposes, and hence to discourage it as far as possible.

The tradition of nationalist history writing in India and its use of history are well-known. It was aimed at creating a sense of pride in India's past in order to compensate for the low esteem in which the country and its culture was held by the colonial rulers (as distinct from the rare breed called the Indologists). Simultaneously, it tried to justify India's claim for freedom by arguing that the wherewithals of the qualities or institutions considered desirable, e.g. democracy, individualism, national unity had existed in the country *before* the arrival of the British, and any weakening was in large measure due to the influence of the British.

This uncritical and somewhat romantic view of history had obviously to yield once India became free. But the change has been accompanied by a sea-change in the attitude to history in the west. The 19th century view of history was, basically, to justify and rationalise the European domination of the world, (i) by emphasizing certain intrinsic superior qualities of the West, i.e., rationalism, individualism, spirit of enterprise, humanism or secularism etc., and (ii) the lack of these superior qualities by the black, brown or yellow races or the peoples inhabiting the Afro-Asian land mass. With decolonization following the Second World War, and the growth of new centres of power outside Europe, the 19th century view of history could no longer be maintained.

How is world history being used today and to what use history is sought to be utilised in history? We cannot try to carry out a review of western history writing in the limited scope here, except to say that by far and large, the Eurocentric view of history has not really been abandoned, despite a definite trend of studying other non-European civilizations in a more sympathetic manner, and assessing the impact of the west in a more modest manner. Also, in place of empires, peoples, their lives and thought, behaviour etc. are being given greater importance.

In the above context, to what use is history being used, or sought to be used in India? Government desires, and it is possible to sympathise with its point of view, that history should teach love for the country, respect for the various people who made India their home and their contributions to the fabric of Indian civilization. At a second remove, government also desires that the unity and stability of India, democratic values, secularism and a rational temper, and national integration should also be upheld by the historian. Since all these are closely related to the imperative need of India forging ahead as a united polity, the ideas of government are shared by many historians. The question is, how to uphold these ideas without doing violence to or distorting history?

As is well known, every age puts its own questions to the past. Hence, the past has to be constantly re-interpreted. Such a process is always attended by pitfalls and controversy. The specific questions which the historian has to raise today are related to India's unity and development, as also its place in the world comity, i.e., its contribution to the growth of human civilization, and the factors responsible for its phases of stagnation and growth. This has made it necessary to determine the phases of development of Indian society, and the factors of growth or lack of it in each phase. The question immediately arises whether India passed through the same phases of slavery and feudalism as Europe did upto the 15th century, and whether it had any potentialities of developing a capitalist system independently? Also, the precise extent to which colonial rule aided or retarded such a development. While these questions are still very much in the realm of controversy, it has led to a more intensive study of social structures and developments in different parts of the world. To that extent, the intense phase of emphasizing the "uniqueness" of India, and hence eschewing any comparative studies is passing.

The problem of development has also given a new dimension to Indian historical studies. With the rise of linguistic states, each state or linguistic cultural area is seeking the roots of its cultural identity. Thus, there has been a renewed interest in the growth of regional studies. The question has also been raised, within regions and between regions, why certain regions/areas, sections/communities develop/adapt more rapidly to the needs of modern society and technology than others? These are questions which can only be answered on the basis of detailed socio-cultural, economic, and a whole host of related factors. Not only regional, but local, urban and village studies have drawn sustenance from this line of study.

Questions have also been raised about the roots of Indian democracy, the Indian understanding of secularism, the role of science and technology and its impact on society; in other words, the precise balance between the spiritual and the temporal.

The new historical studies are also intended to create a spirit of critical, rational understanding of the nature of Indian society and of its functioning and growth. The earlier concerns of unity and integrity have not been discarded, but are seen in a broader perspective of ebb and flow.

Thus, history is no longer seen as representing a unilinear

line of development, or progress or whatever word one likes to use for progression. The movement of history is a much more complex one, needing a combination of macro and micro studies and the insight provided by diverse disciplines. We have only begun this arduous march in India.

6

NEHRU THE HISTORIAN

In his last work, *The Discovery of India,* written in the Ahmadnagar Fort prison in 1944, Nehru says:

"I cannot write academically of past events in the manner of a historian or scholar. I have not the knowledge or equipment or training; nor do I possess the mood for that kind of work."

Was this merely Nehru's modesty, and we should take serious note of Nehru as an historian? Or should we take his words at face value, and consider his major works, *Glimpses of World History* (1934, 35) and his *Autobiography* (first published 1936), and the *Discovery,* more as milestones in Nehru's intellectual development than serious history?

It was with these ideas in mind that I reopened the pages of books I had read during the course of the national struggle. My first impression was that despite his modesty, Nehru was, if not contemptuous, impatient with the historians of his times (with some exceptions, Gibbon being one of them). He makes it plain that for him history did not mean heaping facts upon facts in an impersonal, lifeless manner. This obviously was a departure from the German school of historiography which was still fashionable in those days. The business of the historian, it was believed, was not to interpret or establish linkages, but to present facts which would speak for themselves. That was not the way Nehru saw history. For him, the past was integrally related to the present and the future. "... the past is ever with us and all that we are and have comes from the past," he says. "We are its products and we live immersed in it. Not to understand it and feel it as something living within us is not to understand the present."

For Nehru history was thus "a living process", a continuum linked to the present, and "influencing the future, partly determining it." However, he refused to accept the philosophy of determinism which is often confused with Marxism. Nehru admired Marx for his scientific outlook on history but he did not feel sure that the complexity of human life and history could be framed in any hard and fast rules and systems. He was drawn to the Marxian "dynamic concept" of history and felt that it left room for an individual's contribution to the process of social change. However, social forces remained more important than individuals. While rejecting the concept of history providing lessons to teach, Nehru felt it was possible to learn from history by "trying to discover the forces that move it."

But there is also a psychological aspect to Nehru's approach to history. He explains that all his life he had trained himself for action. But life in prison was "actionless". For Nehru, history was both "imagined action", and a preparation for future action. This also makes his approach to history intensely personal. As he explains in the *Discovery:*

"Inevitably, my approach will often be a personal one; how the idea grew in my mind, what shapes it took, how it influenced me and affected my action. There will also be some entirely personal experiences which have nothing to do with the subject in its wider aspects, but which coloured my mind and influenced my approach to the whole problem."

Thus, Nehru, the action-oriented individual, and Nehru, the historian and student of social change, constantly intrude on each other. That precisely is the charm of Nehru's historical writing. Also its limitation.

The essence of history, for Nehru was change. He says in the

Glimpses, "What is history, indeed, but a record of change? And if there had been very few changes in the past, there would have been little of history to write."

Nehru traces this process of change in all its aspects—social, economic, intellectual, cultural in various periods and climes. Part of the "voyage of discovery" he undertook was to link himself with the past, and to place India in time. This implied a rebuttal of the highly Eurocentric view of history which was then the fashion in the West, and which even H.G. Wells had not been able to escape in his *Outline of World History.* Tracing the ascent of man, and the antiquity of civilization preceding the Greco-Roman civilization, Nehru finds much in common between Greece, Iran, India and China. "Greeks and Indians and Chinese and Iranians were always seeking a religion and a philosophy of life which affected all their activities and which was intended to produce an equilibrium and a sense of harmony." This, he says, was reflected in every aspect of life—in literature, art and institutions, and produced "a sense of proportion and completeness." That is why Nehru rejected the notion of a fundamental difference between the Orient and the Occident. He found it "vague and unscientific, without much basis in fact." The difference was really based on the industrialization of Europe and America in which respect Asia was backward. "This industrialization is new in the world's history", and he presaged that as it spread, it would "change the world more than anything else has done."

This comfortable notion of automatic progress, once nations were free and could order their affairs, dates Nehru, since it preceded the growing realization of limits of development, the growth of new forms of technological neocolonialism, and the sharply growing disparity between and within nations. But his attempt to see World History not within the framework of the West, and the conclusion he drew that as an Indian he was the inheritor not only of all that India achieved but what man had achieved anywhere in the world, were important conclusions. Nehru's approach to history was not national, but international in the true sense of the word. It was, in a sense, a continuation of the Indian concept of *"Vasudhaiva kutumbakam."*

Revolutions—the French, the American, the Russian and all the other in the offing, attracted Nehru. He did not see in them a break with the past, rather the result of long processes of evolution. Also, he was thrilled to see the movement of tens and hundreds of thousands of people. For Nehru, the people were not only the stuff of history, he felt a unique empathy with them. They did not move at the bidding of agitators, but represented unconscious social forces. History did not necessarily move in the direction aimed at by conscious actors: there were unintended consequences in history. "Imperialism produces nationalism." But this was hardly novel. For Nehru was merely echoing the Hegelian-Marxian idea of "thesis-antithesis" or of action producing its own reaction. But it induces in Nehru a sense of "mystery" and he wonder about human affairs. He candidly confesses: "Often as I look at this world, I have a sense of mysteries of unknown depths." Thus, a spirit of wonder is reflected in Nehru's writings. He talks of unconscious "race memory", and of the "complex and mysterious personality of India", some aspects of which he could not fathom.

After his aerial survey of the world in the *Glimpses,* in the *Discovery* Nehru comes back home to India. There is much in India that Nehru finds exhilarating and oppressive. He thunders:

"India must break with much of her past and not allow it to dominate the present. Our lives are encumbered with the dead wood of this past; all that is dead and has served its purpose has to go", he warns. "But that does not mean a break with, or a forgetting of the vital and life-giving in that past."

Nehru searches avidly for the deep springs of the vital, life-giving source which was the secret of the remarkable continuity of India's civilization. Nehru traces it in the unity and diversity of India, its deep tolerance and efforts to synthesize divergent elements, its flexibility and adaptability that helped in the absorption of foreign elements, its intellectual freedom and the strength of its social institutions. Nehru places the first synthesis between the Aryans and the non-Aryans, the last, the result of Turko-Afghan incursions during Mughal rule. Between the 6th and 10th centuries A.C., India passed through a phase of sterility where the original impulse seems to dry up.

India became more and more insular mentally as also in her foreign contacts. It was this outlook which led to the decline of science, and India's conquest by the foreigners. The Turko-Afghan invasions gave a new challenge. The foreigners became rapidly Indianized, and a new synthesis was arrived at in various fields. The sufi and bhakti saints played a role in this, though he makes manifest his reservations about mysticism: it was "not a rigorous discipline of the mind but a surrender of mental faculties and living in a sea of emotional experience."

It is easy to pick holes in some of Nehru's arguments, and to say that he either over-estimated the "essential unity" of India before the arrival of the British or did not adequately understand the forces of religion. In fact, it is possible to argue that the partition of the country, carried out under foreign auspices, does not vitiate any of the arguments of Nehru about the essential cultural unity of Hind-Pakistan.

Nehru is not on equally strong grounds when he traces the evolution of caste, and bases the stability of Indian life on village panchayats, caste and the joint family. A lot of work has been done on these aspects since Nehru wrote. The facile assumption that the panchayats continued to function uninterruptedly, and that wars and other developments had no impact on the tenor of village life is no longer accepted. There were phases in the development of society in which the villages were deeply affected. Caste has been linked more closely to the evolution of society in ancient India rather than a process of fushion between Aryans and non-

Aryans. Nor is Nehru's belief that growth of industrialization and education in India would erode the caste system been borne out. Yet we are far from arriving at a consensus regarding the role of social institutions in the growth and preservation of Indian civilisation and culture.

Not all that Nehru has written can stand the test of time. But the essence of what Nehru has said—the joy of life in Indian civilization as depicted in song, dance, sculptures, music—even works on sex; our early ancestors' spirit of enquiry in all aspects of life and beyond, and their bold speculations, the combination of spritualism with materialism, the advancement of science and the gradual atrophying of the critical faculties on account of the growth of religious obscurantism and growing insularity of mind and cutting off of outside contacts are aspects which engross the reader and still pose a challenge to historical scholarship.

To be able to hold the attention of the readers almost half a century or more after the works were written is no mean tribute to Nehru. It is something for which any academic historian would be proud. What Nehru tries to inculcate through his writings is above all a sense of history. Ignoring of history "produced a vagueness of outlook, a divorce from life as it is, a credulity, a wooliness of mind where fact was concerned." On the other hand, what Nehru wanted to achieve through history and the scientific method was "a greater appreciation of facts, a more critical faculty, a weighing of evidence, a refusal to accept tradition merely because it is tradition." This challenge persists.

7

THE INDIAN NATIONAL MOVEMENT AND CONCEPT OF SECULARISM

"India cannot cease to be one nation, because people belonging to different religions live in it. ... If the Hindus believe that India should be peopled only by Hindus, they are living in a dreamland. The Hindus, the Mahomedans, the Parsis and the Christians who have made India their country are fellow-countrymen, and they will have to live in it only for their own interests. In no part of the world are one nationality and one religion synonymous terms; nor has it ever been so in . India."

M.K. Gandhi, *Hind Swaraj* (1908)

"I am convinced that the future government of free India must be secular in the sense that the government will not associate itself directly with any religious faith but will give freedom to all religious functions .... any government of India which infringes this rule of religious freedom takes upon itself a grave responsibility ... "

Jawaharlal Nehru, to Ghanshyam Singh Gupta, 1945, *Selected Works*, XIV, p. 102.

These two quotations bring out the two major concerns of India's leadership during the course of the national movement, viz., the nature of India's nationhood, and the basis on which its unity could be preserved. It was obvious from the outset that unlike western countries such as Britain, France, and later Italy and Germany, which had emerged as nation-states, India was inhabited by people speaking diverse languages and professing diverse faiths. This plurality which had always been accepted in India, and which is referred to in the pillar inscriptions of Ashoka, asking people of one faith not to interfere with someone else's faith, was the basis on which British rulers and administrative historians denied that India was a *nation,* and thereby denied it the right to exist as an independent, united *state.*

Sir Syed only echoed these views when he said that India was "peopled with different nations." "Consider the Hindus alone. The Hindus of our Province (modem U.P.), the Bengalis of the East, and the Mahrattas of the Deccan, do not form one nation," he said in a speech at Meerut.[1] "The concept of the Muslim *qaum* of India, irrespective of linguistic differences, forming one nation was a later development. For Sir Syed, the Muslims were a numerical minority which needed safeguards from the British. But these alone were not enough; the Muslims also needed the goodwill and co-operation of the major community, the Hindus. Thus, Sir Syed was not really the advocate of a two-nation theory as he had often been made out to be.

During the early phase, the concept of a break-up of India either on a linguistic or religious basis was unthinkable for any section of leaders. The concept of secularism arose in this context. It sought to mediate between the interests of various communities, and postulated a united Indian state where the followers of any religion would neither be favoured nor discriminated against. Thus, unlike Europe, secularism in India arose not so much in the process of conflict with organized religion, as an attempt to unify the followers of different religious faiths in their struggle against the British by

[1]A.M. Zaidi (ed.) *Evolution of Muslim Political Thought in India,* New Delhi, S. Chand, 1975, i. p, 38.

making it the premise of a united free India. This has to be borne in mind while analyzing the nature of the concept of secularism in India. Simultaneously, Indian cultural traditions and historical experience cannot be lost sight of.

The concept of secularism, as it evolved in Europe since the Renaissance, comprised principally of three strands:

(i) Religious toleration including the right to publicly practice or preach religious ideas and beliefs;

(ii) Equal access to public offices, including the highest, to votaries of all religions.

(iii) Secular education including the concepts of humanism and rationalism, and struggle against all forms of obscurantism, super-naturalism, irrationalism, etc.

The concept that religion should be treated essentially as a personal affair and concern itself only with the spiritual and moral welfare of the individual, leaving all aspects of secular life to the state developed only by the middle of the 19th century. Even then, there was a bitter struggle in many countries, such as France, Italy, etc., regarding the extent to which education should be under the *control* of the state. While the control of the state over education has increased, the *influence* of the Church shows little signs of diminishing.

In India, the impact of the concept of secularism was seen first in the field of education. The Wood's 'Education Despatch of 1854', often called "The Magna Carta of Indian Education", laid down that the education provided by government should be "exclusively secular."

For the nationalist leaders of the times, "secular education" was a safeguard against the Christian missionary institutions which then dominated the educational scene.[2] Western education, which was a synonym for secular education, was also considered a liberating force. As Gokhale said

[2]"... at that time, the Mission institutions maintained four times as many pupils as the Government schools ... Schools under Hindu or Muslim establishments by contrast were few." (D.E. Smith, *India as a Secular State,* OUP, London & Bombay, 1963, p. 342).

in 1906: "The greatest work of western education in the present state of India is not so much the encouragement of learning as the liberation of the Indian mind from the thraldom of old world ideas, and the assimilation of all that is highest and best in the life and thought and character of the West."[3]

The struggle for secular education soon merged with another struggle—the struggle for social reforms in order to establish a rational society based on the principles of equality and justice. This implied removing the worst iniquities of the caste system, improving the position of women, etc.

Both the struggle for secular education and social reforms were tied up with the question of a united, free India. The early nationalist leaders who had faith in the democratic bona fides of the British, were convinced that once they had been able to purge the Indian society of its age old superstitions and backwardness, the British Government would readily agree to a free India, even though such a development may take centuries.

Thus, the struggle for secularism had three interconnected aspects—the realization of a united, free India; modern secular education, and an egalitarian society based on justice. Although the precise formulation of these objectives varied from time to time, according to political exigencies as also the value system of the leaders, there was remarkable continuity in the objectives themselves. This element of continuity must not be lost sight of even though we may designate the early phase as the phase of liberal secularism, the Gandhian phase as one of sarvodaya secularism, and the period of Nehru as one of radical secularism.[4] Also, each

[3]*Speeches of Gopal Krishna Gokhale,* ed. G.A. Natesan, Madras, 1916, p.279.

[4]Ravinder Kumar, "The Secular Culture of India" in Occasional Papers on History and Society, Nehru Memorial Museum & Library, N,). XVIII, November 1984 *(mimeo).*

phase was a phase of intense controversy, and the phases over-lapped, with earlier attitudes persisting side by side with new ones.

In 1905, the Congress demanded "a beginning in the direction of free primary education." In 1906, the Congress defined national education as a system of education—literary, scientific and technical—which was "suited to the requirements of the country, on national lines, and under national control."[5] It may be noted that the Congress made no reference to the contentious issue of secular education. Even earlier, Ranade had said that moral and religious precepts were necessary in all schools, but the type of those institutions had to be left to the Indians. However, it should be clearly understood that neither Ranade nor Gokhale were averse to religious education. Ranade declared, "When the people themselves are able to take care of their own education, they will, establish regular religious classes in their schools."[6] While Tilak argued for religious education since "secular education, alone is not enough to build up character," he wanted to use education to build up pride in India's past.[7] Many of the liberal thinkers such as Ranade, Agarkar, Gokhale, etc., felt that the more important task was that of "the liberation of the Indian mind from the thraldom of old world ideas."[8] Advocates of both secular and religious education were, however, emphatic in supporting the development of western science and technology in the country.

Thus, Ranade and Tilak really represent two moods of the Indian bourgeoisie which wanted a modem state and also to hold on to its old world values; the former implied

[5]See A.M. Zaidi, ed.. *The Encyclopedia of the Indian National Congress,* relevant volume.

[6]M.G. Ranade, *Miscellaneous Writings,* Bombay, 1915.

[7]See D. Keer, *Lokmanya Tilak: Father of Our Freedom Struggle,* Bombay, 1959, pp. 53-59.

[8]*Speeches of Gopal Krishna Gokhale,* ed. G.A. Natesan, Madras, 1916, p.279.

western education, science and technology; the latter, religious education and all that went with it.

These divergent moods were later to be crystallized in the person of one individual, Gandhiji.

In accordance with his dictum "Religion must govern all life", Gandhi could hardly support a purely secular education. At the same time, by religion he did not mean adherence to dogma or the outer forms of religion. Nor did he counter-pose religion to reason. Thus, he declared, "Everything has to submit to the test of reason, and, in the long run, it will be found that any other method will lead us to trouble." (*Harijan*, Feb. 15, 1942). In fact, he asserted, "A *Veda* text must be rejected if it is repugnant to reason and contrary to experience."

Hence, Gandhi compromised by saying that since the secular state could not provide religious instructions for every denomination, "Such instruction is best given at home." The most he would allow was to provide tutors for the instructions to the denominations, provided they paid for them. (*Harijan*, 16 Jan. 1938).

Whatever Gandhi's motives, his attitude towards religious education encouraged various religious bodies, such as the Arya Samaj which espoused the slogan "back to the Vedas", to become active in the field of education. This, in turn, aggravated religious tensions between the major communities, the Hindus and the Muslims.

Meanwhile, different religious minorities—the Muslims, the Christian, the Sikhs, etc., reached in different ways to the concept of modem, secular education. Perhaps, the most serious crisis was faced by the Muslims who earlier had large representation at various levels of the administration. As is well known, the education imparted in the *maktabs* during the medieval period included both religious and secular subjects. Only a small proportion of those educated in the *maktabs* had gone. on to higher seminaries *(madrasa)* in order to follow the profession of theologians *(maulvi)*, judges *(qazi)*, etc. The decision in 1837 to dispense with Persian as the official language in revenue and judicial matters, followed by the decision in 1844 to make knowledge of English an essential qualification for government service above a level, came as a big blow to those institutions where Arabic and Persian texts were taught through the Urdu medium. As government jobs for students in the *maktabs* shrank, two divergent trends appeared. One was the experiment of Sir Syed Ahmad, of imparting modern education through the English medium, but combining it with religious instructions to meet orthodox opposition. The other experiment was the one at Deoband where the religious component was further strengthened, along with an effort to reassert the fundamentals of Islam without compromising with Imperialism. The Deobandi *ulemas,* while orthodox in their approach to religion and secularism, sided with the nationalist leaders in the struggle against British Imperialism. But reassertion of Islam and emphasis on the religious aspect of education was part of a broader movement which is testified to by the fact that in U.P. and Bihar alone, the number of *maktabs* doubled during the second half of the 19th century.[9]

Thus the growth of secular education, which was resorted to mostly by the Hindus and the Parsis, especially those living in the coastal areas of the country, accentuated religious tensions, and created new types of regional divides which were reflected in the nationalist movement during the subsequent period.

It should also be noted that the British, while formally adhering to secular education, were not at all averse to the growth of religious influence in the educational system of the country. Their interest in helping Protestant Missionary societies to dominate education has been noted already. In the context of the establishment of Annie Besant's Hindu College at Banaras in 1899, the Home Secretary, Hamilton, wrote to Curzon that emphasis on religious education would help to "break the Hindu educated party into two sections holding widely different views" and that such a division

[9]See Mushirul Haq, *Islam in Secular India,* Simla, 1972, pp. 30-31.

would "strengthen our position against the subtle and continuous attack which the spread of education makes on our present system of administration."[10]

II

Regarding social reforms, also, although the Age of Consent Bill which had raised such a storm in 1889 was passed, Tilak won a pyrric victory in this field also. The Congress discontinued from 1891, the practice of holding the meeting of the Social Reform Conference at the same venue as the Congress. The Sharda Act of 1914 raising the age of consent for girls from 12 to 14, was proposed by a private member, and remained virtually a dead-letter. Thus, the Congress virtually conceded the point that a state ruled by foreigners had no right to interpret religious texts and pass legislation on that basis, as also Tilak's point that since the orthodox elements were in a majority, it would be impolitic for the Congress as a representative body to side with the reformers.

Gandhiji's advocacy of reforms ameliorating the position of women, especially women's education, abolition of purdah, widow remarriage, etc., and his denunciation of untouchability as "a sin", began a new chapter in the struggle for a rational, just society. The fundamental point was that for Gandhiji, these issues were not to be regarded as religious issues, but social issues which affected all. The reforms were to be effected, above all, by educating public opinion. The national movement itself was a powerful lever in bringing about many attitudinal changes. In this way, Gandhi tried to disarm orthodox opposition, and in winning over to his side the reforming elements among the various communities. However, he could not break the alliance of the orthodox and the feudal elements which looked to the British for

[10]See Suresh C. Ghosh, *Indian Nationalism: A case study for the First University Reform by the British*, Vikas, 1985, pp. 22-23.

protection and support.

Gandhi was also keen to ameliorate the position of the untouchables whom he renamed *harijans* or God's people. His main emphasis was on improving the social status of the *harijans* for which he supported a programme of removing social barriers against their entry into Hindu temples, communal eating, and getting rid of other social taboos. He emphasised that *charkha* and *swadeshi* were means of giving employment to the *harijans,* women, and members of the minority community, but did not take up the question of land redistribution although the *harijans* formed the largest section of the landless peasants. This is clear from the Karachi Congress session of 1932 which included, in fundamental rights, "equal access to use of public roads, public wells and all other places of public resort", i.e. temples, to all citizens, but remained silent on the question of redistribution of land. Nor was Gandhi in favour of reservations for the *harijans,* in services or educational institutions. In fact, he undertook a fast in 1931 to frustrate a British design to further fragment the national movement by providing separate electorates for the *harijans,* in addition to the Muslims.

Despite limitations, the long-range repercussions of Gandhi's support to social reform should not be underestimated. Not only was he able to effect a wide stirring of social opinion, he was able effectively to isolate the orthodox elements among the Hindus. The reform of Hindu society by legislation after independence would have been impossible but for these two conditions. The Hindu Code Bills which along with successive Acts should be seen against this background. They placed Hindu women legally on par with men regarding right of property, adoption, etc., abolished polygamy and provided for divorce. The opposition of the orthodox elements, aided and supported by the President, Dr Rajendra Prasad,[11] was defeated on the basis of the earlier

[11]S. Gopal, *Jawaharlal Nehru, A Biography,* Oxford University Press, ii, 1979, p. 155.

stirring, and the massive mandate which the Congress, headed by Nehru, received from the electorate in 1950. Whether, in practice, the women were able to enjoy legal equality is, of course, an entirely different matter, and should not be lost sight of. But the acceptance of the idea of legal equality was itself a step forward.

A secular society postulated a common civil code for all its citizens, irrespective of race or religion. The framers of the Indian Constitution, included the ideal of a common civil code in the Directive Principles, but shrank from implementing it for fear of Muslim opposition. Like the Hindu orthodoxy which based itself on *Dharmashastras* backed by the Revealed Books, the *Vedas,* the Muslim orthodoxy took its stand on the *sharia* which had the sanction of long usage, and was supposed to be based on the revealed word of God, the *Quran.* Earlier Muslim rulers, the Turks and the Mughals, had not in practice, accepted this stand of the *ulema:* they had claimed and were accorded the right of making secular laws *(zawabit)* which supplemented, and sometimes even circumscribed the *sharia.* Thus, the *sharia* laws for theft, adultery, etc., were not enforced. Even laws of inheritance were sometimes not applied, the ruler himself apportioning the property of a deceased noble among his heirs according to his likes and dislikes. But the disintegration of the Mughal empire, and weakening of secular authority led to a reassertion of the Muslim orthodoxy. In consequence, the efforts of some Muslim thinkers, such as Sir Syed, Chiragh Ali, Amir Ali, etc., to pave the way for social reform among the Muslims by opening the way for *ijtihad* or a critical application of the *sunna* or public opinion was largely frustrated. It has been rightly observed that the educated Muslims were suspected of being pro-British, and ready to "sell any traditional values for Western or Hindu cultural commodities."[12] On the other hand, the *ulema*

[12]Fazlur Rahman, *Islam,* London, 1966, p. 214, quoted by Mushirul Hasan, "Some Aspects of Muslim Social Reform", in *Muslims* in *India* ed. Zafar Imam, Delhi, 1975, p. 224.

who continued the tradition of being anti-British, were not prepared to countenance any interference with the *sharia* which, according to them, covered every aspect of life.

Face to face with this dilemma, in fact, eager to win over the *ulema* to their side in the national struggle against the British, the nationalist leaders adopted from the beginning an ambivalent attitude towards social reform among the Muslims. As early as 1887, Badruddin Tyabji, the President-elect of the National Congress, said:

> "... we, Musalmans, have our own social problems to solve, just as our Hindu and Parsi friends have theirs, yet these questions can be best dealt with by the leaders of the particular communities to which they belong."

In course of time, this attitude hardened into a definite policy, giving an edge to the orthodox elements over the moderates, and making the question of social reforms a religious or communal issue, rather than a secular, national issue.

The question whether in a secular state religious minorities would have the right to maintain their own personal laws as a long as they liked, or whether there would be a uniform civil code was sought to be resolved by the Congress. In order to reassure the Muslims as well as the Sikhs, the Congress Working Committee, while spelling out the rights of the religious minorities resolved that "Personal laws shall be protected by specific provisions to be embodied in the Constitution."[13]

III

We have emphasized that for the Indian leaders, the concept of secularism was a means of keeping the country united, despite differences of religion, language, race, etc. This postulated a certain distance between secular power and

[13]See A.M. Zaidi (Ed), *The Encyclopedia of the Indian National Congress.*

the religious leaders, broad toleration to those professing different religions and speaking different languages, and a ruling class drawn, as far as possible, from diverse segments. These conditions were fully replicated during the Mughal period. Even an orthodox ruler such as Aurangzeb could not deny broad religious toleration to the people on the basis of the Quranic injunction "To you your religion, to me mine." He also rejected the concept of dismissing Hindus from the services. Recent study shows that the proportion of Hindus including Rajputs and Marathas rose from 24 per cent under Shah Jahan to 33 per cent during the latter part of Aurangzeb's reign. Nor did he allow the clergy to interfere in political affairs, though he sometimes used clergymen to further his political objectives: witness his seeking a *fatwa* from the Chief Qazi justifying his imprisonment of his father, Shah Jahan, who was the reigning monarch, and dismissing the qazi who refused to give such a *fatwa*.

Thus, a *de facto* separation of political authority from religion, and a distance between secular and ecclesiastical authority was a part of the Indian tradition. This may explain why the European concept of secularism, i.e., separation of state from religion found ready acceptance, as long as it did not affect the practice of religion as such, i.e. in the social and moral spheres. And that is where the difficulties began, as we have tried to show.

Just as the concept of a composite ruling class, consisting of people drawn from various religious groups, was integral to the thinking of the nationalist leaders, so was the concept of allowing the different languages of the people to develop, and in order to ensure that, organize administrative units, viz. the provinces on the basis of language. The situation had crystallized to the point that in December 1917, the idea of linguistic states was keenly debated and approved at the Congress session. In her Presidential Address, Mrs. Besant observed, "Sooner or later, preferably sooner, provinces will have to be redelimited on a linguistic basis." In

1920, when Gandhiji drafted the new Congress constitution, he based it on linguistic units. Gandhiji declared, "I regard this constitution, with a certain measure of pride. I hold that if we could fully work on this constitution, the mere fact of working it will bring us *Swaraj*."

The Congress sessions at Lahore in 1929 and at Karachi in 1931 form a water-shed in the conceptualisation of the national secular state in India. At Lahore, the Congress declared complete independence to be its objective. At Karachi, the rights of the people including the religious minorities were sought to be defined. These included freedom of conscience, and the free practice of religion "subject to public order and morality," and that no disability would attach to any person of religion, caste or creed "in regard to public employment, office of power or honour of the exercise of any trade or calling." S. Gopal rightly points out that this was "the first breakdown, in concrete terms, of the concept of secularism in the Indian context."[14] The fundamental rights included "religious neutrality on the part of the State". Explaining the resolution in the open session, Gandhi said, "Swaraj will favour Hinduism no more than Islam, nor Islam more than Hinduism. But in order that we may have a state based on religious neutrality, let us from now on adopt this principle in our daily affairs." But simultaneously, he said, "It is meant to indicate to the poor inarticulate Indian the broad features of Swaraj or Ram Raj."

The question regarding the rights of the minorities continued to be debated in the Congress even after the Karachi session. Apart from reiterating that "joint electorates shall form the basis of representation in the future constitution of India," in 1932 at Bombay, the Congress added an important section on minority rights, viz., that "the cultures, languages and scripts of the minorities of the different linguistic areas shall be protected." Most of these rights were

[14]S. Gopal, "Nehru and Socialism", in *Occasional Papers on History Society*, Nehru Memorial Museum & Library, No. XLII, May 1987, p. 12.

later incorporated almost wholesale into the Indian Constitution.

During the period, Gandhiji clearly defined his position regarding the position between state and religion. Writing in the *Harijan* on 22-9-1946, he said,

> "I swear by my religion. 1 will die for it. But it is my personal affair. The state has nothing to do with it. The state will look after your secular welfare, health, communication, foreign relations, currency, and so on, but not my religion. That is everybody's personal concern."

This did not, of course, define the position at all. What about social welfare, justice for the weaker elements? Would the state remain neutral about their welfare, or intervene?

For Nehru, *swaraj* meant a modem state based on science, technology and modem industry. He contrasted the method of religion which was based on emotion and intuition which it applies "to everything in life, even to those things which are capable of intellectual inquiry and observation," It allied itself with vested interests and "encourages a temper which is the very opposite to that of science."

This implied that a secular state would wage a resolute struggle against all forms of "intolerance, credulity and superstition, emotionalism and irrationalism."

* * *

Thus, it would be clear that the concept of a secular state contained within it a deep division of opinion regarding the attitude of the secular state towards religion, towards a common civil code and education aimed primarily at combating superstition, intolerance, irrationalism, etc. The Indian Constitution approved by parliament in 1949 was, therefore, a compromise document where no reference was made to secularism, much less define it, and the basic issue of a common civil code was relegated to Directive Principles. In the field of education, a lacuna was left that no religious instructions shall be provided "in any institution *wholly* maintained out of State funds". (Article 28, Emphasis mine).

Thus, the Constitution, while it marked a definite stage in the struggle for the establishment of a secular state, also marked the starting point for a more intensified struggle for the realization of a secular state, both in form and content.

8

HISTORICAL BACKGROUND TO THE RISE OF THE BHAKTI MOVEMENT IN NORTHERN INDIA

After the rise and growth of Buddhism in the country between the 6th century B.C. and the 2nd century AD., the medieval *bhakti* movement was undoubtedly the most widespread, far-ranging and multi-faceted movement that appeared in India. The *bhakti* movement influenced almost the whole country at different times, and had a definite impact not only on religious doctrines, rituals, values and popular beliefs, but on arts and culture as well. In turn, these had an impact on the value structure of the medieval state and the ruling classes. At a certain stage of its development in some regions, the *bhakti* movement was sought to be used as a platform by forces opposed to the centralizing Mughal state. In the cultural field, the growth of regional languages, devotional music, dance, painting, sculpture etc., became closely related to the *bhakti* movement.

The *bhakti* movement can scarcely be called a mass movement in a strict sense, for its objective was individual salvation or mystical union with God rather than a change in the living conditions of the masses, except indirectly. Likewise, it can hardly be called a single movement, barring in the broad, doctrinal sense of a movement which emphasized divine grace as a means of attaining salvation or nearness to God with the help of a guide or *guru.* Even within this compass, there were often wide differences regarding the nature of relationship of the devotee with God, the attitude towards the scriptures and the traditional faith, as also towards the society and the ruling authority. Commenting on the teachings of Ramanand, Tara Chand noted that they "gave rise to two schools of religious thought, one conservative, and the other radical."[1] Such variations were, by no means, confined to the north. While the southern movement of *bhakti* was fundamentally egalitarian in spirit, it hardly denounced the caste system, or brahmanical privileges as such. However, the *Virashaiva* movement, which followed the path of *bhakti* and came to the forefront during the 12th and 13th centuries, adopted a strongly radical and heterodox attitude.[2] The movement also differed from one region to another. Thus, in the Punjab, an essentially quietist movement became a vehicle for the expression of popular sentiments on a wide range of subjects, and provided a basis for men and women of diverse classes and backgrounds to come together, and act against what they considered "tyranny".[3] Hence, the historical background of the rise of *bhakti,* the factors contributing to its growth and spread, its variations in different regions, and its impact on society, politics and culture have to be studied in detail. However, we are attempting here a delineation of some general features that characterised the *bhakti* movement, or the trend towards it in northern India.

[1]Tara Chand, *Influence of Islam on Indian Culture,* Allahabad, 1946, p. 145.

[2]Tara Chand, *loc. cit.,* p. 116-24; "Virasaivism" by Kumar-Swamiji in *The Cultural Heritage of India,* Calcutta, 1957, IV, pp. 98-107; Arun P. Bali, The Virsaiva Movement" in *Indian Movements: Some Aspects of Dissent, Protest and Reform,* S.C. Malik (ed.)I.I.A.S., Simla, 1978, pp. 67-77.

[3]In the case of the Sikh movement, a distinct organisation was set up by Guru Govind for the purposes of action. This was a break from the earlier organisational pattern common to the various sects broadly adhering to *bhakti.*

That the philosophy and framework of *bhakti* had been developed in the centuries before the Christian era, and were furthered in the succeeding centuries by the rise of *Mahayana* Buddhism, and later by the worship of Narayana and Vishnu, are too well-known to be repeated here. Although the worship of Vishnu began to spread under the Gupta rule (4th-6th centuries A.D.), it is questionable whether *bhakti* had acquired a genuine popular base by that time. Till then, the works pertaining to *bhakti* were invariably found written in Sanskrit. A genuine popular movement could hardly have expressed itself in a language which was the preserve of the elite, especially of the *brahmans* who were identified with and were the chief upholders of a ritual and a set of doctrines that largely excluded the people, or kept them at a distance, and accorded all kinds of privileges to the *brahmans.* Our understanding of the subject is, however, limited to some extent by the comparative neglect of *apabhramsha* literature in our Universities and centres of learning. Although *apabhramsha* was nearer to the languages of the people than Sanskrit, and was used by the Jains and others for a long time for religious and secular purposes, we do not know enough about its secular forms, orientation, value structure etc. On the basis of our present knowledge, we may not be far wrong in drawing the conclusions that *bhakti* in its popular form rose and flourished for the first time in south India from the 6th century onwards.

The rise and growth of *bhakti* in its popular form between the 6th and 10th centuries in south India rather than in north India—where it had its early development—needs some explanation. Efforts have been made to trace the process by which *bhakti* travelled from the south to north India, and a key role in this has been assigned to Ramanand, who lived at Kashi and whose period of work is supposed to cover the last quarter of the 14th and the first half of the 15th centuries. Latterly, the rise of the *Varkari* saints of Maharashtra and the growth of *Sahajayana* in Orissa and eastern India have been emphasized as links in the northward movement.

Two questions arise here. First, the links between the north and the south had never been broken, despite what has been called the process of political disintegration in north India after the death of Harsha (7th century A.D.). It is now known that the death of Harsha was followed by the rise of powerful extensive empires, such as the Gurjara-Pratihars, the Rashtrakutas and the Palas in north India which contended with each other for the control of Kanauj, or in reality for the control of the upper Ganga valley and adjacent areas, such as, Malwa. The movement of armies implied the existence of communications. Nor were the southern products, such as sandal wood, cloves, etc., found wanting in the north. The close link between the south and the north in the cultural field was underlined by the tradition that to establish a school of thought in India a *digvijaya* i.e., travel and discussion-bouts or *shastrartha* in different parts of the country was necessary. It was in pursuit of this tradition that Sankara (c. 8th century) is credited with a triumphant *digvijaya* in his short span of life of 32 years, and the setting up of *matha* in different parts of the country, such as Badrinath, Dwarka etc. The example of Sankara was followed by many others, namely, by Ramanuja and Nimbarka. From north India also, many *Nathpanthi sadhus* are credited with travelling to south and western India and setting up their centres. There was a lively exchange of Sanskrit works also.[4]

Under the circumstances, if popular *bhakti* is, as has been generally accepted, an off-shoot of the popular *bhakti* movement of the south, it is difficult to explain why there was a time lag of almost five hundred years between the two. As is well known, the *bhakti* movement in the south reached its climax in the 10th century. Thereafter, it gradually moved into the grooves of the traditional Hindu religion, i.e., it accepted the *varna* system, the superiority of the *brahmans*

[4]According to Sukumar Sen (*Cultural Heritage, loc. cit.*, IV, p. 283), the usual haunt of Gorakshanath was the shade of a *bakula* tree at Vijayanagar.

and their rituals. In north India, the *Varkari* movement began with Namdeo in the second half of the 14th century, Kabir's popular monotheism in the 15th century and popular Vaishnavism, which upheld the worship of Krishna and Rama, in the first half of the 16th century.

The question is: was this time lag accidental? In that case, a much closer similarity between the philosophy, ethics, ritual and social outlook of the two movements would have to be established than has been done so far. According to present thinking, Ramanand is considered to be a crucial link between the southern and the northern movements. His *guru,* Raghavanand, is linked to the *Sri Sampradaya* of Ramanuja, while Kabir and some of the *ashtachhapa* poets associated with the Vaishnavite movement, are believed to be his disciples.[5] Unfortunately, Ramanand is a shadowy figure and not much is known about his life and works. His most significant contribution, it is asserted, was the opening of the path of *bhakti* to all, irrespective of caste. He thus departed from Ramanuja, who had tried to establish a careful balance between the *Dharmashastras* and popular *bhakti* by espousing *prapatti* which had been advocated by Nath Muni earlier and which was open to all, while restricting *jnana, karma* and *bhakti* as the prerogatives of the upper castes.[6] What were the factors which propelled Ramanand to bring about this far-reaching change? Was it the outcome of a desire to counter the influence of the *Nathpanthis*

[5]It has been argued by David N. Lorenzen (in "Evaluation of the Kabir Panth," a paper presented at the International Congress of Human Sciences in Asia and North Africa, Mexico, 1976, mimeographed) that there is little relationship between Kabir and Ramanand, and that the claim of Kabir's being a disciple of Ramanand was a later development, designed to bring his followers into the traditional fold. Tara Chand *(loc. cit.,* p. 151), empahsizes that "Kabir's teachings were shaped by Sufi saints and poets." However, Hazari Prasad Dwivedi *(Kabir,* Delhi, 1971, pr. 45-56) has stressed his indebtedness to the *Nathpanthis.*

[6]Bhandarkar, R.G., *Yaisnaoism, Saivism and other Minor Sects,* London, 1913, p. 57; Radhakrishnan, S., *Indian Philosophy,* London, 1962, i, p. 221.

who had already opened their doors to all, irrespective of caste? Whatever the causes, the change can hardly be credited to Ramanuja or to the southern *bhakti*.

Conceptually, it is now agreed that a mystical movement, or a movement based on the philosophy of grace *(prasada)*, is not peculiar to anyone country or region, but could grow independently in different countries or regions on the basis of concrete conditions prevailing there. The failure of a popular movement of *bhakti* to grow in northern India between the 6th and 14th centuries (and its rapid growth thereafter), has therefore, to be sought in the concrete social, economic, political and cultural conditions obtaining in the region, rather than to undertake a search for inspiration from outside as its causative factor. This applies as much to the growth of a popular movement of *bhakti* in the south,[7] Hence, there need not be any considerable difficulty in accepting that the popular *bhakti* movements in the south and the north orginated and grew in their own particular circumstances. However, both remained within the broad framework of Indian culture, and shared many philosophical concepts, ethical and aesthetic ideas etc.

In north India, the dominant features of the period between the 7th and 12th centuries have been identified as the growing weakness of the state; the growth of the power of local landed elites and their decentralising authority by acquiring greater administrative, economic and political roles; the decline of towns; the set back to trade, especially long distance trade, and the alienation of land to the *brahmans* in larger proportions than before.[8] The period is also noted for the rise of the Rajputs. There has been considerable controversy among

[7]The ideas of Weber and Grierson, trying to link the growth of popular *bhakti* with Christian monotheism, and Dr. Tara Chand's arguments linking it with Islam *(Influence of Islam, loc, cit.,* pp. 106-8) are too well-known to be repeated. here. Behind them lay the diffusion theory of culture which modem anthropolgists do not accept.

[8]R.S. Sharma, *Indian Feudalism* c. 300-1200, Calcutta, 1965, pp. 263-73.

historians about the origin of the Rajputs. However, there appears to be a fair consensus that they were drawn from miscellaneous castes, including *brahmans,* aboriginal tribesmen and foreigners who had settled in the country.[9] The manner in which they became 'Hinduized' or were assigned the status of Rajputs is still not clear in detail, but can be surmised from analogous developments during the later medieval period. Thus, those sections which had control over land or gained political authority at the local and regional levels were often successful in gradually rising in the *varna* scale. Conversely, those who lost control over land or local authority often sank in the *varna* scale.[10]

However, apart from control over land and political authority, a higher *varna* status could not be acquired without the support and backing of the *brahmans.* The emergence of the Rajputs in north India represented a tacit alliance between those who controlled land and possessed political authority, and the *brahmans* who were the legitimizers, so to speak.[11] In return for granting recognition to the various ruling elements as Rajputs or *kshatriyas,* the *brahmans* received generous grants of land and money for their sustenance, and for building and maintaining temples. The growth

[9]For a recent review, see B.D. Chattopadhyaya. "Origin of the Rajputs: The Political, Economic and Social Processes in Early Medieval Rajsthan," *Indian Historical Review,* Delhi, III, No.1, July 1976, pp. 59-82.

[10]The example of the Marathas who, in general, were not classified as *kshatriyas* before the 17th century is an index of the former, while the case of the Meenas of Rajasthan who had been owners of land at one time but gradually sank in the *varna* scale signalizes the latter. For a fuller discussion see Satish Chandra, "Social Background to the Rise of the Maratha Movement during the Seventeenth Century," in *Medieval India: Society, the Jagirdari Crisis and the Village,* Delhi, 1982, pp. 139-46.

[11]*Cf.* Tara Chand, " ... the ascendency of the Brahmans in the social life of India began in the Gupta period, and was completed when the foreign immigrants were received into the Hindu social system ... the Rajputs paid the price of their elevation from barbarism to civilisation by accepting and confirming their *[brahmans']* claims of superiority" *(Influence of Islam on Indian Culture,* Allahabad, 1946, p. 131).

of mangificent temples during the period was an index not only of a resurgent Hinduism but, even more, of the newly acquired power and wealth of the *brahmans*. The *brahmans* enjoyed many other privileges, too: they were appointed as *raj-purohitas* and often asked to advise on various matters of *dharma* and polity. On numerous occasions they were employed on diplomatic missions. They were also assessed land revenue at a concessional rate—a tradition which continued upto Mughal times and even later.[12] The prestige which the *brahmans* enjoyed was shown in a classic example: the rulers of Mewar, traditionally considered the leading house in Rajput society, designated themselves not as rulers, but as only the priests of Ek Lingaji, who was the real ruler. Thus, Rajput rulers stood forth as protectors of *brahmans*, the cow etc., and of the four-fold division of society which was thought to be an integral part of *dharma*.

It may be argued that this was not a new situation, but one which had, in a general manner, prevailed in Hindu society during the earlier period. That is just the point one should remember. The *Dharmashastras* (generally representing the *brahman* or upper caste views) pointed to one direction, political realities to another. According to the *Dharmashastras*, every Hindu ruler was *ipso facto* bound to protect *dharma* which included protection of *brahmans*, to obey the *Dharmashastras* and to uphold the *varna* system. However, since the time of Ashoka, rulers in north India, with the exception of the Sungas, had either been supporters of Buddhism, or even if they worshipped the gods in the Hindu pantheon, had expressly given freedom and equal respect to all religions, including Buddhism and Jainism. In other words, they were not prepared to stand forth as the open defenders and promoters of the religious ideas and beliefs propounded by the *brahmans*. Even the great Harsha, who

[12]W.W. Hunter, *Orissa*, Vol. I, pp. 33-54, ii 255-56; Dilbagh Singh, "Caste and Structure of Village Society in Rajasthan during the Eighteenth Century," *Indian Historical Review*, Vol. II, No.2, Jan. 1976, pp. 299-311.

was supposed to have been a devotee of Siva, called meetings of the Buddhist Council every year, and at the time of the quinquennial gaherings at Prayag, worshipped in turn, Buddha, the Sun, and Siva. He was also munificent in his gifts to the Buddhists as well as to the *brahmans*.[13]

The Rajput-Brahman alliance represented a departure from this situation. It virtually marked the triumph of a resurgent, aggressively expanding Hinduism. The former is reflected in the writings of Kumarila who tried to revive the Vedic worship, and stridently championed the *varnashram-dharma.* The latter was reflected most clearly in the persecution of both Buddhists and Jains, with many Jain and Buddhist temples being converted into Hindu temples at the instance of the *brahmans* and backed up by the rulers. It was also reflected in the Hinduization of many tribes and the consequent growth of many new *jatis* or subcastes, which had to be fitted into the existing structure by putting forward the theory of *varnasankar,* i.e., the growth of mixed castes.[14] The rise of image worship, of en accompanied by gross superstitions, and the elaboration of a religion of works *(karma)* were other features of the religious ideas of the period.

This socio-religious order was supported and buttressed by the Rajput-Brahman alliance. Thus, any effort to disturb the established social order viz., the *varna* system and the religion of works, would not only have to face the opposition and hostility of the entrenched *brahman* class, but also invited repression at the hands of political authority. This may explain why the early stirrings of *bhakti* in north India did not lead to a broadening of the movement, though at the purely intellectual level, Sanskrit works related to the philosophy and doctrine of *bhakti* continued to be produced. The most notable of these was the *Bhagawata Purana* which

[13]B.N. Sharma, *Harsha and His Times,* Varanasi, 1970, pp. 401-02 and 430-3l.

[14]R.S. Sharma, *Social Change in Early Medieval India (c. A.D. 500-1200),* Delhi, 1969.

was written most probably in north India, but a southern origin cannot be ruled out. The tradition of intellectual freedom could not be denied as long as it did not lead to social action. At the grass-root level, it is possible to discern the rise of a number of dissident or heterodox movements during the period. In this context, reference many be made to the spread of Tantrism and *Shakii* worship, and the rise of the *Nathpanthi* movement and the *Sahajayana.* The origins of Tantrism go deep, but we need not concern ourselves here with its origins, or early development. Nor are we concerned with the different schools of Tantrism which often differed from each other. The spread or reassertion of *Tantrik* ideas during this period is testified to by the large number of extant works. It is noticeable that Tantrism, and the worship of the goddess *(Shakti)* was more popular in the eastern part of India—an area dominated by Buddhism for a long time. This also implied that in this area, Brahmanism and the caste system did not have such a strangle-hold. The *Nathpanthi* movement, sometimes considered to be an offshoot of Tantrism, orginated in east U.P. on the borders of Nepal and Bihar and gradually spread to the northern and western parts of India. What is noteworthy is that often *Tantrik* and *Nathpanthi* ideas were expounded by preachers called *siddhas* who generally were not *brahmans,* but were drawn from the lower orders of the society. Also, that anyone, irrespective of caste, creed or sex could be initiated into the *Tantrik* or *Nathpanthi* orders.[15] Further, that the *siddhas,* while proclaiming *mukti* or release as the goal, had the immediate object of gaining control over nature through the regimentation of bodily senses and the use of magical formulae and esoteric practices. Thus, it was believed that the *siddhas* and *yogis* could fly through the air, see at long

[15] Avalon, A., *Principles of Tantra,* London, 1914, Ch. xvii, p. 352. See also Bagchi P.C, *Studies in the Tantra,* Calcutta, 1939, Dasgupta, S.B., *Obscure Religious Cults as Background to Bengali Literature,* Calcutta, 1946, and *The Struggle for Empire,* (Vidya Bhawan Series V), 1957, pp. 404-13.

distances, be at more places than one, etc. Whatever the validity of these claims, they had a definite influence on the masses. Later on, we see similar claims being put forward on behalf of the *sufi* saints. Popular credence to these claims sometimes put the *Nathpanthis* and *yogis* in an advantageous position *vis-a-vis* the *brahmans.* Nor, as we have noted, was anyone excluded from being initiated into these orders on the basis of caste. In fact, we have reference of women from the category of 'untouchables' being accepted as *guru,*[16] It is difficult to say how widespread was the influence of these movements or sects. The appeal of Tantrism apparently remained limited on account of its very esoteric nature which, to some extent, was a device to escape social and political persecution. This and the use of forbidden foods and drink by the *Tantriks,* and the advocacy by some sects of a type of free love as a stage to higher knowledge etc., enabled the *brahmans* to brand the whole system of Tantrism as 'immoral'. The state also looked upon the *Tantriks* with suspicion and ill-concealed hostility.[17] The *Nathpanthis,* who under Gorakhanath, adopted a high moral tone, tried with some success to meet the brahmanical attack, and set up their centres in different parts of north and western India, and even in some parts of the south. They provided a base for the growth of popular monotheism and the *bhakti* movement in north India later on. But their influence also remained limited. There were many points of difference between the north and the south during this period. In the

[16]Jayasi, *Padmauat,* V.S. Agrawal (ed.), Jhansi, V.S. 2018, No. 38/448.

[17]In the *Dashkumarcharit* of Dandin, there are a number of references to *Aghoris* and *Tantriks* being slain by the ruler for actions which were against *dharma,* and for endangering the state. Jayasi (38/448) also warns Ratan Sen. against the magico-religious practices of the *Tantriks,* saying that even the famous Raja Bhoj had been deceived, i.e., had lost his throne due to these *Tantrik* practices. For the hostile attitude of the *Lokayatas* (i.e., *Tantriks)* and the *Sahajiyas* towards the ruling classes of the time, see Chattopadhyaya D., *Lokayata: A Study in Ancient Indian Materialism,* Delhi, 1981.

south, the feudal process of encroachment on land and power by a hereditary, landed class had not apparently advanced as far as in the north. Nor was there any close concordance between the landed classes and the *brahmans*. The social structures also differed in a marked manner. A *kshatriya* caste hardly existed in south India, the two main castes being the *brahmans* and the *shudras*. The *brahmans* were also relatively smaller in numbers as compared to the north. In consequence, the *brahmans* were not as powerful and influential in the south as they were in the north. In the relatively simpler, less hierarchical society, a popular movement of *bhakti* could grow more easily in the south. It should also be remembered that the early targets of the *bhakti* movement in the south were not so much the *brahmans* and their hide-bound rituals as the Buddhists and Jains who held a dominant position at many of the southern courts at that time. The ousting of the Jains from the Pandya, the Chola, the Hoyasala and the Kalachuri courts at the instance of the *Nayannars* and *Alwar* saints, and the efforts of these popular saints to combat the Jain and Buddhist ideas at the popular level, suited the *brahmans*. That also explains the role of the temples in the growth of the *bhakti* movement in the south. These, apparently, are the reasons why some modern writers are inclined to look upon the southern movement of *bhakti* as an "Hinduizing" movement which, in the long run, strengthened and not weakened the caste system. Still, in the immediate context, the *brahmans* in the south had to accept the right of the *shudras* to preach, and to have access to the *Vedas*.[18]

The advent of Islam in northern India, and the overthrow of the Rajput states by the Turks towards the end of the 12th century unleashed powerful forces which paved the way for the growth of *bhakti* as a popular movement in the

[18]See, for instance, M.G.S. Narayanan and Veluthat Kesavan, "Bhakti Movement in South India," with a select bibliography, in *Dissent, Protest and Reform, loc. cit.*, pp. 33-66.

subsequent centuries. As we have noted, the Rajput-Brahman alliance had dominated the scene in north India during the preceding five centuries, and was responsible for the maintenance of the existing socio-cultural order based on the *varnashram-dharma,* supported by a religion of works *(karma).* The violent end of the Rajput-Brahman alliance removed a big obstacle in the growth of popular heterodox movement i.e., movements opposed to the *varna* system and the religion of works. The prestige and influence commanded by the *brahmans* received a severe setback with the coming of Islam. The *brahmans* had often presented the images worshipped by the credulous people not as symbols of God but as if the images themselves were gods who could be commanded by the *brahmans,* and would reward the faithful, and cast down those who doubted their power and potency. These images were broken and trampled under foot by the heathen Turks, and the *brahmans* and other servitors of the temples killed or dispersed. Yet no harm befell the Turks. Materially, also, the *brahmans* suffered, losing the wealth and properties commanded by many of the temples.

Although the Turkish rule in north India was well-established by the first quarter of the 13th century, the rise of *bhakti* in a popular form in the region hardly antedates Kabir, who is assigned to the 15th century. This delay is generally accounted for by the stunning effect of the Turkish conquest and the continued violence and warfare, and the resulting social instability in the initial phase. The Turkish conquest itself was followed by the onslaught of the Mongols who brought about large scale death and destruction in the areas under their sway, which included Kashmir, Multan and the Punjab upto the river Beas. Resistance by the displaced Rajput rajas, and invasion of western and southern India by the Turks continued apace. However, the violence and bloodshed was accompanied by a slow, imperceptible process of regeneration which came to the surface in the 14th century. The period of regeneration can broadly be dated to the rise of the Khaljis and the Tughlaqs to power.

Under their rule, the narrow Turkish domination was replaced by a ruling class which had a broader social base among the Muslims. The linking of the Delhi Sultanate with the sea ports of Gujarat on the one hand, and its expansion towards the south on the other; and the end of the Mongol menace, freeing the Punjab and Kashmir from their fearsome rule and reintegrating them with the rest of the country opened the way for expansion of trade with central and west Asia. Under the Tughlaqs, internal administration acquired stability, and efforts were made, with some success, to expand and improve cultivation. An index to the new situation was the first tentative though largely unsuccessful, efforts made by Muhammad bin Tughalaq in inducting Hindus into the central ruling apparatus.[19] This was also the age of Amir Khusrau. Amir Khusrau's pride of being an Indian, his praise for all that was good in India and his romanticization of the marriage of Dewal Devi of Deogir with Khizr Khan, the son of Alauddin Khalji, shows that the Turkish ruling class was beginning to take roots in India. Also this period saw the rise to prominence of the great *sufi* saint, Nizamuddin Auliya, who was respected by Muslims and Hindus alike. Perhaps, it was this trend of growing mutual adjustment which the historian, Ziauddin Barani, dubbed as "*jahandari*" i.e., a situation in which the state was only formally Islamic, permitted many practices which were opposed to the *sharia* and accorded not only freedom of worship but respect to the non-Muslims.[20] Barani lamented that even at Delhi, the capital, Hindus went in procession, beating gongs and cymbals, and passed beneath the walls of the palace to immerse the idols in the river, and the Sultan, on his own admission, was powerless to

[19]Barani, *Tarikh-i-Firuzshahi*, p. 505.

[20]Barani, *Fatawa-i-Jahandari*, tr. as *Political Theory of the Delhi Sultanate* by M. Habib, A. Jahan, Allahabad n.d., Advice XI.

interefere with them.[21] While the precise extent of the freedom of worship and public observance of festivals, ceremonious religious practices etc., varied from ruler to ruler, there is little doubt that the non-Muslims enjoyed a considerable degree of religious freedom.

We do not have any detailed study of the interaction between the two major communities, Hindus and Muslims, during the period. From available evidence, it would appear that the first beneficiaries of the diminished influence of the *brahmans* were the *Nathpanthi yogis.* This sect seems to have reached the height of its prestige and influence during the 13th and 14th centuries, and was powerful enough even in the 16th century to merit the barbs of Tulsidas. The biography of Shaikh Nizamuddin Auliya of Delhi by Hasan Sijzi and the *Malfuzat* of many *sufi* saints suggest that there was continuous contact between the *sufi* saints and the *yogis,* apparently *Nathpanthi yogis,* and Jain saints *(yatis).* The use of Hindi devotional poetry in the *sama* or musical gatherings of the Chishti saints is well-known. This had reached such a point by the 15th century that a writer, Abdul Wahid Bilgrami, had to justify it by providing *sufi* allegorical meaning to such terms as "Udho", "*murli*", "Gopis", "Ras-Lila" etc.[22] Unfortunately, we have little information about the writers of these *'Hindavi' bhakti* songs or their contents.

At the higher, philosophical level, between the 10th and 13th centuries, there seems to have been little follow up of the work of al-Biruni. But a change can be discerned from the beginning of the 14th century. Thus Zia Nakhshabi (d. 1350) is credited with taking up a number of Sanskrit works for translation into Persian. The work of translation into Persian apparently continued under Firuz Tughlaq and Sikandar Lodi, both reputed to be orthodox, even bigoted

[21]Barani, *Tarikh-i-Firuz Shahi,* p. 216.

[22]Abdul Wahid Bilgrami, *Haqaiq-i-Hindi,* Hindi tr. by S.A.A. Rizvi, Kashi, V.S. 2014. See also *Rushdnama,* Hindi tr. by S.A.A. Rizvi and S. Zaidi as *Alakhabani,* Aligarh, 1971.

rulers. Although the Sanskrit works translated consisted mostly of stories and works on music, sex etc., works on religion could not be completely excluded.[23] Thus, we can presume that by this time a small but knowledgeable set of people, familiar both with Sanskrit and Persian, and with the basic religious ideas of Hindus and Muslims, had come into being. This was the background which led to the production during the 14th, 15th and subsequent centuries of a large number of works in Hindi, using popular stories, legends or fables, combining them with *sufi* mysticism on the one hand, and with Hindu mythology and philosophy on the other. The earliest of these works available to us so far is Mulla Daud's *Chandayan,* which significantly is dated in 1379, i.e., when the work of translation from Sanskrit into Persian had started. While the poetical works of these *sufi* saints do not show any deep knowledge of Hindu philosophy, they reflect popular attitudes and the extent to which mysticism, basing itself on the imagery of carnal love, was providing a common platform for the followers of the two leading religions in the century, Hinduism and Islam.

To what extent could we consider *bhakti* in its popular form in north India a result of the loss of power by the

[23]Zia Nakhshabi's *Tuti Namah,* based on the Persian translation of a Sanskrit work, was well-known. He seems to have taken special interest in translations from Hindu i.e., Sanskrit sources, and his works include a translation of *Kok Shastra.* The earliest Persian treatise on Indian music was the *Ghunyat-ul-Munya,* written in 1374-75 for Malik Shamsuddin Abu Raja, a leading noble of Firuz Tughalaq, and governor *(naib)* of Gujarat. The standard Sanskrit works made available to the author include *Bharata Sangit Ratnawali* etc. Abdul Aziz Shams Baha-i-Nuri translated Varahamihira's work on astronomy, *Brihatsamhita,* at the instance of Firuz Tughalq under the title *Tarjuma-i-Barahi* (I.O., MSS. Ethe. 1997). (S.M. Ikram, *History of Muslim Civilisation* in *India and Pakistan,* Lahore 1961, pp. 173-84; *Ghunyat-ul-Munya,* Pers. text, ed. by Shahab Sarmadee, Delhi, 1978).

landed classes, as suggested by Max Weber?[24] We have already suggested that it was not so much the support of the displaced feudal elements, but the loss of power and influence by the *brahmans,* and the resultant freedom for the growth of the heterodox, anti-caste movements to grow that cleared the ground for the development of popular monotheism. Also, the popular *bhakti* movement seems to have grown, at least in the initial phase, in the atmosphere of the cities rather than the countryside. The displaced rajas and *thakurs* did not live in the new, growing cities, but had retired to their forts and *garhis* in the countryside. Hence, they could have made little contribution to the growth of *bhakti* in the initial phase. Perhaps we may consider more relevant for our purposes Weber's concept of *"ressentiment",* or resentment by those who had been assigned a low position in society, due either to the existing socio-economic system, or to the value system supported and upheld by the religious leaders.[25] An apocalyptic movement, such as *bhakti,* attracted these elements by promising them not only the prospect of release *(moksha),* but also a higher status to the elect (the *bhaktas)* even in the phenomenal world. Obviously, such sentiments could not grow as long as the old value system, i.e., the set of ideas, doctrines and practices propounded by the *brahmans* held sway. Hence, the crucial element, again, was

[24]"A salvation religion [such as, *bhakti*] developed by socially privileged groups within a nation normally has the best chance of becoming permanent when demilitarization has set in and when the nation has lost either possibility of political activity or the interest in it. Consequently, salvation religions usually emerge when the ruling classes, noble or middle class, have lost their political power to a bureaucratic, militaristic imperial state .... This does not mean that salvation religion arises only at such times. On the contrary, the intellectual conceptions may sometimes arise without the stimulus of such anterior conditions, as a result of unprejudiced reflection in periods of dynamic political or social change." (Max Weber, *The Sociology of Religion,* Eng. tr. by Ephraim Fischoff, Boston, 1964, pp. 122-23).

[25]Max Weber, *Sociology of Religion,* pp. 97, 110-11.

the clearing function of the Delhi Sultanate, and of the *Siddhas* and *Nathpanthi* saints in undermining the hold of the *brahmans* on the mind and imagination of the people.

It has been argued that *bhakti* grew in the north as a kind of a defence mechanism to save the Hindu society from the immediate threat of subversion from Islam and the challenge posed to it by the Islamic doctrines of egalitarianism, brotherhood and simplicity. There is little evidence to show that during the 13th and 14th centuries the Hindu society was in any imminent danger of subversion due to the appeal of Islam. Even in the immediate vicinity of Delhi, the imperial capital, the overwhelming majority of the population remained Hindu. Evidently the Muslim doctrine of "brotherhood" did not have as much appeal as might have been expected, perhaps on account of the glaring social and racial disparities rampant in the Muslim society in India. In fact, on account of the strong sentiments of racial superiority among the Turks, and their emphasis on "purity of blood" and "fitness of only high born people for high office," the converts from the lower castes among Hindus continued to feel discriminated against. Also, materially the converts could hope to gain only marginally by securing government employment of a low grade. Economic life, in general, continued to remain in the hands of Hindus. Hindus, in fact dominated even at the local levels of the government. Nizamuddin Auliya, who had his fingers on the pulse of the people, said sadly; "Many [Hindus] know Islam to be a true religion, but they do not accept it." and that "they [Hindus] have excluded Islam from their hearts as a hair is discarded from flour [while kneading it]."[26]

This is not to deny the impact of Islam in other ways. The Muslim emphasis on monotheism, on the role of the *pir,* and on mystic union with the "beloved" coincided with many aspects of the Hindu thinking and, by a process of symbiosis, quickened the heterodox movement in that direction. The remarkable similarity in the thinking of the

[26]*Fawaid-ul-Fuad*, pp. 150, 195-97.

sufis and the popular monotheistic saints, including their opposition to the orthodox elements belonging to the two faiths, was both a cause and an effect. However, this process was by its very nature insidious and slow, and hence difficult to be pinned down within a chronological framework.

While analysing the political factors responsible for the growth of *bhakti* in its popular form, the continuing prestige and influence of the *brahmans,* who still presided over the normal functions of life: birth, death, marriage etc., should not be underestimated. The *brahmans* could still use the forces of tradition and "susperstition", which were yet quite strong. That is why Kabir, undoubtedly the most powerful figure among the popular monotheistic saints in the *bhakti* movement, concentrated his fire on the common *brahmans,* using "that most potent weapon, ridicule."[27]

These developments were aided, even conditioned by economic and social factors. As is well-known, the Turkish empire in India, which extended over the entire northern India including Gujarat, could not have survived without a high degree of centralization. This centralization, in a larger measure, was based partly on the *iqtadari* system and partly on the ability of the Turkish rulers to move rapidly from one part of the country to the other. The *iqtadari* system led to the evolution of a ruling class which was more dependent on the ruler, and which could be easily transferred from one place to another since the nobles were not allowed to acquire ownership rights over land, and thus strike local roots. This ruling class did not live in the countryside, like the *thakurs,* and *zamindars,* but resided in the towns located at strategic points, and extracted the rural surplus through their agents and with the help of the *zamindars.*

It has been argued that the growth of popular monotheism in north and north-west India was aided by the

[27]Savitri Chandra, "Indian Social Concepts in the Latter Half of the Sixteenth Century," p. 35 *infra.*

concentration of agricultural surplus. in the hands of the Turkish ruling class, the development of towns, and the growth of the artisans along with the emergence of new technologies, such as the making of the dome and the arch, the horse-shoe and the ironstirrup, the production of high· quality glass, growth of tailoring etc., and the Persian wheel, as also by the movement of the Jats to the Punjab and the upper Gangetic doab, and their conversion from pastoralists to agriculturists.[28] While the precise impact of the new techniques is still a matter of debate among scholars, we may accept the general proposition that the growing class of artisans in north India during the period was not content with its position in the traditional Hindu society, and that many among the artisans were inclined to support the egalitarian, monotheistic movements sponsored by saints like Kabir, Nanak, Raidas and Dadu. However, the appeal of these radical thinkers was not confined to the artisans. Popular monotheistic movements, such as the *Nathpanthi* movement, predated the establishment of the centralized Turkish state. Also, the lower order in general was dissatisfied with the position accorded to it in traditional Hindu society, and favoured heterodox movements and movements which voiced sentiments of protest and dissent. The growth of a centralized Turkish state and the introduction of new products in the expanding markets directly benefitted the class of traders and merchants. The merchants, too, were not happy with the social status assigned to them in a society dominated by *brahmans* and the feudal classes represented by *kshatriyas.* The continuing support extended by the trading communities to Jainism in western Rajasthan and Gujarat, as also in south India, was an index of this attitude. That Nanak was a *khatri,* a class specializing in trading and government service in the Punjab, is another

[28]Irfan Habib, "The Historical Background of the Popular Monotheistic Movements of the 15th-17th Centuries," *Ideas in History,* Bisheshwar Prasad (ed.), Bombay, 1969, pp. 6-13.

pointer. Perhaps at the lower level the master-craftsman and the trader had developed many common bonds.[29]

Thus, the popular monotheistic momements were complex movements with multi-class support. While we may broadly call them popular in the sense that they reflected attitudes and aspirations of the people to a certain extent, they actually tried to draw their support from a wide social spectrum. Hence, it would be misleading to call them simply as "lower class movements." It is, however, possible to find in them the focal points of popular discontent under specific historic circumstances.

The 16th and 17th centuries witnessed a striking resurgence of popular *bhakii* in northern, eastern and western India, generally focussed around the worship of Rama and Krishna as incarnations of Vishnu. These movements to a considerable degree, put in the shade the earlier movements of popular monotheism, except in some areas in the Punjab and Rajasthan. We have yet to assess the social and economic background, and the historical significance of this second phase of the *bhakti* movement so to say, or popular *(saguna) bhakti* as distinguished from the earlier movement which has been called radical monotheism. Was the "success" of *saguna bhakti* in large parts due to its being more traditional, and hence aroused less hostility from the orthodox *brahmans?* Was its appeal specifically more rural, as compared to the earlier movement which drew its support mostly from city-based artisans and traders? If so, why did the Jat peasantry of the Punjab rally under the banner of Sikhism, while the Jat peasantry of the Agra-Mathura region came under the influence of the Krishnite school of *saguna bhakti?* Or, as it has been argued by Niharranjan Ray, did Tulsidas's "revivalism" base itself on the re-assertion of the *zamindars* under the Mughals, and on the revival of the prestige of

[29]In this context, see Marx *(Capital,* Moscow, 1959, iii pp. 329-31) who postulates a situation where "the merchant turns the small masters into his middlemen."

the *brahmans* following Akbar's "liberal" policy of entering into a dialogue with them?[30] It might also be postulated that the *brahman* successors of Tulsidas systematically emphasized the traditional and ritualistic aspects of Tulsi's teachings at the expense of his non-conformist and humanistic views, thus making him, in course of time, a symbol of conservatism.[31]

We are at present, unable to answer these and other attendant questions. But the triumph of *saguna bhakti* over the more radical school of radical monotheism in the Gangetic valley may, to some extent, be considered as the triumph of the conservatism of the countryside over the latent radicalism of the towns. This, in turn, should be viewed in the context of the relatively slow growth or stagnation of the, Indian society and economy during the 17th and subsequent centuries. However, considerably more research work will be needed for a proper understanding, in an historical perspective, of the growth of *bhakti* movement in different regions, as also its subsequent stagnation and decline. The ideas put forward above are meant to be an aid to such a detailed study.

[30]Niharranjan Ray; *The Sikh Gurus and the Sikh a Tradition,* Patiala, 1977, pp. 23-25.

[31]For a similar development in the case of Chaitanya, see Tapan Raychaudhuri, *Bengal under Akbar and Jahangir,* Delhi, 1966, pp. 119-142.

9

INTERACTION OF BHAKTI AND SUFI MOVEMENTS IN SOUTH ASIA

In the course of its rise and spread, Islam came in touch with all the major religious movements of the world—Christianity, Judaism, Zoroastrianism, Buddhism and Hinduism. While relations with the religions prevailing in Europe and parts of Western Asia remained adversarial for a long time, in South Asia, after an initial period of conflict, relations between Islam and the religions of the area were marked by mutual understanding and tolerance, although elements of conflict and disharmony were never totally absent. The spirit of mutual understanding, tolerance and cooperation were, to a large degree, promoted by the rise and spread of Sufi and Bhakti ideas in the region. This spirit of cooperation coincided with the broad interests of the mass of the people, as also with sections in the ruling classes. Cultural developments, especially in the field of the creative arts, such as literature, architecture, music and painting also promoted this process of rapprochement.

Much has been written about the rise of the Bhakti movement in India, and of the Sufi movement in West and Central Asia and the adjacent areas which need hardly be repeated here. While the concept of wonder, which is the basis of mysticism, is inherent in man, the concept of grace combined with the concept of love. between God and the created being is a later development: It is found in the later portions of the Gita, and was a specific feature of Sufism almost from the beginning. Both the movements were well developed before an active process of interaction began following the incursion of the Turks in the region from the eleventh century onwards. (I am excluding Sindh because of insufficient research on the region, and my own ignorance about the developments there.) Their interaction grew till it reached a climax in the sixteenth century. However, its impact was so considerable that it shaped popular minds and attitudes till the end of the eighteenth century, when new conditions were created with the advent of colonialism.

Although the Bhakti and Sufi movements have been amongst the most widespread and long lasting popular movements in the region, and have deeply influenced the moral, spiritual and cultural life in the subcontinent, as also state policies, they have, with some notable exceptions, been generally studied in isolation. The division of the subcontinent into three separate countries—Pakistan, India and Bangladesh—has to some extent, compounded this tendency.

At the outset it may be useful to mention some of the notions which have arisen largely on account of inadequate understanding of the two sides, which, in our opinion, has tended to inhibit rather than promote a comparative study of the two movements. Foremost among these is the notion that in some ways, one was a by-product of the other. Thus, it has been argued that the fundamental concept of unity between God and the created beings, the concept of divine grace as a means of liberation, and of the relationship of love between them was the outcome of Christian, and even more of Vedantist influence.[1] On the other hand, it has been asserted that emphasis on monotheism, human equality and love and opposition to a religion of works was due to the

[1]RA. Nicholson, *Studies in Islamic Mysticism*, Cambridge 1967; R.C. Zaehner, *Hindu and Muslim Mysticism* (University of London, 1960), to mention two of the latest.

influence of Islam.[2] Even more harmful was the notion that both Sufism and Bhakti developed in hostility and opposition to each other, the basic tenet of the Sufi saints being the conversion of Hindus peacefully, while the Muslim rulers and mullahs wanted to use force for the same purpose.[3] On the other hand, it has been argued that the main objective of the Bhakti movement was to reform Hinduism (even by accepting some Islamic notions) so as to defend Hinduism more effectively against the onslaught of Islam.[4] A third notion which has a number of variations is that the objective of both the Bhakti and Sufi saints, or a section among them, was to bring about a kind of an amalgam between Islam and Hinduism or, at any rate, to weaken or destroy their uniqueness, and that these attempts were resisted and fought by the orthodox elements of both the religions, aided by political elements, and were ultimately defeated, leading to the evolution of new political forms, including partition.[5]

The purpose of any cross-cultural study is not to try and demonstrate the superiority of one over the other—an approach that has often vitiated western study of 'oriental' civilisations, but to establish their specificity, inner dynamics, and nature of interaction with other similar or dissimilar civilisations. Islam, which was a simple religion, and originated in a relatively less developed region, had to interact with a number of developed civilisations in its neighbourhood—the Greco-Byzantine civilisation, the Egyptian civilisation, the Sassanian civilisation and the Indian

[2]Tara Chand, *Influence of Islam on Indian Culture* (Allahabad 1946, written 1922): Yusuf Husain, *Glimpses of Medieval Indian Culture* (1957).

[3]See P.R. Chaturvedi, *Uttar Bharat ki Sant Parampara* (Allahabad 1951).

[4]'One group (of Hindu thinkers) accepted what was congenial to it in the new spiritual system while the other group adopted a few elements from the spiritual structure of the dominant race in order to strengthen Hinduism and to close a few fissures which had widened and to make it better able to withstand Islam.' (S.M. Ikram, *History of Muslim Civilization in India and Pakistan*, Lahore 1961, p. 202).

[5]Aziz Ahmad, *Studies of Islamic Culture in the Indian Environment* (reprint, Oxford, 1966).

civilisation, with China in the background. It had necessarily to borrow from them, but what it borrowed was quickly given a stamp of its own within a religio-moralistic framework and socio-political structure. Within a period of two centuries, the process of borrowing had come to an end and Islamic civilisation stood as an independent, self-confident, even arrogant civilisation, so much so that its conquests began to be combined with a civilisational mission. This is an important factor in understanding the nature of interaction between Islam and the neighbouring civilisations in the period after the tenth century.

Similarly, Hinduism has had a unique capacity to borrow and assimilate external elements, and even absorb them, without losing its identity. The Muslims in South Asia, on the other hand, have been afraid of losing their identity and uniqueness, thus looking upon the process of assimilation with suspicion.

From the eleventh to the fifteenth century, it would appear that as far as the Indic region is concerned, the main interaction between Sufism and Hindu mysticism was through the yogic movement. Yogic practices, such as control of breathing *(pranayama),* postures *(asanas, mudras),* and ascetic practices leading to states of semi-consciousness or ecstasy *(samadhi, maha-sukha) were* common among the Buddhist, the Jain *yatis,* the Hindu *siddha* and Yogis, who were all called *jogis* by the Sufi writers. The most influential and widespread among the *jogis* were the *Nathpanthis* who had their main seat at Gorakhpur in modem east Uttar Pradesh. Although claiming a long list of preachers called *siddhas* who preached their doctrines, *Nathpanthi* ideas were systematised by Gorakhnath. The *Nathpanthi jogis* established centres all over the region, including south India. From their headquarters at Peshawar, and travelling in pairs, they became familiar figure in Central and West Asia. Interest in Yoga in Islamic circles, particularly among Sufis is shown by the translation of Patanjali's *Yoga-sutra* into Arabic by Al Biruni, and *Amrita-Kunda,* a work based on *hath-yoga,* into Arabic by

Qazi Rukunud Din Samarqandi and then into Persian by Shaikh Muhammad Ghaus Shattari (906-970/1500-1 to 1562-63).[6] In consequence, many yogic practices, such as control of breathing *(habs-dam)*, penances, etc., were familiar to Sufis before Sufism entered South Asia. In the Indo-Pakistan region, the presence of *jog* is in the *jamaat-khanna* of Sufis is referred to in the context of Shaikh Safiud Din Gazruni of Sindh, Baba Farid, Nizamud Din Auliya, Nasirud Din Chiragh Delhi, etc. From the reference it would appear that their presence in the gatherings of Sufis was considered quite normal.[7] The interaction of the Sufis and *Jogis* is more significant than has generally been realised. Control of the senses through yogic practices was a recognised stage in the realisation of mystical union. It also implied the ability to rise above space and time, and acquiring miraculous powers, including the power to predict the future and to cure. This, and the reputation of the leading Sufis as holymen enhanced their popularity. Many of the *Jogis* were wandering saints who could not only share esoteric knowledge, their presence in the *khanqahs* and the *jamaat khanas* added further to the prestige of the Sufis among the Hindu masses ..

Apart from this, both Sufis and *Jogis* were, till this time, considered to be representatives of the masses as against the classes. This image was heightened by their adopting a life of poverty and resignation, though this was departed from by some of the *silsilahs* and individual saints. To begin with, the Sufis were those who were disenchanted with the state and society of their times and were opposed to any association with them. In consequence, they had to face persecution. Later, on account of the growing popular esteem of the Sufi saints, the rulers and the ruling classes tried to use them for their political purposes and private benefit. This led to a certain ambivalence in the position of

[6]S.A.A. Rizvi, *A History of Sufism in India.* (Delhi, 2 Vols. 1975, 1983) i.335.

[7]*Ibid.*, 323, 335.

the Sufi saints and *silsilahs,* some becoming closely associated with the state, and some retaining an attitude of aloofness. We see this process at work in the northern regions of the Indian sub-continent during the thirteenth and fourteenth centuries.

In this context, the position of the *Nathpanthi siddhas* and *Jogis* in Hindu society needs to be understood. Most of the *Nathpanthi siddhas* and *jogis* belonged to the low-castes *(sudras).* They opposed the caste-based inequalities, denounced the religion of works favoured by the Brahmans, and did not favour image worship.[8] In consequence, they were denounced by the Brahmans who accused them all of following licentious practices, eating foods considered taboo and even practising necromancy, etc. The elliptical language often used by these sects, and neglect of the popular language, *Apabhramsa,* in which many of the popular saints preached, is another cause of ignorance about them. Like the early Sufis, the *Jogis* were feared and sometimes persecuted, being accused of plotting against the state. However, this section could forge ahead in considerable measure due to loss of prestige and power suffered by the Brahmans, and the collapse of the Rajput Brahman alliance following the Turkish conquest, in consequence of which they were no longer in a position to suppress the growth and spread of dissenting movements.[9]

There were other factors in the coming together of the Sufis and the *Jogis.* The *Jogis* broadly accepted the authority of the Vedas, and the six schools of Hindu philosophy. They accepted the Vedanta philosophy, and considered the phenomenal world to be *maya,* 'not real'. However, their object was *not* merger with the Supreme Reality, but liberation from time and space, and existence of the soul as a separate nomad, while conscious of the eternal and all-encompassing

[8]Hazari Prasad Dwivedi, *Kabir aur Kabir Panth* (Allahabad 1965) 138, 51.

[9]See supra pp. 113-19.

nature of Brahma.[10] Since Islamic thinking emphasised the fundamental difference between God and His created beings, and the Sufis, even while upholding the concept of *tauhid* could not go against it, there were many points of coincidence between the Sufi concept and the concepts of the *Jogis.* Thus, the *Siddha Siddhanta Paddhati* of Gorakhnath demonstrated the relationship between *dvaita* (non-dualism) and *advaita* (dualism) by using the analogy of water and the bubble which was also used in the *wahdatal-wujud* concept favoured by the Sufis.[11]

Nevertheless, the role of the *Jogis* in establishing closer understanding between Hinduism and Islam should not be overestimated. The *Jogis* were themselves recluses following a difficult and esoteric path which could hardly be followed by the average householder. Also, the Brahmans continued to preside over the day-to-day rituals and functions. They also discharged the task of education and dissemination of knowledge and culture. Hence, they continued to have considerable influence and hold on the masses.

The fifteenth century saw the rise of popular *Bhakti* and popular Sufism in the country and a broadening of the contact between the two religions, Islam and Hinduism. Among the popular Sufis were those who generally developed no organised school of theory or praxis by way of a *silsilah,* often resided in comparatively remote rural cities *(qasba)* and villages, and lived and interacted with the people of the area by adopting their language, idiom and even customs. Such saints were widely scattered and had little or no literature, and have therefore not received adequate scholarly attention. However, a few who had been initiated into *silsilahs* but did not rise high in the hierarchy have left behind works written in local languages. A diligent search, and publication of their works is a necessary prelude to a deeper study of

[10] A.C. Dasgupta, *A History of Hindu Philosophy* (Cambridge 1951); R.C. Zaehner, *loc. cit;* 9-11.

[11] A.K. Bannerji. *Philosophy of Gorakhnath.,* (Gorakhpur, n.d.) 69; Rizvi, *loc. cit;* i. 333-4.

their works. Some progress in this field appears to have been made in the case of Hindi, Bengali, Punjabi and Rajasthan.[12] Since I am not familiar with all these works, I am using the Hindi works of this genre as a case study. In recent years, a number of such works written in Hindi have been published, while many others[13] have been listed but are yet to be published.

On the basis of the few that have been published, a few broad generalisations may be made:

(i) These popular Sufis tried to propagate Islamic ideas by presenting God as eternal, immutable, formless, beyond. comprehension, and the creator as well as the cause of everything. He was immanent in everything *(sarva vyapi),* yet not part of anything. However, to put their concepts across, the poets used the words Gosain, Niranjan, Parmeswar, Onkar, Alakh, Vidhata, etc. for God.

(ii) While praising Muhammad 'who was the beloved of everyone', Mulla Daud, author of the first of these works, *Chandayan,* who was linked to Nasirud Din Chiragh Delhi, refers to the Vedas and Puranas as revealed books, like the Quran. Sometimes, the word 'Puran' is used as a synonym for 'Quran'. Likewise, the word *dharma* is used as 'the true path'.

(iii) The author not only shows familiarity with many Hindu popular beliefs and legends, but refers to them with respect. Thus, the Ganga washes sins; the first four Caliphs are called pandits, i.e. men of learning and piety; Indra is called the lord of heaven *(swarga),* and Vasuki of the netherworld *(patala);* the world is

[12]For a preliminary study, see Shyam Manohar Pandeya, *Madhya Yugin Premakhyan,* (Allahabad 1992) (2nd rev. ed); Rizvi. *op. cit.* i 351-8, ii, 437-57.

[13]See appendix given by Savitri Chandra, 'Sea and Sea-Faring as Reflected in Hindi Literary Works during the 15th to 18th centuries' in K.S. Mathew (ed), *Studies in Maritime History* (Pondicherry 1990), 90.

pictured as resting on *meru parvata,* etc.

(iv) The lack of animosity towards Hindu beliefs and practices is also shown by lauding justice as implying equal treatment to Hindus and Turks *('Hindu-Turk-duhu sam rakhai')*[14], respect shown to Brahmans as soothsayers, ambassadors, etc., including reference to Sanskrit as a 'pleasing' language. Nowhere is image workship or the religion of works condemned. In fact, there are references to worship and festivities in temples.[15] But it is clear that all except the path of love is considered irrelevant.

(v) The ideal devotees are the *Jogis* who are followers of Gorakhnath, and pursue a path of love. They pursue the path of love despite all trials and tribulations. Even princes become *Jogis* for some time to attain their objective. This was the main message of the Sufi poets. They take great pleasure in describing in elaborate detail the beauty of their beloved, identified with the supreme soul. The *nakh-shika* (top-to-toe) descriptions of Chanda in Mulla Dauds *Chandayan* seem to have been popular because they were incorporated in their writings by all later Sufi writers. Needless to say, such descriptions were a common feature with Hindu *Bhakti* poets, at least from the time of the twelfth century *Gita Govinda.*

The impact of the rise of *Bhakti* movement in the northern parts of the subcontinent from the fifteenth century onwards, and its impact on Sufi writings in Hindi, particularly from the sixteenth century onwards, needs a separate study. As is well known, the advocates of the path of *Bhakti* or loving devotion to God were broadly divided into two—the *nirguna* or those who advocated devotion to an attributeless god, and the *saguna* or those who chose Krishna or

[14]*Chandayan,* ed. M.P. Gupta, Agra, 1967, Nos. 1-7, 14.

[15]Malik Muhammad Jaisi, *Padmavat* (ed. V.S. Agarwal) Chirgoan V.S. 2012, Nos. 185, 191, 197, 207-16.

Rama, considered forms of Vishnu, as the object of their devotion.

A lot has been written about Kabir, Nanak and Dadu, the three leading *nirguna* saints of the times. Kabir was a seminal figure who not only summed up all that had gone before him in the field of devotion in the region, but became virtually the starting point of a new trend of thinking. Although efforts have been made to project Kabir as following in the tradition of Ramanand[16] he seems to have borrowed freely from the teachings of the *siddhas* and the *Nathpanthis* as from the Hindu scriptures. He was also associated for long with the Sufis. It is from the *siddhas* that he borrowed his contempt of the Brahmans for their cant and hypocrisy. He strongly denounced asceticism, fasting, bathing in rivers and becoming sanyasins without a sense of personal devotion to God. He also laid emphasis on a sternly ethical code of life both for guru and the householder. Criticism of laying emphasis on the externalia of religion was not confined to the Brahmans, but extended equally to the Muslim Shaikhs and mullahs for their empty insistence on *roza, namaz,* etc.[17]

An even more important aspect of Kabir's teaching was his emphasis on human equality. He denounced inequality based on caste, station, race or wealth, and criticised the wealthy and the powerful for their pattern of life. This strain is

[16]See Charlotte Vaudeville, *Kabir,* Vol i (Oxford 1974), 110-17.

See also David N. Lorenzen 'Evaluation of the Kabir Panth', paper presented at the International Conference of Human Sciences in Asia and North Africa, Mexico, 1976, and his 'Kabir Panth and Social Protest' in Karine Schomer and W. Jr. McLeod (eds.), *The Sants: Studies in a Devotional Traditional of India.* (Delhi, 1987), 265-80.

According to S.M. Ikram, both Kabir and Dadu were Muslims, but were absorbed more in the Hindu system of thought and sainthood with the success of the *naqshandiyya mujaddiya* order and the increase of orthodoxy among Muslims (Ikram, *Muslim Civilisation in Hind-Pakistan,* 201).

[17]Savitri Chandra, *Social Life and Concepts in Medieval Hindi Bhakti Poetry,* Delhi 1983,47-61.

largely missing in the writings of the Sufi saints of Hindi for whom God was the creator of everything. According to them He created the rulers and the slaves, and the rich and the poor.[18] This resignation was not for Kabir. He voiced the sentiments of the poor and the oppressed. He wanted a change in their lives but suggested no way to do so. Perhaps he hoped for a change in attitudes through his message of love and fortitude. This problem was faced by his successors also.

Kabir was strongly opposed to reliance on religious authority and revealed scriptures. For him the only true path was reliance on constantly repeating the name of the One God whom he identified as Rama, Hari, Govind, Allah, Khuda, Sahib, etc. Tara Chand says that Kabir's mission was to 'preach a religion of love which could unite all castes and creeds'. He goes on to say, 'Kabir's was the first attempt to reconcile Hinduism and Islam; the teachers of the south had absorbed Muslim elements, but Kabir was the first to come forward boldly to proclaim a religion of the centre, a middle path ...'[19]

With all respect to Tara Chand who was a pioneer in exploring the impact of Islam on Indian culture, I would like to express my disagreement with this assessment of Kabir's mission. Kabir certainly believed that God is one, and different religions were, therefore, different paths to Him. His own path of love and devotion to God was one which could be followed by all, *irrespective of their religions.* His message was therefore meant for all, like the Sufis to whom he was clearly indebted.

What Tara Chand calls Kabir's middle path was expressed even more clearly by Kabir's follower, Dadu (d.1603). Dadu calls his path the path of *nipakh* or non-sectarianism. He

[18]Jaisi, *Padmavat,* No.3: '*Kinhesi koi thakur koi dasu*' '*kinhesi koi bhikari koi dani*', See also Qasim Shah, *Hans Jatoahar Bhasha,* (Lucknow 1969) (ed.) Nos. 4-5.

[19]Tara Chand, *Influence of Islam,* 150, 165.

rejected all revealed scriptures—Vedas, Quran, and the six schools of Hindu philosophy, depending wholly on personal devotion, love and repetition of the name of the one, true God. But this did not imply any attempt to set up a new religion, for he sadly confessed that in a world divided among sects, only rare ones were 'non-sectarian.'[20]

Of all the *nirguna Bhakti* saints, Nanak was influenced the most by Islamic and Sufi ideas. This is not surprising because the area where he preached, the Punjab, was the highway of communication with the Islamic world, and the seat of many Sufis from the eleventh century. Amongst these, his debt to Baba Farid and his successors, whose poems were incorporated in the Guru Granth Sahib, was the greatest.

The ideas and precepts of Guru Nanak are too well known to be discussed in detail here. Like Kabir, Nanak emphasized the essential equality of man. Almost alone he advocated giving an equal status to women 'who were the mother of men', and denounced *sati*. He was strongly opposed to caste-based inequality, and identified himself with the lowly *(neech)* and the poor. He laid great stress on a sternly ethical code and the conquest of the sense and ego *(humai)*, but did not favour the ascetic path. Be opposed the formalism of both Hinduism and Islam, and denounced idol worship and the doctrine of incarnation. These, as we know, are two major points of difference between Islam and Hinduism. However, he upheld the belief in the transmigration of souls, something which orthodox Sufis denounced as *hulul*.[21]

The position accorded to the Guru Granth Sahib, and the position of the Guru who almost paralleled the position accorded to the Prophet of Islam, were other points of comparison. There are also many points of comparison with the Sufis regarding Nanak's concept of God and the relationship with the individual soul. However, this was a

[20]Savitri Chandra, *Samaj aur Sanskriti: Sur, Tulsi aur Dadu ke Vishesha Sandarbha mein*, (Delhi, 1975), 210-23.

[21]J.S. Grewal, *Guru Nanak in History* (Chandigarh, 1969).

point about which there was hardly any difference between the Sufis and *nirguna Bhakti* saints. The *Bhakti* saints talked of *maya* in a general sense, emphasising the transitory nature of the world, and its illusory character as compared to the inner world of the senses. But in their concept of *Bhakii* or love between the individual soul and God, they accepted Ramanujam's view of qualified monism *(visistadvaita)* as compared to Sankara's pure monism. This was much nearer to the Sufi concept of *wahdat-ul-wujud.*

Although Nanak's ideas ultimately led to the establishment of a new religion, Sikhism, it is possible to discuss whether that was Nanak's objective at the outset, or whether Nanak's mission was 'the unification of the Hindu and the Musalman' by first 'end(ihg) the conflict of religions'.[22] The Sufis, the *Nathpanthi Jogis,* and the *nirguna sants* among whom Nanak may be included, formed separate but overlapping concentric circles, with the overlap varying. in each case. What is significant is not the attempt of a merger of the two religions—something never attempted seriously by anyone, but the emergence of a large measure of understanding and harmony between the two religions in which the Sufis, the *Jogis* and the *nirguna* saints played a definite role.

The Sufis also interacted with the more traditional stream of Hindu thinking represented by the Vaisnavites up to the fifteenth century. The main interaction in the Indo-Gangetic valley between the Sufis and the Vaisnavites was with the *sahajiyas,* about whom enough is not known. They were spread all over the region, the Maithili poet, Chandidas, being one of those who favoured them. The *sahajiyas* symbolically used the love between Krishna and Radha as the proto-type of the relationship that should exist between God and the individual soul. Hindi *dohas* dealing with this theme were popularly used in the *sama* gathering of the Chistis. and the wide knowledge and acceptance of concepts such as Krishna, Radha, *gopi, murli* etc., is sought to be explained and

[22]Tara Chand, *Influence of Islam,* 168.

justified by Abdul Wahid Bilgrami in his *Rushd Nama* or *Alakhabani.*[23]

The sixteenth and seventeenth centuries saw a number of new trends which have yet to be fully assessed and understood. From the middle of the sixteenth century, non-Muslims began to be incorporated in increasing numbers in the highest echelons of government. Although the beginning of such a trend can be traced back to the Lodis, not to mention the abortive attempt of Muhammad bin Tughluq in this direction, this trend gathered force under Akbar, beginning with his campaign in Gujarat, and then in the Punjab and Kabul areas. However, at the religious level, the attitude of harmony and understanding which had been developed earlier, gradually came under strain. Developments during the sixteenth century are important for understanding these apparently contradictory trends. From the time of Akbar, Khwaja Muinud Din Chishti and Shaikh Salim Chishti were virtually made the patron saints of the Mughals. Thus, Akbar succeeded in doing what the Khaljis and the Tughluqs had not been able to achieve earlier. Similarly, the *naqsbandis* were closely associated with , the Timurids in Central Asia from the time of Khwaja Ubaidulla Ahrar. The conquest of India by Babur gave considerable impetus to the *naqsbandiya* order. Not only did the order spread in the region, 'many *naqsbandi* Sufis who migrated from their homeland in Transoxiana to Agra obtained high posts in the civil and military administration'.[24]

The liberal outlook of Akbar, based on the concept that different religions were different paths to the same God, and his non-sectarian approach based on *sulh kul* were broadly endorsed by the Chishti and Qadiri Sufis. For some time, even the *naqsbandis* kept quiet. Thus, a large number of liberal Sufis, far from keeping aloof from the state, became virtual extensions of the state, and their doctrines became

[23]S.A.A. Rizvi, *Alakhbani,* (Aligarh, 1971).

[24]Rizvi, *History of Sufism,* ii. 181.

almost a part of official policy. In this situation, opposition to the state, or dissatisfaction towards it, or even fissures within the ruling class were likely to be reflected in opposition to the official 'liberal' doctrine, and support to more fundamentalist ideas.

There was a somewhat analogous development in the field of *Bhakti*. The challenge posed by the growing popularity of the *nirguna* saints, the gradual recovery of self-confidence by the Brahmans and the slow spread of the thinking of the Alwar and Adyar *Bhakti* saints of South India, led to new forms being given to the worship of Vishnu as a personal God who would be prepared to intercede on behalf of his devotees. The objects of this worship were Krishna and Rama. Although antecedents of this doctrine of loving devotion can be traced back to the *Gita,* ascribed to the fifth century A.D. in its final form, and its growth in South India between the seventh and twelfth centuries, its sudden popularity in the Indo-Gangetic plains from the fifteenth century can perhaps, be explained on the basis of the developments outlined above. Also, the Sufi saints and poets, by their incessant propaganda of the path of love, had prepared the ground for the growth of a mass Vaisnavite movement based on the doctrine of love. The Vaisnavite movement had two forms: one, devoted to the worship of Krishna, advocated ecstasy based on *bhajan, kirtan,* etc. in which the symbolism of sexual union was used to denote the ideal relationship between God and the individual soul. Such a union recognised no limitations-whether of caste, race, religion, or status. It proved to be highly popular since it involved little effort on the part of the individual except total surrender. The second was the movement devoted to Rama. It combined love with upholding social propriety and norms, and a stem ethical code of life. The chief exponent of this school of *Bhakti,* Tulsidas, laid, in addition, considerable stress on the need for social and political stability within the framework of which alone religious duties could be properly performed. The basis of this was his belief that the overwhelming sections in society consisted of people with wicked and evil propensities. Hence social, religious and political controls were necessary. Social control implied the maintenance of a reformed caste system in which people did not transgress their prescribed duties. For this, the support of a just, discreet ruler *(niti-nipuna)* and high-minded *(sajjan)* officials was necessary. Their efforts were to be combined with those of a high-minded guru devoted to the public good, gathering around him a selfless band of devotees, among whom there would be no discrimination of caste or station.[25]

Thus, Tulsi prepared the ground for wider cooperation with the Mughal state. This, in turn, was reciprocated by the Mughal state which gave land grants to the leading centres of Bhakti at Mathura, Vrindavan, etc. However, Tulsi's own approach was fundamentalist or traditionalist in the sense that he based his teaching on the scriptures which, along with the Brahmans, were to be respected and were to be regarded as the bedrock of religion. He also strengthened and revived the tradition of image worship, the deity being worshipped and treated with the deference due to a person of high station. The tradition of reincarnation was automatically reaffirmed. These provided an opportunity to the orthodox mullahs to reinforce their prejudices against Hinduism, although it was clear that rapprochement and good relations between Islam and Hinduism could not be predicated on the latter giving up what it considered some of its essential features.

For the present, the symbolism of love and beauty was more important than the difference of theory and praxis. The ecstatic stream of love and devotion flowing from the *saguna Bhakti* poets had a deep impact on the masses and the classes. Hindi poets propounding these views began to be accorded official position at the Mughal court, along with

[25]Savitri Chandra, *Samaj aur Sanskriti* 9-13, *Social Life and Concepts,* 87-94.

Persian poets. Mughal nobles, such as Abdur Rahim Khan-i-Khanan, also composed poems devoted to the love of Radha and Krishna.

A lot has been written about the orthodox opposition to Akbar's liberal policies which gathered force during the seventeenth century, spearheaded by the *naqshbandi* Shaikh Ahmad Sirhindi. The point at issue was whether in a state headed by a Muslim ruler, all religions and their followers were to be given an equal status, and if so, whether this would not weaken the uniqueness of Islam and the special position of its leaders, the *ulema,* thereby jeopardising their mission of converting all people to what it considered the truth. This controversy found reflection also in the dispute between lbn-i-Arabi's concept of *wahdat-ul-wujud* and the concept of *wahdatul-shuhud* put forward by Shaikh Ahmad Sirhindi. The discussion about the relationship between the Absolute and being, and whether the phenomenal world was real, i.e. a creation, or merely an extension of God was not new. What was new was Shaikh Ahmad Sirhindi's claim to be the renovator *(mujaddid)* of Islam, from whom even the mystical members of the Sufi hierarchy were to receive grace. The question of interaction with the Hindus did not arise, because the *Mujaddid* advocated no association with them. He wrote that by meditation and self-mortification the infidels could cleanse their baser selves but not their hearts.[26]

The exaggerated claims of the *Mujaddid* were not accepted by the other Sufi orders, or by Jahangir or Shah Jahan. Nor did the influence of the *wajudis* decline, even though Aurangzeb sought the blessing of the *Mujaddid's* son, Shaikh Muhammad Said, during his Qandhar campaign in 1652 and extended favours to him.[27] Interaction between the Hindu *Bhakti* saints and the Sufis continued mainly through the Chistiya and Qadiriya *silsilahs.* In this, the association of

[26]Rizvi. *op. cit*. ii. 208.

[27]*Ibid,* 243.

Jahangir with Jadrup Gosain; and of Dara with Mullah Shah, Shaikh Muhibullah, Miyan Mir, the wandering mystics, and the Hindu saint Baba Lal 'are well known. It is difficult to say that Dara's assertion in the *Sirr-i-Akbar* and *Majma-ul-Bahrain* of the fundamental unity of God, of the Vedas being the *loh-i-mahfuz* mentioned in the Quran, and of all religions being different roads to the same God would have been able to create a new climate of interaction had Dara not have been the heir apparent, leading to his defeat by the more orthodox Aurangzeb who used Dara's *bidat* to rally orthodox support around himself.

The nature and extent of the Sufi and Bhakti interaction during Aurangzeb's reign needs careful study. Although Aurangzeb himself was more interested in *fiqh* than mysticism, he paid respect to the Sufi saints, especially the *wajudis* whenever he passed by the mausoleum of one. Also, he did not prevent his sons, Muazzam and Azam, and other members of the family from consorting with liberal Sufis, so much so that Muazzam and Azam were suspected of harbouring Shiite tendencies. Jahanara and later, Aurangzeb's daughter, Zebunnisa who held court at Delhi from 1679 to her death in 1702, patronised liberal Sufis, many of whom had close contacts with Hindus, or were well versed in Hindu philosophy and Hindi poetry. Among these was the governor of Delhi, Aqil Khan, who was also a scholar and composed many romances such as *Masnavi Man-wa-Mahar* or *Manohar wa Madhumalti, Masnawi Shama-toa-Parwana* or *Padmavati*, etc.[28]

Sufi writers continued to write *masnavis* in Hindi. Many of these, written during the first half of the eighteenth century, have come to light. Prominent among these are Usman's *Chitravali*, Shaikh Nabi's *Gyandeep*, and Jan Kavi's numerous works *Ratnavali, Katha Kamalata, Laila Majnu*; Qasim Shah's

[28]Nurul Hasan Ansari, *Farsi Adab ba Ahd-i-Aurangzeb* (Delhi, 1969) 7-11, Satish Chandra, 'Cultural and Political Role of Delhi, 1675-1725' in R.E. Frykenberg (ed) *Delhi through the Ages* (O.U.P. 1986) 208-9.

Hans-Jawahar etc. Many works broadly dealing with romances, were also written in Rajasthani, often based on popular legends such as *Dhola-Maru, Bisaldeo Raso* and *Prem Prasad.* Thus, the *masnawis* of the Sufis were received into a framework which was popular and familiar. This explains their continued popularity.

Apart from the *Pusti margi sampradaya* of Vallabha in whose tradition was the Krisnite poet, Surd as, and those founded by Chaitanya and Tulsi, a number of popular sects flourished during this period and the succeeding century. Of these, Tara Chand has referred to a number of sects which continued the tradition of seeking a via media between Islam and Hinduism. Prominent among these were Dharnidas and Pran Nath, founders of the *Dharni* sect; Jagjivandas, who reorgnaised the *satnami* sect which had suffered defeat at the hands of Aurangzeb or organised one with similar aims; Bulla Das who was a Kunbi by caste, and many others.[29]

At the political level, too, the close association of the state with Islamic orthodoxy came to an end within half a dozen years of Aurangzeb's death, and many of the discriminating practices adopted by him, such as *jizyah,* came to an end. The Syed Brothers, who dominated the court of Delhi from 1713 to 1719, adopted a liberal policy towards the Rajputs, Marathas and the Hindus generally. Thus, from the time of Jahander Shah (1712), Mughal emperors and nobels took part in Hindu festivals such as Dasehra and Holi, with Basant Panchami being celebrated on a grand scale at the court.[30]

Despite their sharp differences, both *wujudis* and *shahudis* strongly denounced the *ulema* for their hypocrisy and worldliness. In the Urdu poetry of the times, which became

[29]Tara Chand, *Influence of Islam,* 197-212 .

[30]Satish Chandra, *Parties and Politics at the Mughal Court: 1707-40,* Delhi, (3rd ed. 1979), 260-1; Z. Malik, *The Reign of Muhammad Shah 1719-48,* Asia, 352.

popular both among the Muslim and Hindu elite and the urban sections, the Shaikh was portrayed as the 'hypocrite', and the *zunnardar* (Brahman) as a symbol of being faithful despite adversities. It was in this atmosphere that Shah Waliullah, considered the greatest theological thinker of the time, tried to set out a new ethical moral code in which sectarian controversies were at a discount. While denouncing many of the practices taken over from the Hindus' as un-Islamic, he 'admitted that the essence of all religions was the same and all of them enjoined a similar code.' He also tried to reconcile *wujudi* and *shahudi* doctrines, thereby legitimising ideas and practices denounced by the *Mujaddid.* In fact, earlier, Mirza Mazhar Jan-i-jahan, a Sufi *naqshbandi* poet, had come to the same conclusion as Dara, viz. that the Vedas were revealed books, and hence the Hindus could not be identified with the *kafirs* of Arabia. In his opinion, there was little difference between idol worship and *tasawwar-i-shaikh* or concentration on the mental image of the preceptor.[31]

Thus the eighteenth century, while a period of political strife, was not a period of growing religious controversies and conflict, but one in which the dominant trend was continuation of the efforts at compromise and understanding which had been promoted in no small degree by the Sufis, the *Jogis* and the *Bhakti* saints. Simultaneously, efforts to instill a life of piety and a stem moral code, purging it of immoral and licentious practices on the one hand, and of un-Islamic (i.e. Hindu) practices on the other, continued.

In assessing the history of the religious movements in the sub-continent during the medieval period, quite apart from the role of the religious leaders, it has been usual to contrast the policies of Akbar and Aurangzeb or, earlier Muhammad bin Tughluq or Firuz Tughluq as broad and liberal or narrow-based and orthodox' from one point of

[31]*Hujjat-ul Allah-al Baligha,* tr, into Urdu, N. Ismail Godhravi, 222; S.A.H. Rizvi, *Shah Waliullah and His Times* (Canberra, 1980).

view, and from another, as compromising Islam or of strengthening it. In the process, the carefully crafted, gradually evolved policies of Jahangir and Shah Jahan have tended to be overlooked. Both these rulers tried to satisfy the orthodox *ulema* about their concern for the *sharia* and their due share in the government, without, at the same time, allowing them to flex their muscles, weaken the alliance with the Rajputs, or pursue policies which might create a sense of discrimination among the Hindus. Unfortunately, this compromise was wrecked by factionalism in the nobility, lack of its credibility among the masses and the intelligentsia, and the rivalry between Dara and Aurangzeb, and their own individual orientations. In the ultimate resort, however, it was neither the policy of Akbar nor that of Aurangzeb, but the compromise worked out by Jahangir and Shah Jahan which prevailed during the eighteenth century and continued during the nineteenth. Whether this has any lessons for the present, it is difficult to say. Of course history rarely repeats itself or moves in a straight line but in elliptical even mysterious ways. That is why history is history and there is no end to it.

10

REASSESSING AURANGZEB

For a long time, Aurangzeb has been a kind of bugbear in Indian history with opposite and sharply divided opinions put forward regarding his motivations, the real purpose of his policies, and their impact both on the empire and the larger society. Unlike an earlier ruler, Muhammad-bin-Tughlaq who, like Aurangzeb, tried to extend the frontiers of his empire to the natural; geographical limits of India, there is near unanimity about the personal character of Aurangzeb—his single-mindedness of purpose, his dedication to his mission as a ruler, his personal valour and skill as a military leader, and his aversion to a life of ostentation, leaning rather to simplicity almost bordering on asceticism.

The point at dispute is his motivation. Was his real purport, as Sir Jadunath Sarkar suggests, the establishment of a truly Islamic state *(dar-ul-Islam)* in India which implied 'the conversion of the entire population to Islam and the extinction of every form of dissent...' (Sarkar, *History of Aurangzeb*, Calcutta, 1928, iii, pp. 249-50). In that case, the personal qualities of Aurangzeb, his dedication and singleness of purpose, become a negative point rather than an asset.

On the other hand, some Pakistani historians such as Ishtiaq Hussain Qureshi (formerly of St. Stephen's College, Delhi) argue that in a Muslim state, power must be retained firmly in the hands of the Muslims, and the unity of the Muslims who had the ultimate responsibility for the defence of the state maintained by a rigid adherence to the orthodox creed, the *sharia*. Qureshi concludes, 'It was a crime to lull the Muslims into believing that the maintenance of the Empire was not their prime responsibility. Even more disastrous was. the encouragement of the feeling that toleration implied the belief that all religions were merely different goals all equally good, of reaching the same God, *(History of the Freedom Movement*, i, p. 34).

Thus, for Sir Jadunath Sarkar, Aurangzeb had singly the largest responsibility for the breakdown of the Mughal empire because he alienated the Hindus, and expanded the empire till it fell under its own weight. For Qureshi, Aurangzeb battled in vain to undo the damage done to the empire by Akbar's liberal policies, and his admitting Hindus to the top services. Unfortunately for Dr. Qureshi, his theorisations about the motives of Aurangzeb have been blown sky-high by research which shows that far from being reduced, the number of Hindus in the services during the latter part of Aurangzeb's reign were larger than ever before, rising from 24 percent under Shah Jahan to 33 percent in 1689. It is clear that Dr. Qureshi was more concerned with defending the policies of the ruling class in Pakistan than analysing the real motivation and policies of Aurangzeb.

Nationalist historians, such as Dr. R.P. Tripathi, have argued that all the actions of Aurangzeb were based on political considerations, and his apprehension that the Hindus had become seditious and were opposing his attempts to establish and strengthen all-India unity by absorbing in his empire the Deccan as well as the areas dominated by the Marathas. This approach implies a laborious explaining away of Aurangzeb's various acts of intolerance and bigotry.

Recently, some efforts have been made to lay more emphasis on the social and economic factors to explain the rise of Muslim and Hindu communal lobbies in the country during the 17th century, and their impact on politics. In particular, emphasis has been laid on widespread unemployment among the Muslim clergy, the growth of a

Muslim middle class which wanted better opportunities or preference for itself both in government service and private trade, and the growth of a jagirdari crisis in consequence of the income of the state falling short of expectations or requirements. In other words, the religious reaction is considered to be an integral part of a deeper socio-economic-cum-administrative crisis.

A slow realisation has therefore come that Aurangzeb cannot be seen in terms of black or white, for he was a complex character. He ruled for almost 50 years over the largest empire India had seen since the days of Ashoka. Both the geographical range and the time span implied policies which were often contradictory as well as subject to shifts in view of changed situations. Aspects of Aurangzeb's policies where sharply different opinions have been expressed by historians are:

— his policy towards temples, reinstitution of the poll tax *(jizyah)*, and towards the Hindus generally;
— his break with the Rajputs;
— his policy towards the Marathas, especially Shivaji;
— his decision to annex the Deccan kingdoms.

Without attempting to go into the details of all these aspects, we shall only note the present academic position.

Temples

It is well known that right at the beginning of his reign, Aurangzeb reiterated the position of limited, toleration set out in the *sharia,* i.e. that while new churches, synagogues, temples and so on, cannot be permitted in opposition to Islam, old places of worship can be repaired because 'buildings cannot stand forever'. There is little evidence to show that this led to a wave of temple destruction. In fact, it was only in the eighth year of his reign, in 1665, that Aurangzeb ordered the destruction of such temples in Gujarat which he had ordered to be destroyed when, as a prince, he had been viceroy of the province, but many of which including the temple of Somnath, had been rebuilt subsequently.

The argument of Sarkar, followed by S.R Sharma, that around this time Aurangzeb issued an order for the general destruction of temples has not been accepted because no copy of any such order has been found, and has been referred to by no contemporary observer, except Saqi Mustaid Khan who wrote half a dozen years after Aurangzeb's death. On the other hand, evidence has been cited to show that Aurangzeb continued to grant land and other favours to non-Muslim places of worship (for example, the famous temples of Vrindavan, the Sikh shrine at Dehra Dun).

How, then, to explain the destruction of the temple of Vishwanath at Banaras, and a number of temples at Mathura, Thatta, and so on? A simple explanation would be that this was simply an example of his orthodoxy: it had been brought to the notice of the emperor that both Hindus and Muslims used to come from far-off places to study under the brahmans at these places. R.P. Tripathi's argument that these places had become centres of sedition finds no contemporary corroboration.

On the other hand, it does appear that Aurangzeb had begun to look upon the preservation of prominent temples as a kind of guarantee of good conduct on the part of the Hindus of the area. Thus, places of worship began to be treated as fit objects of reprisal in case of misconduct or rebellion. This was applied to Bir Singh Deo Bundela's temple at Mathura when the Jats of the area rose in rebellion, and in Marwar when there was conflict following the death of Maharaja Jaswant Singh. But this policy seems to have been modified after the conquest of Bijapur and Golkonda in 1687. Hardly any Hindu temples were broken in the South despite continued conflict with the Marathas.

Jizyah

Jizyah or poll tax had been abolished by Akbar in 1564. It was revived by Aurangzeb in 1679, in the 22nd year of his reign, on the ground that it was *wajib* (compulsory) according to *sharia*. No one accepts any longer Sarkar's theory that Aurangzeb's purpose was the forced conversion of the Hindus by instituting this measure—the indigent, women and children, the physically handicapped and government servants being exempt. Though burdensome for the poor, its incidence was too light for the middle and upper classes, being resented more as a mark of discrimination.

The question is, if the measure was purely an orthodox measure, why did Aurangzeb wait 22 years before reinstituting it, despite repeated demands by orthodox sections? Nor was the measure merely economic in nature because Aurangzeb had exempted many taxes levied earlier, and earmarked the proceeds of *jizyah* for charity. I have suggested elsewhere[1] that the measure was both political and ideological in nature. It was ideological in the sense that it marked out Aurangzeb as an orthodox Muslim King. It rallied the clergy to his side by providing them jobs as *amins* or (collectors) of *jizyah*, with the (unintended) opportunity of extorting illegal sums in the process. Politically, Aurangzeb hoped that this would help in rallying Muslim opinion behind him, not only in his conflict with the Rajputs and Marathas, but even more in his looming conflict with the Muslim kingdoms of the Deccan.

In 1705, Aurangzeb 'suspended' *jizyah* in the Deccan on account of war and famine in the area. But war and famine had been endemic in tile south for a long time. Was this an admission of failure on Aurangzeb's part, or should it be seen in conjunction with Aurangzeb's effort around this time to come to terms with the Marathas by agreeing to Shivaji's swarajya, and the grant of sardeshmukhi (though not chauth) of the Deccan? Sufficient debate on the point has not yet taken place because of the belief popularised by Sarkar, that the religious policy of Aurangzeb, as it crystallised

[1]See Satish Chandra, 'Jizyah and the state in India during the 17th century', *Journal of the Economic and Social History of the Orient*, Vol. II, No.3 1968, pp. 322-40.

around, 1679, was rigid and inflexible. Similarly, many of the so-called 'puritanical' measures of Aurangzeb are being examined in this perspective, viz., as a communal reaction to a complex socio-economic reality.

Fall-out with the Rajputs

Recent studies refute the idea that Dara was a friend of the Rajputs on account of his liberal religious views, and that Aurangzeb was, on account of his orthodoxy, inimical to them. In fact, Aurangzeb was fully aware of the importance of the Rajputs, and carefully cultivated the leading Rajput rajas, especially the rulers of Udaipur and Amber, in view of the inevitable civil war after the death of Shah [ahan. As it was, only Maharaja Jaswant Singh of Marwar and the Hadas fought against Aurangzeb and that, too, more on account of Shah Jahan than Dara.

Aurangzeb excused Jaswant Singh for his double treachery, and had good relations with the Rajputs during the early part of his reign, with Mirza Raja Jai Singh emerging as one of his principal advisors. The breach with Rana Raj Singh came about not because of Aurangzeb's orthodoxy, or the Charumati affair, but because of a desire on the part of the Rana to playa larger role in Rajput affairs. The background to this was the steady erosion of the predominant position once enjoyed by Mewar, and the rise to prominence of other Rajput states—the Rathors, the Kachhawas, the Hadas who were considered inferior or subordinate to them by the Sishodias of Mewar.

The death of Jaswant Singh of Marwar, and the escheat of the state by Aurangzeb was interpreted by Sarkar as a part of Aurangzeb's policy of the forcible conversion of the Hindus, and depriving the Hindus of an efficient head to oppose this policy. Recent researches[2] show that the escheat of

[2]See for instance, *Jodhpur Hakumat ri Bahi,* eds., S. Chandra. R Sinh, G.D. Sharma Meenakshi, Delhi, 1976.

the state was part of a regular policy of doing so whenever there was a dispute about the succession.

An extra cause of the escheat of the state was the recovery of large debts to the Mughal state left behind by Jaswant. The claim for the gaddi between the posthumous sons of Jaswant Singh, and Indra Singh, the grandson of Jaswant Singh's elder brother Rao Amar Singh whose claim had earlier been passed over by Shah Jahan, divided the court and led to an acrimonious dispute. Aurangzeb toyed with the idea of partitioning the state between the two contenders on the model of the division of Bundi and Kotah by Shah Jahan. The solution would have been an invidious one, and Raj Singh of Mewar stepped in to oppose partition, and support the sons of Jaswant Singh. The subsequent history of the conflict—the flight of Durga Das, the triumph of Ajit Singh and the subsequent war, are too well known to be repeated.

Aurangzeb withdrew support from Indra Singh, though for reasons of false prestige, but refused to accept Ajit Singh's claim, leading to a debilitating civil war. That this was unwise may be readily conceded. But it is less clear that an earlier settlement of the dispute would have had an impact on the conflict with the Marathas, or on the war in the Deccan.

The Marathas and the Problem of the Deccan

The problem of the Marathas and the Deccan, although two separate problems, had largely fused by the time of Aurangzeb's accession, and hence need to be examined almost as one. Together they constituted the most intractable, long lasting and convoluted problem, combining geographical, societal, ethnic, cultural and political aspects which kept shifting their focus. Sarkar's theory that the annexation of the Deccan was the 'sleepless ambition' of the Mughals is not accepted. Though historical and cultural traditions implied that the Mughals move towards the Deccan, they consciously tried to limit the expansion of their territories to the south even while claiming sovereignty over the entire country.

The position was complicated by the rise of the Marathas which had become noticeable during the first half of the 17th century. Both Jahangir and Shah Jahan recognised the importance of the Marathas in the Deccan and tried to recruit them into Mughal service, but with limited success. With the weakening of the Deccan states, many nobles—Habshis, Deccanis and Marathas (including Shahji, the father of Shivaji) tried to carve out their own sphere of domination (the word 'independence' had little meaning in those days where authority was directly proportionate to the length of one's sword). This forms the political background to the rise of Shivaji. The coming of Aurangzeb hardly changed the situation. Nevertheless, the rise of the Marathas under Shivaji has been sought to be explained in terms of a religious reaction to Aurangzeb's policies (Sarkar, Sardesai), the assertion of a Maratha sense of nationality (Ranade, Sardesai), peasant lure for plunder (Irfan Habib), and societal factors, including hopes of rising in the *varna* hierarchy (Irawati Karve, Satish Chandra).

The first Mughal noble who tried to look at the Maratha and Deccan problems in an integrated manner was Mirza Raja Jai Singh who advocated a policy of befriending and isolating the Marathas in the context of a forward policy in the Deccan. Aurangzeb who, as a prince, had been an advocate of a strong forward policy in the Deccan, did not really agree with the Mirza Raja, not only because he distrusted Shivaji (he was a past master in changing sides) and placed a low value on his alliance (later, Jahanara called him 'a petty bhumia'), but also because he was afraid that the Deccan could not be won without committing large armies which could not be placed under a nobleman, much less a prince (his own rebellion against Shah Jahan was an example). Nor could he afford to go to the Deccan personally, as long as Shah Jahan was alive, and the Persian threat on the frontier persisted.

Aurangzeb's logic was sound, and in accordance with earlier Mughal practice. Why did he suddenly embark upon a policy of annexing the Deccan upto Jinji, not with the support of the Marathas as Jai Singh had postulated, but despite them? Was he afraid of the entire Deccan falling under the domination of the Marathas if the Mughals continued to mark time? After the death of Shivaji in 1680, and the rise to power of the brothers Madanna and Akhanna in Golkonda, such a 'possibility seemed hardly feasible, except that the Deccani states and the Marathas, while fighting each other, would have constituted a strong anti-Mughal coalition.

That the conquest of the Deccan was the consequence of a shortage of jagirs is also not warranted. In fact, if we are to accept the version of the contemporary observor, Mamuri, who was echoed by Khafi Khan, the conquest of the Deccan aggravated the crisis of the jagirdari system, with the influx of large numbers of Deccanis and Marathas, creating acute unemployment among the khanazads, the sons of old Mughal nobles. Was Aurangzeb, therefore only concerned with grasping more territory—'a heap of stones' as the contemporary Bhimsen alleged? If so, this was itself a change, for Aurangzeb had earlier rejected such adventures in Deccan.

Was Aurangzeb actuated by the desire to control the European who were exploiting the weak states in the Deccan for extracting all kinds of concessions, including the setting up of arms factories? Or, was Aurangzeb merely concerned with bringing under his control areas where handicraft production and exports had expanded the fastest during the preceding half century? A simplistic explanation that has been put forward is that in a feudal-militarist state, expansion is the norm, unless countered by a counterveiling force.

Anyhow, in none of these speculations does religion or Aurangzeb's orthodoxy figure anywhere. Thus, emphasis on Aurangzeb's religious policy is slowly giving place to a deeper study of socio-economic, intellectual, cultural, geographic (regional) and political factors. These studies tend to show neither a hero nor a villain, but a somewhat rigid and unimaginative politician who failed to understand the societal problems at work in the country, and often took recourse to religious slogans in order to meet complex socio-economic and political problems.

Contrarywise, it has been argued that the Mughal decision to undertake the annexation of the Deccan was itself an index of a deep-seated crisis within the empire. There has been a fair (though inadequate) debate regarding the nature of this crisis—whether it was essentially internal (with structural factors, class relations, the nature of the ruling classes and the state) factors playing a crucial role, or whether it was being deepened/impelled by external factors (influx of silver and the growing monetisation of the economy, growth of internal and foreign markets, growing inflation, etc.).

Thus Aurangzeb is no longer regarded primarily as an orthodox fundamentalist, intent on instituting in India a truly Islamic state as he saw it, or a communalist whose narrow, illiberal views hastened the downfall of the empire, or one who battled incessantly against forces of disintegration while he tried manfully to establish an all-India empire. More and more he is seen as the representative of an old order which was unable and unwilling to recognise, much less face the stirrings and incipient growth of a new socio-economic system.

FURTHER READINGS

1 Sir Jadunath Sarkar, *History of Aurangzeb* (5 volumes), Calcutta, 1912-30, 2nd revised, enlarged editions, 1928-52.

2 Zahiruddin Faruki, *Aurangzeb and His times*, Bombay, 1935, reprinted, Idarah-i-Adabiyat-i-Delhi, Delhi, 1972-80.

3 S.R. Sharma, *The Religious Policy of the Mughal Emperors*, 1940, 2nd ed., Bombay, 1962.

4 I.H. Qureshi, *The Muslim Community of the Hind-Pakistan Sub-Continent*, Karachi, 1947.

5 K. Kanungo, *Dara Shikoh*, Calcutta, 1952.

6 Satish Chandra, *Parties and Politics at the Mughal Court (1707-40)*, Aligarh, 1959, 3rd ed., Delhi, 1979.
7 S.A.A. Rizvi, *Muslim Revivalist Movements in Northern India in the Sixteenth and Seventeenth Centuries*, Agra, .1965.
8 M. Athar Ali, *The Mughal Nobility Under Aurangzeb*, Bombay, 1966.
9 Yohanan Friedmann, *Shaykh Ahmad Sirhindi; An Outline of His Thought and a Study of His Image in the Eyes of Posterity*, Montreal, 1971.
10 J.F. Richards, *Mughal Administration in Golkonda*, Oxford, 1975.
11 Satish Chandra, R. Singh. C.D. Sharma (eds), *Marwar Under Jaswant Singh: Jodhpur Hukumat-ri-Bahi*, Meerut, Delhi, 1976.
12 Muzaffar Alam, *The Crisis of Empire in Mughal North India: Awadh and the Punjab 1707-48*, Delhi, 1986.

ARTICLES

1 M. Athar Ali, 'Religious Issues in the War of Succession', *PIHC'*, 1960.
2 Irfan Habib, 'Agrarian Causes of the Fall of the Mughal Empire', *Enquiry*, Nos. 2 & 3, 1960.
3 M. Athar Ali, 'Causes of the Rathor Rebellion of 1679', *PIHC*, 1961.
4 Satish Chandra, 'Some Factors Leading to the Break Between Aurangzeb and Rana Raj Singh', *Proceedings of the Indian History Congress, (PIHC)*, 1965.
5 Satish Chandra, 'Jizyah and the State in India during the 17th Century' *Journal of the Economic and Social History of the Orient*, Vol. XII, No.3, 1969.
6 Muzaffar Alam, 'Some Aspects of the Changes in the Position of the *Madad-i-Ma'ash* Holders in Awadh, 1676-1727, *PIHC*, 1974.
7 M. Athar Ali, 'The Passing of Empire: The Mughal Case', *Modern Asian Studies*, Vol. 9, No.3, 1975.
8 P. Hardy, M.N. Pearson and J.F. Richards, Articles on the Decline of the Mughal Empire, *Journal of Asian Studies*, Vol. XXXV, No.3, 1976.
9 Satish Chandra, 'The Deccan Policy of the Mughals—A Reappraisal (ii)', *Indian Historical Review (IHR)*, Vol V. Nos. 1-2, 1979.
10 Shireen Moosvi, 'The Deccan and the Economy of the Mughal Empire', *PIHC*, 1982.
11 Satish Chandra, 'Religious Policy of Aurangzeb during the later part of his Reign—Some Considerations', *IHR, Vol. XIII*, Nos. 1-2, 1987.
12 R.A. Alavi, 'The Temples of Vrindavan and their Priests during the reign of Aurangzeb.' *PIHC*, 1988.

11

AURANGZEB—A CRITICAL REVIEW

Aurangzeb's long reign of 49 years (1658-1707) was marked by strong, highly Personalized rule during while the empire was expanded to the east, north-east and the Deccan, reaching almost upto the geographical limits of India. At its height, it comprised the areas from Kashmir in the north to Jinji in the South, and from Kabul in the west to Chatgaon in the East. The empire disintegrated rapidly after Aurangzeb's death, and there is considerable controversy regarding the extent to which Aurangzeb's policies and acts of omission or commission contributed to the process. Recent controversies may be grouped around the following:

(i) his policy towards temples reinstitutioning of the poll-tax *(jizyah),* and other discriminatory practices which tended to alienate the Hindus;

(ii) his breach with the Rajputs who were considered the sword arm of the empire;

(iii) his expansionist policies, especially in the Deccan;

(iv) his inability or unwillingness to come to terms with the Marathas, a rising power; and

(v) growth of an administrative and agrarian crisis,

Religious Policy: Early in his reign, Aurangzeb reaffirmed the position laid down by the *sharia* that while new churches, synagogues,· temples and so on cannot be permitted "in opposition to Islam," old places of worship can be repaired because "buildings cannot stand for ever." It was in pursuance of this policy that *farmans* were issued (which are extant) to the brahmans at Banaras and Vrindavan, assuring them that local officials would not be allowed to interfere in their repairing old temples. In 1665, a number of Hindu temples in Gujarat, including the temple of Somnath, which Aurangzeb as a prince and Viceroy of Gujarat had destroyed or bricked up, but which had been rebuilt in the interval, were to be demolished. There is no reason to believe that subsequently Aurangzeb departed from this policy of limited toleration and ordered a general destruction of temples. No such orders have been found, nor is there any reference to them in Aurangzeb's letters or the *Akhbarat*. They are referred to only in *'Maasir-i-Alamgiri,* written after Aurangzeb's death. Moreover, not only did many old Hindu temples continue to exist in different parts of the country, there is documentary evidence of Aurangzeb's renewal of land grants enjoyed by Hindu temples at Mathura and elsewhere, and of his offering gifts to them (such as to the Sikh *gurudwara* at Dehra Dun). However, during the period, Aurangzeb adopted a policy of selective destruction or bricking up of a number of Hindu temples, either as a warning to local Hindu rajas, or as a reprisal for rebelliousness. Thus, some of the famous temples at Vrindavan, Mathura, Kashi and Thatta, etc., were destroyed as a part of this policy. This reached a climax in 1679 when, following the death of Maharaja Jaswant Singh, and resistance on the part of the Rathors as a protest against bringing Marwar under direct Mughal administration pending a decision of the sucession dispute, a number of old standing temples in the area were destroyed or bricked up. However, when the Mughals over-ran the Maratha territory and south India upto Jinji after 1687, the temples in the area were, except in a few isolated cases, left undisturbed, many of them being listed by contemporary writers, such as Bhimsen. Aurangzeb visited the caves of Ellora, and, noting the life-like images and paintings, remarked on the desolation of the place and that it "aroused a sense of warning to those who contemplate the future."

Thus, Aurangzeb's policy towards temples was not uniform, and, apart from the injunctions in the *sharia,* seems to have been influenced, at one time, by his fear (real or fancied) of overt or covert opposition by Hindu rajas and others, and at another, by a desire to mollify and win over the local Hindu elements.

Jizyah or poll-tax was revived by Aurangzeb in 1679 on the ostensible ground that it was *wajib* (compulsory) according to the *sharia.* That Aurangzeb waited for 22 years from his accession to arrive at this well-known, orthodox position suggests that his decision was based as much on political as religious considerations. The tax exempted the indigent *(dhimmi nadar),* women, children, the handicapped and government employees. The incidence of the tax was light for the rich, but was burdensome for the poor. In the rural areas, it was collected as a part of land revenue and all its proceeds earmarked for charity. Administered by *qazis,* it provided them an opportunity to amass money. Insistence on its personal collection in the towns was found harrassing, specially by merchants. In a number of towns, there was mass protests against it. However, though discriminatory, it was not designed to force non-Muslims to convert to Islam. Nor did it fundamentally alter the character of the state. Aurangzeb's hope that by reviving *jizyah* he would be able to rally Muslim opinion behind him, especially in the context of a likely contest with the Deccani Muslim states, remained largely unfulfilled. Thus, his chief Qazi, Shaikh-ul-Islam, son of Qazi Abdul Wahab, refused to give a *fatwa* that war against brother Muslim states was legitimate. *Jizyah* was not to the liking of many nobles who repeatedly forwarded requests for temporary remission, much to the annoyance of Aurangzeb. Finally, in 1705, Aurangzeb was forced to suspend *jizyah* in the Deccan, "on account of war and famine in the area." Significantly, it coincided with serious efforts on his part to come to terms with the Marathas.

Aurangzeb's efforts to help Muslim traders by charging them half the customs duty due from others had little beneficial effect, and was abused. Nor were efforts to reserve certain posts, such as *diwans* in crown-lands, and *peshkars* very successful, the Muslim nobles themselves protesting against it. The order had to be modified and remained virtually a dead letter. Restrictions on public celebrations of Holi in Ahmadabad, and certain practices during Diwali were of a moral and administrative nature.

The Rajputs: At the time of his accession, Aurangzeb had established cordial relations with the leading Rajput rajas, Mirza Raja Jai Singh of Amber, Mahraja Jaswant Singh of Marwar, and Maharaja Raj Singh of Mewar. He also pardoned and conciliated the rulers of Harauti and Bikaner who had opposed him. But a coolness in the relations developed after some time, specially after the death of Jai Singh (1666) who was one of the close advisors of Aurangzeb. However, an open breach occurred only after the death of Jaswant Singh towards the end of 1678. Since the Raja had no surviving male heir, the *gaddi* of Marwar was claimed by a number of contenders, the strongest claimant being Indra Singh, a grandson of Jaswant Singh's elder brother, Amar Singh. After considerable hesitation, and after it march to Ajmer, Aurangzeb finally decided to grant the *tika* of Jodhpur to Indra Singh. Simultaneously, he moved in the direction of partioning the state, a smaller proportion, consisting of the parganas of Sojat and Jaitaran, being granted to two posthumous sons of Jaswant Singh. This policy was resented by a strong group among the Rathor nobles, whose claim was backed up by the Rana of Mewar, leading to an open breach and war in which both Marwar and Mewar became involved. Failing to subdue Mewar, and faced by a rebellion by his son, Prince Akbar, Aurangzeb retraced his steps. He had earlier removed Indra Singh. In an agreement made with Maharana Jai Singh in 1681, a vague promise was given of granting *mansab* and *raj* to Ajit Singh, one of the surviving sons of Jaswant Singh, when he came of age. Meanwhile, Marwar remained under Mughal control. Mewar was vacated, but forced to surrender four parganas in lieu of *jizyah.* These terms satisfied neither Mewar nor Marwar. In consequence, there was disaffection, and hostilities continued. In 1698, Ajit Singh was given a *mansab* and parts of the state were granted to him. But Jodhpur remained under Mughal control.

The desultory warfare in Rajasthan was a drain on Mughal resources. Though the Hadas and the Kachhawahas continued to serve the Mughals in comparatively junior positions, the breach with some of the most influential sections of the Rajputs was a political and moral failure, on Aurangzeb's part. It was also reflective of a certain rigid frame of mind which manifested itself in more than one instance.

North-west, North-east, East and the Deccan

Even before his breach with the Rajputs, the Mughals had to face a serious rebellion on the part of the Afghan tribesmen living in the passes between Peshawar and Kabul. These uprisings (1667, 1672-76), and a threat of a Persian invasion absorbed Aurangzeb's attention, and had a definite impact on his policies in the north-east and the Deccan.

After his accession to the throne, Aurangzeb had embarked upon a vigorous forward policy, mainly in the north-east and east of India. Kuch-Bihar was annexed (1663), and efforts were made to oust the Ahom rulers from the Assam Valley and to annex it. After initial successes, the Mughals were faced with stiffening Ahom resistance. After two decades of debilitating warfare in swampy terrain and an hostile environment, the Mughals lost Gauhati and had to agree (1681) to a partitioning of the valley, with the river Manas as the boundary.

The Mughals had greater success in recovering eastern Bengal upto Chatgaon from the Magh ruler of Arakan, and in containing the Magh and *firangi* piracy which had largely laid waste the areas in east Bengal on both sides of the river upto Dacca. The main event was the capture of Chatgaon by the Mughal governor, Shaista Khan, in 1666. This not only led to the re-population of east Bengal, but the growth of its legendary industrial products, (muslin), and the expansion of its trade, both upland and coastal upto Gujarat.

In the Deccan, at first Aurangzeb adopted a policy of limited expansion, his objectives being displacement of Shivaji from the Mughal border, possibly at the expense of Bijapur, and of recovering the Nizam Shahi areas granted to Bijapur by Shah Jahan by the treaties of 1636. The latter effort succeeded, but the former did not. In 1668, Aurangzeb recovered Sholapur, the last Nizam Shahi territory ceded to Bijapur by the treaty of 1636. Earlier, Aurangzeb had seemingly approved, but, in fact, not extended the needed support to Jai Singh's grand programme of conquering Bijapur in alliance with Shivaji, that being a preclude to the conquest of Karnataka and the entire Deccan. Aurangzeb had, perhaps in view of his involvement in the north-west, preferred a policy of nibbling at the Deccani states. However, this had led to the emergence of a grand anti-Mughal alliance of the Deccani powers, including Shivaji. The leading role in forging this alliance was played by the brothers, Madanna and Akhanna, who dominated the affairs of Gokonda from 1672 to the verge of its downfall in 1684.

A more vigorous, forward policy in the Deccan began after 1676. However, successive invasions to conquer Bijapur and Golkonda between 1676 and 1680 failed on account of the united opposition of the Deccani powers, and the limited resources at the disposal of the Mughal Viceroy. Only Shivaji who plundered both the sides gained. Thus, a crisis point had been reached in the affairs of the Deccan, even before Aurangzeb came to the Deccan in 1681 in pursuit of his rebel son, Prince Akbar.

In the remaining twenty-six years of his life, Aurangzeb ceaselessly campaigned in the Deccan. Efforts to break the united front of the Deccani powers and the Marathas having failed, in 1684 Aurangzeb finally decided to deal with Bijapur and Golkonda before he could concentrate all his attention on the Marathas. In the process, he besieged and captured Bijapur (1686) and Golkonda (1687), captured and executed the Maratha king, Sambhaji (1689), and tried to extend the Mughal dominion over the Karnataka upto Jinji. But he was successful only partially, on account of opposition from the local elements and the activities of the large roving bands of Matathas which disrupted Mughal supplies, and seriously interfered with the Mughal process of consolidation of their rule in the Deccan.

The Marathas

The Marathas, thus, posed an intractable problem which successive Mughal rulers, including Aurangzeb, were unable to resolve. From the time of Jahangir, efforts were made with limited success to enrol important Maratha sardars into the mansabdari system. Unlike the Rajputs, the Marathas did not have well-established rulers with definite territories, and a strong sense of kinship loyalties. Various Maratha sardars contended with each other, and with the Deccani rulers and the Mughals, and were quick to change sides, for their own advantage. Lack of trust on both sides vitiated the effort of Mirza Raja Jai Singh to reconcile Aurangzeb to Shivaji, a rising power. Thus, Shivaji's visit to Agra (1666), his disappointment with Aurangzeb regarding the *mansab* granted to him, and his subsequent escape from jail only deepened mutual distrust.

In his dealings with the Marathas, including Shivaji, Aurangzeb consistently underestimated their power and potential. He refused to treat with Sambhaji after his capture (1689), and executed him, confident of his military strength to overcome the Maratha bid for *swarajya.* Thus, he recklessly extended the Mughal lines of communications upto Jinji, without first winning over the Marathas, or dealing with the Maratha roving bands which continually gained in strength and striking capacity, taking advantage of local disgruntled elements and absorbing many disbanded (Muslims) soldiers of the erstwhile Deccani states. Efforts at this stage to induct Maratha sardars in the nobility had little impact on the situation. Hence, after 1699, Aurangzeb concentrated on capturing the leading Maratha strongholds to bring the Marathas to their knees. This proved costly, led to the untold suffering of the beseigers, and was ultimately a failure since it left the countryside, including towns, outside his zone of operations and at the mercy of the Maratha roving bands. It was only in 1703 that Aurangzeb offered to treat with the Marathas by restoring Shivaji's *swarajya* to the captive prince, Shahu, and the grant of *sardeshmukhi* of the Deccan to him. But these efforts collapsed, largely on account of the unacceptable Maratha demand of *chauth* for the six subahs of the Deccan, and Aurangzeb's lack of trust in the Marathas.

Administrative and Agrarian Crisis

Aurangzeb's problems were aggravated by the declining efficiency of the Mughal administrative machinery, and growing factionalism in the nobility. Some contemporary writers trace these to the refusal of Aurangzeb to award harsh punishments, on account of his adherence to the Islamic law "so that no fear and dread of punishment remained in the hearts of jagirdars, faujdars and zamindars." More germane was the growing gap between the real and the paper income of the jagirs which had come to a head during Shah Jahan's reign, leading to a reduction both of *zat* (personal) salaries, and of the obligation of the number of troops and mounts to be maintained. The reduced efficiency of the mansabdars became apparent in the difficult situation in the Deccan. Efforts to induct Deccani nobles and Maratha sardars in the nobility after 1687. deepened the crisis. The new elements were unfamiliar with the Mughal system of administration with its cumbersome checks and balances. They could neither collect the land-revenue due, nor deal with the Maratha roving bands. On the other hand, the influx of the Deccanis and Marathas into the Mughal service upset the existing equations in the nobility, leading to heightened factionalism, and an acute shortage of job opportunities for the sons and sons-in-law of the old jagirdars *(khanazads),* since Aurangzeb imposed a virtual ban on the appointment of new jagirdars. Shortage of productive jagirs, and the resulting corruption led to a crisis in the working of the jagirdari system and was the basis of growing factionalism in the nobility.

While trade and industry, including foreign trade continued to expand in India during the reign of Aurangzeb, agriculture seems to have stagnated in large areas, leading to a growing crisis of financial resources, and pressure on a section of the cultivators. The rise in prices, largely on account of the influx of silver, had unforeseen consequences which have yet to be fully assessed. There were heightened local conflicts and sporadic outbreaks, such as the Jat and the Satnami revolts in the Agra. These and other conflicts at the local level have also to be seen in the context of the struggle for acquiring superior landed (zamindari) rights by certain sections including caste groups. The conflict in the Punjab with the Sikh gurus had a long history. Under the leadership of Guru Govind, the Sikhs attempted to carve out a separate state, largely at the expense of the Hindu rajas in the Punjab hills. This soon broadened into a conflict with the Mughal officials of the areas.

Despite his emphasis on the *sharia,* and efforts to appease and utilise the *ulema* for his ulterior motives, Aurangzeb did not allow the clergy to dominate him. Nor was the fundamental character of the state changed, remaining, in essence, a broadly liberal Islamic state as it had emerged during the reign of Shah Jahan. In an exchange of bitter correspondence with Shah Jahan, Aurangzeb asserted that "Sovereignty signifies protection of the people, not self-indulgence and libertinism." In the letters addressed to his sons, justice is upheld as the highest ideal of kingship, not defence of the faith or punishing infidels. In fact, discharging the duties of sovereignty and necessary worldly tasks are designated "truly religious." Again, Aurangzeb made no effort to abandon the concept of a composite ruling class drawn from Muslims and Hindus, and from diverse ethnic and regional elements. Thus, during the latter part of his reign, the proportion of Hindus in various grades including the highest is the mansabdari system increased to about 30 per cent.

Called popularly a *zinda pir* (living saint) on account of us piety and simple style of living, it would be far from truth to believe that Aurangzeb's personal expenses, and those of his chief queens, was met by the sale of his copies of the Quran and the stitched caps made by him: these were no more than well recognized acts of piety. Orthodox and puritanical by temperament, Aurangzeb tried to put down practices which he considered contrary to the *sharia,* such as the use of intoxicants, stamping of *kalma* on the coins, celebration of *nauroz,* recourse to astrologers, use of costly clothes, banning of music in court, discouragement of the liberal arts such as painting, and encouragement of religious studies, etc. However, Aurangzeb largely failed in his puritanical approach, the dominant ethos of the nobility remaining sensual and eclectic, favouring the liberal sufis, and the eclectic traditions of poetry. The most significant achievement of Aurangzeb in this field was the compendious collection of *fatawas* or religious decrees, under the title *Fatwa-i-Alamgiri.* Aurangzeb was himself widely read, and was a stylist of some distinction. Collections of his letters remained a favourite reading in Persian studies for a long time after his death.

While Aurangzeb's reign marked the territorial climax of the Mughal state, it cannot be gainsaid that he left behind an empire which was deeply distracted by conflicts, a near empty treasury, a deeply factionalized nobility, and a growing sense of disillusionment with the government among wide sections. But he strengthened the traditions of an all-India sovereignty in the house of the Mughals which persisted for a hundred and fifty years after his death.

12

IMPACT OF CENTRAL ASIAN INSTITUTIONS ON STATE & SOCIETY IN MEDIEVAL INDIA (10TH - 14TH CENTURIES)

Important changes in the structure of society and government took place in West Central Asia and Northern India between the 10th and the 14th centuries. In India, with the disappearance of a centralised state after the decline of the Gupta Empire, and particularly after the downfall of the Gurjar-Pratihar empire in the 10th century, political authority in north India was fragmented. A number of states arose in which many of the functions of government were transferred to grantees. These grantees stood midway between the peasants and the ruler. They not only collected land-revenue from the areas assigned to them but discharged miscellaneous administrative duties. Usually, though not always, they had definite military obligations for the service of the state. Again, some held personal grants of a hereditary nature without any definite military responsibilities. In Rajasthan the latter were called *bhaum.* While the first type of grant was not hereditary at first, there seems to have been a strong trend towards its becoming hereditary. The military aspect of the grant was also emphasised, though the precise nature of the military obligations imposed upon the grantees are not clear.

The growth and development of the *bhoga* system (it may be so called in order to avoid an unnecessary controversy whether the term 'feudal' could be used to designate the pattern of society mentioned above) has some interesting parallels with the *iqta* system in West Central Asia.

Whatever may have been the early origins of the *iqta* system, scholars are inclined to believe that it emerged towards the end of the Abbasid period, and that it "was systematised during the Seljuq period, and was accompanied by a major change in the theory of land ownership."[1] A.K.S. Lambton connects it with the growth of mercenary armies which replaced the citizen armies of early Islamic times. On the other hand, Becker considered *iqta* "an administrative and bureaucratic system charged into a military system as the result of an attempt to meet a military problem when the gold economy had broken down". The third element in the system may be steady Turkoman tribal inroads, and the growth of the tribal concept of land as the common property of the tribe represented by the tribal chief.[2]

There have been several types of *iqta* in west Central Asia. The early type was the *tamlik* or hereditary type in which the *iqta* was considered almost the private property of the grantee. The Seljuqs emphasised the state *(mustaghall)* type of *iqta* in which no hereditary rights were conferred on the grantee. It is believed that. while the *mustaghall* type of grant was at first both administrative and military, the military aspect was steadily emphasised due to the growing importance of the military element. A third type was the personal grant in which neither the administrative nor military aspect was emphasised.[3]

It is remarkable that the *bhoga* system developed in India more or less during the same period and under similar conditions. Central authority was weakened after the

[1]A.K.S. Lambton, *Landlord and Peasant in Persia,* O.U.P., 1953, p.49.

[2]*Ibid.* pp. 53-64.

[3]C.E. Bosworth. *The Ghaznavids,* Edinburgh, 1963, pp. 41-42.

disintegration of the Gupta Empire and there is weighty evidence to show that the use of coined money declined in Northern India during the period.[4] The Rajputs rose into prominence during the same period. The origin of the Rajputs is still a matter of controversy among scholars. The arguments of Tod and Crooke in favour of the foreign origin of some of the Rajput tribes are well known.[5] It has been pointed out that the *agnikula* legend on which Tod had based many of his arguments was in fact concocted during the 16th century. But this still does not explain the sudden emergence of the Rajputs during this period. It is well known that big tribal movements took place in Central Asia during the period and that these tribes were pressing down

[4]L. Copal *(The Economic Life of Northern India)* has surveyed the coinage system between 700-1200 A.D. exhaustively. While pointing out the relative scarcity of gold coins during the period and the rise of the price of gold relative to silver (p. 131), the author relates these to (i) the decline of trade with the west, and (ii) the drain of gold coins to West Asia by way of loot, ransom and penalty imposed by the Muslims (p.217).

He is further of the opinion that "the feudalisation of the state structure that, took place in the period would have dispensed with much of the need for the higher denominations of coins ... "(p. 217). Here cause and effect are combined, with one reacting on the other.

See also R.S. Sharma, *Indian Feudalism;* B.P. Mazumdar, *Socio-Economic History of Northern India 1030 to 1194 A.D.;* Pushpa Niyogi, *Contributions to the Economic History of Nrothern India 10th-12th Centuries A.D.,* (Calcutta-1962).

[5]Col. J. Tod. *Annals and Antiquities of Rajasthan 1823* (reprinted 1957), Ch. VI; V. Smith, *Early History of India,* 3rd ed. pp. 407-415.

Many historians have sought to refute Tod. See *Rajasthan Through the Ages,* ed. D. Sharma, Bikaner 1966, pp. 103-106, et. seq. Ojha, quoting Manu, included the Yavans, Sakas, Pahlavas etc. in the Kshatriya races: Dr. D. Sharma thinks that a number of Rajput princes were originally Brahmans, but does not attempt to refute the argument that some of the tribes may have been foreign in origin. (Recently, the matter has been reviewed at. length by B.D. Chattopadhyaya in "Origin of the Rajputs: The Political, Economic and Social Processes in early Medieval Rajasthan", in *The Indian history Review,* New Delhi, Vol III, No.1, 1976, pp. 59-82).

constantly into Khurasan, Kabul, Sindh, Multan and other adjacent areas. Whatever the origin of the Rajputs, there is, however, no dispute that their social concepts were predominantly based on clan-tribal ideas. This is obvious from the manner in which they settled on the land. Land was considered as the property of the clan, which consisted of warriors headed by a number of families. For purposes of administration and providing sustenance to the body of warriors, tracts of land were allotted to these clan leaders. The state was collectively the property of these clansmen, and both they and the ruler were related by ties of blood. The ruler was thus only first among equals. In accordance with this theory, the assignments were not hereditary, and the normal Hindu laws of property of equal partition among sons did not apply to them. They could be resumed for not performing the military services stipulated, or for disloyalty, and the grant had to be confirmed by the ruler whenever a son succeeded his father. In practice, however, the grant was considered hereditary. Generally, the clan leader in turn assigned parts of their grant for the maintenance of an individual warrior and his horse (this grant was called a *chursa* or hide) or to military leaders, their grant being called *patta.* For special services, such as loss of life in battle, small hereditary grants of land called *bhaum* were made.[6]

The Rajput system was thus not in essence different from the Turkish tribal system and has many similarities with the *iqta* system. In fact, but for the continuous changes in the personnel of the ruling sections consequent on the repeated Turkoman incursions, the *iqta* system may well have become hereditary in West-Central Asia. That there was a strong trend towards heredity in the *iqta* system even

[6]For the Rajput system, Ted's *Annals* (pp. 107-172) is still useful. See also *Gazetteers of Rajputana* 1891; P. Saran, "The Feudal System of Rajputana," in *Studies in Medieval Indian History,* Delhi, 1952, pp. 1-23.

under the Delhi Sultanate is well known,[7] Thus, the basis of the politico-military organisation of the Turkish tribes and of the Rajputs is the same. The circumstances of the development of the system has some striking parallels.

In essence, the problem facing the Rajputs and the Seljukids and their successors was the same viz., how to provide stability to the ruling groups and, at the same time, to pay for a centralised possibly merecenary army? The manner and the circumstances in which the Rajputs and the Central Asian rulers sought to solve these twin problems merit deeper study. It is difficult, in our present stage of knowledge, to assert that the Rajput system was influenced at any stage by the Seljuqid or Ghaznavid ideas and practices. However, it is necessary to emphasize here that the remarks of al-Biruni about the insularity of the Hindus and their lack of interest about countries outside India has often been accepted too literally.[8] Al-Biruni's remarks apply, perhaps, to the Brahmans with whom he carne into contact. Elsewhere, we find Indian merchants of the West Coast and South India journeying over the seas to Persia, the Red Sea and South East Asia and even settling down there.[9] There were many points of contacts between the Turks and the Rajputs over a period of a hundred and fifty years. The Kabul and Habul areas remained under the rule of the Hinduized Kabulshahis and later, under the Hindushahis till the end of the 10th century; Punjab and Multan remained under Ghaznavid control from the 11th century onwards and Sindh had been under Arab control much earlier. We find evidence of brisk trade of horses between north India and the Sulaiman

[7]The attempts of Balban and Alauddin to resume the *iqta* of the Shamsi *iqtadars* who considered their grants to be hereditary are well known. (Barani, *Tarikh-i-Firuz Shahi,* Bib., Ind. pp. 61-64). For Firuz Tughlaq, see below.

[8]See al-Biruni's *Indica,* tr. Sachau, reprint S. Chand, Delhi 1952, ii pp. 134-35 (Chapter On that which Especially concerns the Brahmans), pp. 22-23.

[9]See L. Gopal, *loc. cit.,* pp 119-160.

mountains which were famous as a breeding centre for horses.[10] Some Arab writers of the 9th and 10th centuries assert that during the period, Indian armies were not paid, but were in the nature of levies which were called together in an emergency, after which they dispersed. This argument can hardly be applied to north India universally, for the same writers go on to describe the numerous forces maintained by the King of Juzr or Gujarat and say that "no other Indian prince has so fine a cavalry."[11] It is possible that the maintenance of loose tribal levies was the tradition of a section of the Rajputs. However, the Gurjara-Pratihar rulers, as well as the Pala rulers of Bengal, and the Rashtrakutas kept large standing armies which included cavalry.[12] The use of cavalry on a large scale during the period appears to be a new development and can only be explained in terms of Central Asian and specifically Turkish influence. By the time of the Imperial Guptas, the horse-drawn chariots of the earlier period had largely disappeared. The Guptas used cavalry against the Huns and this could not have declined after their downfall.

The growing importance of horses during the period is indicated by numerous manuals on horses, e.g. *Asvayurveda* of Gana, *Asvasastra* of Salihotra, *Asvayurveda* of Nakula etc. It was, perhaps during this period also that the use of iron-stirrup and heavy armour, both for horses and horseman became more general.[13] This, in turn, had far reaching

[10]For horse trade, see R.S. Tripathi *History of Kanauj,* p. 244; L. Goral, *loc. cit* pp. 91-116. Somadeva tells us that the soldiers of Uttarapath rode swift horses and carried spears, swords and bows. An official incharge of horses was called *Sadhanika.* (D. Raghavan, "Gleanings from Somadevasuri's *Yasastilaka Champu", Journal Gangadhar Jha Research Institute,* I, pp. 372-73).

[11]Sulaiman, *Silsilat-ul-Tawarikh,* Elliot Vol. I, p. 7.

[12]*Ibid.* p. 4: al Masudi, *Muruji,* I.p.303.

[13]There has been considerable controversy among scholars about the origin and spread of the iron-stirrup, and its impact on changing the ancient art of warfare. For a recent discussion, see Lyn White, *Medieval Technology & Social Change,* O.U.P. 1962, pp. 14-28. It has been argued

consequences on military weapons and strategy, as well on social organisation. How far Rajput military organization changed to adapt to the new conditions is obvious from the fact that the battle of Tarain between Prithvi Raj and Shihabuddin Ghori was mainly a fight of cavalryman armed with bows and spears.[14] In the first battle of Tarain (1191), Prithvi Raj, according to the later account of Firishta, had a force of 200,000 horses and 3,000 elephants and pursued Shihabuddins cavalry upto 40 miles.[15]

In the second battle, Prithvi Raj had a large infantry 300,000 horses and nearly 3,000 elephants as against Shihabuddin Ghori who had 120,000 armoured horsemen. From Firishta's account, it was the superior tactics of the Sultan, and not the absence of a "mobile cavalry" on the part of the Rajputs which decided the day.[16] Thus, the Turks triumphed because of superior generalship, better mounts and training, and because they were more skilled in the method of warfare which the Rajputs had tried to copy. This is not, of course, to imply that these were the only causes of the failure of the Rajputs.

We have suggested above that, contrary to the general belief among Indian historians, the Rajput armies of the 12th centuries whom the Ghorids encountered were not armies mainly of infantry supported by elephants. The change from infantry to cavalry was perhaps due to the influence of the Huns and later even more to that of the Turks. It is significant that even as late as the Mughal times, the Rajputs dismounted from their horses when they were pressed hard,

that although the toe-stirrup surcingle (which could only be used by a sandie-wearing aristocracy) was known in India in the 2nd century AD., the iron-stirrup was not known in Sasanid Iran and seems to have spread from Central Asia from the 7th century onwards.

[14]Firishta, *tarikh-i-Ferishta* tr. Briggs, pp. 175.

[15]Minhaj Siraj *Tabaqat-i-Nasiri,* tr. Raverty, pp. 176-77.

[16]Firishta, Briggs, pp. 176-77. cf Ishwari Prasad, *Medieval India,* 1933, p. 149.

and preferred to fight on foot. This suggests that although they had taken to horses, they were never quite at home in the new mode of warfare it entailed.

The use of horses, both light and arrnoured, on a large scale must have had definite repercussions on the socio-economic and political organisation, as in the case of medieval Europe. Despite the growth of the *bhoga* system, the Rajputs were never able to develop to the *iqta* system which was the basis on which the Turks were able to organise a highly centralised state. In other words, during the 10th and 11th as during the 18th century, the Indians were quick. to accept and adopt foreign modes of warfare, but were not able or willing to change their society and political organisation to suit the new methods.

The Rajput warrior or nobleman became inseparable in course of time from his horse. A horse became a status symbol and has remained so in the rural areas of Rajasthan to this day. Theft of horses was a common cause of conflict among the Rajputs. The manner in which the concept of chivalry grew simultaneously and with the growing importance of the equestrian warrior is also of some considerable interest. A careful study of both literary and epigraphic records of the period would be needed to trace the development of this concept in Rajasthan. Interestingly enough this is also the period in Persian literature when the legend of Rustam-Sohrab and the attendant concept of chivalry is put forward.

It is not necessary perhaps to argue that the institutions which the Ilbari Turks brought into India were not just Abbasid institutions, but Abbasid ideas and institutions which had been considerably modified by the Samanids, the Ghaznavids and the Seljuqids. (In practice, many of these institutions, particularly the land revenue system, had to be modified in the light of the Indian situation and traditions.) But did Central Asian ideas and institutions continue to have any impact on India after Khurasan and the neighbouring areas had been over-run by the Mongols? This is a part of a wider enquiry regarding the impact of the Mongol invasion on Central and West Asia. Without venturing to encroach on the broader field for which I do not consider myself competent, a few remarks may be made regarding the nature of the Mongol impact on Turkish rule in India. In the first place, the constant Mongol attacks further accentuated the militarist aspect of Turkish rule, and placed a premium on those individuals who could provide strong military leadership. Thus, it is significant that both the Ilbari and the Khilji dynasties were over-thrown by men who had been wardens of the north-western marches. We do not know whether the Mongol methods of warfare and tactics had any effect on the art of warfare in India. Perhaps a better idea of the Mongol contribution in this field would help in the further study of this aspect of the problem.

It is probable that it was only during the 14th century when the Mongols had settled down, and ceased to be a serious danger to the Delhi Sultanate, that Mongol ideas and institutions began to exert a larger influence. The most important in this was apparently the *Yassa* of Chingez. According to Ataul Mulk Juvaini, these were "written down in rolls and kept in the treasury of the chief princes. Whenever a Khan ascended the throne or a great army was mobilised or the princes assembled concerning affairs, of state and administration these rolls were produced."[17] They were apparently so well known that Juvaini declined to waste space by describing them in detail.

Earlier in India, Balban had tried to model his court on the old Sassanid rulers. Muhammad bin Tughlaq who was a learned man, and in whose court many Khurasani nobles were to be found, may well have tried to emulate the Mongol Khans, and may, perhaps, have been influenced by the *Yassa.* His attempt to impose examplary discipline in the army and the nobility, and the harsh punishments he meted out

[17]Ataul Mulk Juvaini, *The History of the World Conquerer,* tr. J.A. Boyle, Manchester, 1958, p. 25.

when they failed:[18] his refusal to accord any special privileges to the *ulema*[19] and his attempt to treat all his subjects as equals, irrespective of their religious beliefs, and admitting almost for the first time a number of ordinary Hindus in to the nobility" have strikingly parallels to the Mongol practices and the *Yassa.*[21]

In the field of organisation of the nobility and the army, again, Mongol institutions may have affected Tughlaq institutions. The *amiran-i-hazara* and the *amiran-i-sada* which played a prominent part in Muhammad Tughlaq's reign, were a Mongol institution, and are heard of in India for the first time in Alauddin Khilji's reign.[22] The organisation of the nobility on Mongol lines, was, perhaps, another of Muhammad Tughlaq's experiments which failed, because we do not hear of it during the reign of his successors, Firuz Tughlaq.

The most important development in the field of institutions during the reign of Firuz Tughlaq was the grant of *iqtas* to the regular *(wajahi)* soldiers.[23] and making the *iqta* and positions of the nobles hereditary.[24] It has been assumed that both these measures were the result of the weak character of Firuz, and his incompetence as an administrator. It is possible, however, that the reforms of Firuz Tughlaq were modelled on another great Mongol ruler, Ghazan Khan. In order to settle the land, and to introduce a measure of sta-

[18]Barani, *Tarikh-i-Firuzshahi,* Bib. Ind. p. 472.

[19]Ibn Battutah, *Rehla,* Paris ed. pp. 294-310.

[20]Barani, p. 505; Ibn Battutah, p. 106.

[21]For the tolerant policy of Chingez, see Juvaini, *loc. cit* p.26. Barani emphasises how Muhammad Tughlaq extended a special welcome-to Mughal *amiran-i-tuman* and *amiran-i-hazara* from Mughalistan, and his liberality towards them. (Barani, pp. 462, 494, 499). His experiment on token currency based on Mongol experiments in China are well known.

[22]In 691H/1291-92, Ulugh Khan joined Sultan Alauddin with his *hazara* and *sada* Mughal sardars, The sultan made him his son-in-law, and the Mughals freely inter-married with the Muslims (Barani, p. 219).

[23]Afif, *Tarikh-i-Firuzshahi,* pp. 302-304.

[24]*Fatuhat-i-Firuzshahi,* ed. Aligarh University, p. 22.

bility, Ghazan Khan introduced a series of reforms by which the soldiers were not assigned *iqtas,* but a definite share was made hereditary.[25] The assignments of the nobles, too, were made hereditary.[26] Efforts were also made to found new villages—some of them with the help of slave boys and slave girls—Indians, Abyssinians, Qairovis etc. As a result, we are told, the civil officials acquired vast fortunes derived partly from or at any rate, invested in land. These lands unless conflicated by the state or usurped by rivals were transmitted by inheritance to the owner's heirs.[27] If this was his object, Firuz tughlaq succeeded, for his officials bequeathed large fortunes to their children.[28] The hereditary system of the *iqtas* satisfied the nobles, and created a false impression of peace and tranquility. How fragile this was demonstrated by the invasion of Timur who was the last Mongol invader of India during that century.

[25]A.K.S. Lambton. *loc, cit.* p. 89.

[26]*Ibid* p. 90 That Ghazan Khan was well known in India as a famous ruler is clear from Battutah's story that the mausoleum of Sultan Qutbuddin should be 30 feet higher than that of Ghazan Khan (Battutah, pp 331-327).

[27]A.K.S. Lambton. p. 96.

[28]Afif, *loc. cit.* pp. 296-98.

13

SOME PROBLEMS OF TRANSITION FROM FEUDALISM TO CAPITALISM IN INDIA*

The term "feudal" means different things to different sections of historians. Although neither Marc Bloch nor Lucien Lefebre were happy with the word "feudalism", preferring to apply it only to the fief and things pertaining to it, Fernanad Braude! says, "It is no more logical to use this word to describe Europe between the eleventh and fifteenth centuries than to use *capitalism* of the same society between the sixteenth and the twentieth." He argues that any other label would still mean a society with wide variations, and different from the society which followed.[1] In another anthology on Feudalism, edited by Coulbourne, many of the historians felt that the term was basically a system of military organization and did not even cover the whole of Europe. The application of the term to a non-European country such as India where the system of vassalage did not exist, has raised even more serious objections.[2] However, if feudalism

[1]Fernand Braudel, *Civilisation and Capitalism: 15th to 18th Centuries*, tr. from French, Vol. ii, London, 1982, p. 464.

[2]For a recent debate see *Journal of Peasant Studies Special Issue on Feudalism in Nan-European Societies*, No.2 & 3, Jan./April, 1985; D.N. Jha (ed.) *Feudal Social Formations in Early India*, Delhi, 1987. See also *A. Comprehensive History of India*, Vol. IV part I, Delhi 1992, Appendix pp. 728-39.

is to be regarded as a mode of production as well as of productive relations, its forms, institutional structure and its inner logic of development must be sought for and studied not only in Europe, but also in countries outside Europe. In India, Marxist historians have, for a long time, categorized medieval Indian society as feudal in the sense that power was vested in the hands of a class which subsisted on the surplus produced by the peasant but which did not work on the land itself.[3] On the basis of the works of D.D. Kosambi, R.S. Sharma and others, it is now widely accepted by a large section among Indian historians that such a society was slowly developing in India from the early centuries of the Christian era, and that it assumed a form which can be called definitely feudal from about the 8th century A.D. It is also accepted that this society reached a climax during the 17th century, but signs of a crisis had already made their appearance and that the crisis became more acute during the succeeding century. The break-up of the centralising Mughal empire in the 18th century was an index of this developing economic and social crisis, the crisis being accompanied by political developments such as extended warfare in the Deccan, rise of the Marathas, growth of various opposition movements etc., and finally the British conquest.

The precise nature of the crisis of the Mughal empire has been a subject of controversy among scholars. This problem, and the related question whether feudal economy in India had reached such a state of crisis that it could not continue in the old form any longer, in turn implyies that the pre-requisites of a new society viz., capitalism had been laid are some of the issues which are still being debated by scholars both inside India and outside.

Any discussion on the crisis of feudalism in India or any of its aspects, such as the agrarian crisis or the crisis of the

[3]This is based on Kosminski, *Studies* in *the Agrarian History of England,* Oxford 1956, p. VI. See also S. Nurul Hasan, *Thoughts on Agrarian Relations* in *Mughal India,* P.P.H., New Delhi, 1973, pp.1-2.

jagirdari system should be preceded by a discussion on the feudal mode of production, and the inner mechanics of its development. Unfortunately, the nature of the source material available imposes severe limitations on the Indian economic historian. There are hardly any records available to assess demographic trends, nature of productivity etc. before the 16th century. Nor has any careful study been made of the extent of agricultural cultivation during various periods, the productivity of the *banjar* or the cultivable waste-land brought under cultivation in different phases, etc. Much more diligent study, and inter-disciplinary work will have to be done before we can establish any meaningful inter-relations between these aspects. Micro-studies on a comparative regional basis will also be necessary. The concepts put forward by French and European scholars and the methodologies adopted by them will be of considerable interest to our scholars. In this context, it may be appropriate to pose a few questions.

Assuming that the techniques of agricultural production did not change materially in India during the feudal period due to technological stagnation, that there was plenty of cultivable waste-land available, and that fairly limited in-puts were needed for bringing *banjar* land under cultivation, the question arises: why did agricultural growth and ex-pansion in India proceed so slowly, or, if their were alter-nate periods of relatively rapid growth and stagnation or decline, what was their basis? Generally speaking, the slow development or stagnation in India have been sought to be explained in terms of the magnitude of the feudal rent, and the working of institutional factors, such as the state, the jagirdari system etc. Reference has also been made to the nature of the ruling class, i.e. its indifference to the growth and improvement of cultivation, its rapacity, life style, etc. In these matters, was the Indian feudal class fundamentally different from the European feudal nobility? Thus, conspicuous expenditure has been a part of the life-style of all feudal nobilities. Perhaps the charge of indifference towards agricultural growth levied against the Mughal ruling class (which was perhaps the most "progressive" ruling class thrown up in medieval India) is predicated, in part, on the belief that feudal agricultural production depended in Europe, in the main, on large scale agricultural production, i.e. on the manorial economy which is conspicuous for its absence in medieval India. It is here that Guy Bois's definition of the characteristic feature of feudalism as "small scale peasant production" becomes meaningful.[4] India is almost a classic case of small scale peasant production. To what extent did the normal and extended small scale peasant producers depend on themselves i.e. on internal resources, and to what extent on the state, i.e. external sources? The feudal landed classes in general, i.e. those who were not directly engaged in agricultural production but depended largely on the extraction of feudal rent, certainly had a general interest in expansion and improvement of cultivation. However, nowhere except in limited areas over limited periods (e.g. 18th century England) does the feudal ruling class take a direct and continuing interest in improvement and expansion of agriculture. The Turkish and Mughal classes were no exception to this. Did then, peasant production depend entirely on its resources? In specific terms, was the role of the state largely irrelevant, except negatively for agricultural growth"? I would consider such a stand to be un-Marxist. The state which by far and large was to subserve the interests of the ruling class, had to playa certain positive role in the discharge of this fundamental function, otherwise its exploitative character would become apparent to all, and lead to negative developments. To some extent, the state sought to validate itself in terms of its providing protection without which normal economic life could not be continued. In practice, the forms of protection could be highly

[4]Guy Bois, *Crisis of Feudalism,* National Foundation of Political Sciences Press, Paris, 1976. (English summary by Rodney Hilton in the *Times Literary Supplement,* 8.7.1977).

decentralised, to the sub-regional or village level. In other words, it was the village society itself (with the state power in the background) and its net work of relationships which had to provide for normal production and expansion, and which also acted automatically as a limiting factor. I have argued elsewhere that the structure and stratification of village society played a definite role in this processes.[5] Village society was dominated by land-holding proprietors called *khud-kashi* in official terminology. These peasant proprietors, who cultivated the lands primarily with the help of family labour dominated the village society. The *khud-kashi* owned the pick of the lands in the village, had the use of the village pond, forests common etc., and were assessed at a concessional rate. Sometimes they were collectively held responsible for the payment of land-revenue, even though the ownership of land was individual. The landless labourers and the village artisans, many of whom were drawn from the scheduled castes and in some areas from the scheduled tribes, were dependent on the landed proprietors, both economically and socially. The *khud-kashi* who, in modern parlance, may be called intermediate castes, were unwilling to allow the lower castes to own land, or to settle on new lands. This was an important limiting factor in expansion of cultivation in medieval Indian society which has contemporary relevance. By virtue of being assessed at a concessional rent, and due to caste prejudices, the higher caste elements also sided with the land-holding intermediate castes. Thus, the *khud-kasht* tried to regulate and control the movement of peasants from one village to another. These migrant peasants or *pahis* were not given an equal status with *khud-kashi* even though sometimes the *pahis* brought

[5]Satish Chandra, "Some Aspects of Indian Village Society in Northern India during the 18th Century: The Position and Role of the *Khud-kasht:* and *pahi-kasht, Indian Historical Review,* Vol. No. i. 1974, pp. 51-64; Idem. Some institutional Factors in providing Capital Inputs for the Improvement and Expansion of Cultivation if Medieval India, "*I.H.R.* Vol. III, No.1, 1976, pp. 83-98.

with them their own ploughs or bullocks. Increase in the number of *pahis* in a given region was an index of the growth of a rural crisis. However, with the help of the state, i.e., the Central Government and the *zamindars*, the *pahis* were settled in new territories, or used to resettle villages ruined for one reason or another. In this way, the Central Government acted as a mediator or as a safety-valve so that rural tensions did not reach beyond a certain state.

Historians have so far paid scant attention to the role of caste and village stratification in the development of Indian feudalism and its stagnation or breakdown. In this context, a closer study of demographic trends, the periodicity of famine, pestilence etc. would also help in working out what Guy Bois calls "the rythm of village life." By providing additional capital inputs, the state could accelerate the process of agricultural expansion as apparently happenend in North India during the 17th and the first half of the 18th century. According to Guy Bois's model cited above, this should have led to decline in productivity, decline in feudal rents, decline in prices, and growth of population and poverty. We have little evidence of demographic trends, but we may assume a slow growth of population in the 17th and 18th centuries, as examplified by the settlement of new villages in eastern Rajasthan of which we have evidence. This may apply. to a number of other regions as well. During the second half of the 17th century, prices almost doubled and rose steadily during the first half of the 18th century. They declined during the second half of the century but the causes are still a matter of controversy.[6]

[6]See Irfan Habib, *The Agrarian System of Mughal India,* Asia, 1963; S.P. Gupta, *Land Revenue System of Eastern Rajasthan,* C. 1650-1750 (Unpublished thesis, Aligarh Muslim University, 1974) (Published, Manohar, Delhi, 1986); Dilbagh Singh, *Movement of Agricultural Prices in Eastern Rajasthan During the Second Half of the 18th Century."* (Seminar paper Calcutta 1978, *mimeo.* See also his *The State Landlords and Peasants: Rajasthan in the 18th Century,* Manohar, Delhi, 1990.) Recent evidence drawn from Kotah Records does not support the contention that prices declined during the second half of the 18th Century.

What role did feudal rent play in the above processes? In this context, Guy Bois's theory of a tendency of feudal rents to decline, and decline of productivity and growth of poverty merit a careful study. It is believed that the growth of centralisation in India from the 12th century onwards enabled the Central Government, and through the *iqta* or *jagir* holding nobles, to demand a larger share of the produce from the peasants. The question has been raised whether Turkish centralisation implied limiting the share of the intermediary class of land-holders i.e. the zamindars, or implied pressure on the peasant to part with a larger share of the produce? In a situation where there was plenty of surplus cultivable waste-land, and where there was a relative shortage of cultivators (excluding, perhaps, the low castes), the picture of rising feudal rent is difficult to reconcile. Nor is there any evidence of the tendency of feudal rents to decline unless we were to mean by it zamindari rights which were sought to be curtailed by a centralizing state. If there was relative shortage of manpower in the countryside, how to explain the influx of the peasants into the towns and the rapid expansion of towns in north India, particularly, from the middle of the 14th century onwards? Can this again be explained in terms of the working of the village community, viz., the refusal of the dominant castes to permit the lower castes to be anything other than despised village craftsmen or landless labourers? The growth of towns also presents a problem; the towns expanded rapidly during the seventeenth century. This postulates a certain inflow of rural population into the towns. What were these sections? Did the towns provide some kind of an escape from a state of rural semi-serfdom to the low caste sections there? Famines, and resulting decline in specified regions and periods would also hit these elements the hardest, thus providing an incentive for migration to towns or to other rural areas. The Hindi poet Tulsidas, who was a contemporary of Akbar, refers to the acute problems facing both artisans and cultivators *(qasbi, kisan)* in times of famine.[7]

We may not be able to answer the above question in our present state of knowledge. However, it appears to me that these factors are closely inter-linked to what has been called the crisis of the jagirdari system. Both the mode and the relations of production did not permit a rapid enough growth of agricultural production and this stagnation, in turn, led to growing strains on the landless, the small peasant proprietor, the intermediary zamindar, and finally the nobles representing the Central Government. Within rural society, pillage and assault on the Central Government provided one way out for the growing tensions in rural society.

[7]Tulsidas, *Kavitavali*, p. 96-97, quoted by Savitri Chandra "Social Life and Concepts—As Reflected in the Works of Tulsidas", in *Tulsidas: His Mind and Art*, ed. Dr. Nagendra Delhi 1977, p. 182.

14

SOCIETY, CULTURE AND THE STATE IN MEDIEVAL INDIA: AN ESSAY IN INTERPRETATION

A critical study of the works dealing with sovereignty and religion, growth of society and the economy, and cultural developments are important for our understanding of the evolution of state and polity in India during medieval times. Such an understanding is necessary because basic historical problems are not confined to, but spill from one aspect or epoch to another. In consequence, many contemporary problems have historic roots which need to be analysed, This was a point which Professor Nihar Rajan Ray always emphasized, as also the need to see the holistic picture. The present essay is a humble tribute to Professor Nihar Rajan Ray who refused to divide knowledge into parcellized segments.

Speculation regarding the nature of the state had an old and continuous tradition in India. The *Arthashastra* of Kautilya was the culmination of an older tradition which is now lost. Speculation regarding the nature of the state continued in the Buddhist works, as well in the *Dharmashastra.* The *Mahabharata* which was given a final form in the Gupta period, devoted a canto, the *Shanti-parva,* to state and polity. Later commentators, Parashar, Medhatithi, etc., continued the tradition.

Muslim thinking on the state had a complex evolution, the Islamic ideas crystallizing into the four schools of law around the 9th century which had a powerful influence on the concept of the state. The writings of Abu Yusuf Yaqub (731-98), al-Farabi (d. 950), al-Mawardi (991-1031), al-Ghizali (d 1111), etc. also gave definite shape to the Muslim concept of the state in an evolving situation, viz, the collapse of the Abbasid Caliphate and the rise of de facto independent states, most of them under the newly converted Turks with strong tribal and ethnic/racist predilections. The Indian tradition regarding the state was not completely eclipsed with the coming in of the Turks, but continued in many peripheral areas. Thus, it can be traced in the writing of the Vijaynagar ruler, Krishna Deva; in the Rajasthani *Vigat* and *Khyat* literature, and in Ramchandra Amatya's *Ajnapatra.* This is not to state, however, that the old Hindu tradition remained uninfluenced by the Islamic tradition of "sultanism". Islamic thinking on the state was also influenced by the political concepts and practices of the Iranians and the Byzantinians whom the Arabs had conquered in the first phase or their expansion. Political thinking was also shaped by the *Adab* literature or "Mirrors for Princes". These were mostly written by men of affairs and letters who had learnt in the school of experience. They were less concerned with principles than with the art of government, and laid great stress on "justice and equity in conformity with the limits of Islam combined with a strong element of expediency". Their method was "to introduce traditions and ancedotes by a general statement or aphorism."[1] The *Adab* literature was, to some extent, influenced by the *Panchatantra* which was introduced into Arabic literature by Ibn-al Muqaffa's translation of *Kalila wa Dimna (Panchatantra)* from Pehlavi. With a Persian revival from the 9th century, the early Iranian rulers became the figures around whom many of these

[1]E.I.J. Rosenthal, *Political Thoughts in Medieval Islam,* O.U.P., 1962, pp. 68-9.

legends were woven. justice. equity and political realism were the hall mark of these legends.

The 11th century *Siyasat Nama* of Nizam-ul-Mulk was part of this tradition, and seem to have influenced early political thinking by Turkish rulers in India. However, right from the beginning, the Turkish rulers were aware that they had a number of peculiar problems in India which effected the character of the state. This is fairly clear from the writings of the period. The earliest work dealing with state and polity after the establishment of Turkish rule in India was undoubtedly the *Adab-ul-Harb-was-Shujaat* of Fakhr-i-Mudabbir, written between 1206 and 1236. Barani's *Fatawa-i-Jahandari* which dealt with the same subject, was written in the later half of the 14th century, but remained unknown during the medieval times, although some aspects of his thinking are reflected in his *Tarikh-i-Firuz-Shahi.* Barani's writings provide a valuable index to the attitudes of the Turkish ruling elites regarding the problems of state and statecraft in India.

Although Abul Fazl, writing during the second half of the 16th century, did not write a separate book on state and polity, the *Ain,* which was a part of Abul Fazl's *magnum opus,* the *Akbar Nama,* marks a milestone in the evolution of thinking of the subject during the 15th-16th centuries. The 15th-16th centuries saw important changes in the political structure and cultural ethos of India and the Islamic world, especially Central and West Asia. The rise of the Mongol empire had shattered the concept of a world empire based on Islam, and presided over by an Imam or Khalifa. The Timurids, the Ottomans, the Safavids, and later the Mughals had no need to accept even theoretical allegiance to an Imam or Khalifa outside their states. The Timurids, while accepting the *shara,* were also guided by the *Yassa* of Chingez. This duality in their outlook had a definite impact on their understanding of the nature of the state in India.

Another interesting development during the period was the production of a series of works called *Akhlaq Namas.*

Although based largely on Jalaluddin Dawwani's *Akhlaq-i-Jalali,* these works which set the cultural tone among the Mughal nobility, reflected a shift of consciousness from tribe or ethnicity to certain cultural mores. These values were, to a large extent, reflected in the Persian poetry of the period. The rise of Hindi Riti Kalin poetry during the 17th century represented a parallel trend. Since the Mughal ruling class was by that time more composite in nature, drawn from various ethnic and religious groups, religion could no longer provide a common means of communication between various groups. Of course, religion continued to be important among the mass of the people, and even among the nobles for personal purposes (marriage, birth and death, festive occasions, etc.) The darbar itself provided a secular focus, along with music, painting, the chase, etc. The role of music and poetry—both Persian and Hindi—as a means of communication has yet to be adequately studied In the Hindi Riti Kalin poetry of the period, produced mainly for the upper classes, there was a marked emphasis on love and beauty and fate and duty. An almost inescapable aspect of the former was emphasis on eroticism, along with an undue emphasis on the feminine form. Generally condemned as representing the growing licentiousness of the Mughal ruling class, it should also be seen as providing a non-ideological basis on which the composite Mughal ruling class tried to find a means of communication. This was, to some extent, replicated in Urdu poetry during the succeeding century.

The British were both attracted and repelled by the cultural attitudes of the Mughal ruling class. Many of them tried avidly to copy it by acting as Indian nabobs. The British historians of India, led by James Stuart Milt condemned it as barbaric and degenerate—an attitude accepted uncritically by a wide range of Indian historians towards the early part of the century. Also, British administrative historians paid no attention to studying the development of institutions, such as state, civil society, etc., in India. As is well known, writing in the last quarter of the 19th century, Elliot roundly declared that there was nothing like the growth of institutions in India.[1a] This was the period when the concept "Oriental Despotism" began to be used to characterize almost all pre-British Asian states. The hallmark of this concept was the idea that in these societies, all power and all property vested with the ruler; that there was no hereditary nobility, no written laws to restrain the ruler, and hence no civil society. Religion and custom at best played a limited role. Such a society, it was believed, was a stationary one, power being organised at two opposite poles—an all-powerful ruler, basing himself on a large, standing army, on the one hand, and on the other, a group of atomised villages containing a mass of miserable beings who suffered in silence or rebelled. Thus, there were no linkages between the two poles.

With the withdrawal of the direct political rule of the west, and with many of the former colonies embarking on the path of rapid economic development, the paradigm of a stationary Orient has had to be given lip. However, many of the features included in the concept "Orientalism" are sought to be retained under different nomenclatures. Thus, the concept of the absence of a civic society or of absence linkages between tone mass of the people and the ruling elites (as if these were the features not of a phase as in the West but characterized oriental society in all times), has sought to be maintained by putting forward the idea of a "segementary state" or a "disaggregated society". In some recent writings, it has been argued that the Hindus and Muslims had no concept of a "territorial state", believing in a universal state, as if the medieval Christian state was any different, (pace the Papal Bull dividing the world between Spain and Portugal), and that the medieval state in India, far from being a state which was remarkably successful in

[1a]Introduction to *History of India told by its own Historians*, 8 Vol., London, 1867 etc.

centralizing many sinews of power in its hands, without abolishing the paralocal political entities, was a very weak state, based on "paracellized suzerainties", with strife and warfare *(fitna)* being endemic in the country-side so that the Mughal sovereign controlled little more than some towns and roads![2]

Thus, as soon as co-relations at the world level change, western ideas about the orient, oriental society also change, as if the orient was always a subset of the west.

In order to understand the changing concept of the state in medieval India, it is necessary first to examine the writings of some of the leading medieval Indian historians, especially Fakr-i-Mudabbir, Barani and Abul Fazl, as also some of the leading saints of the period, In other words, to study the state not in isolation but as an essential component of medieval society, its culture ethos, and its economic and social developmental trajectory.

II

In their thinking about the state, Muslim political thinkers were concerned primarily with stability which included social stability. The protection of the existing social order was considered to be one of the prime duties of the state. Justice which implied both protection and punishment was an instrument for the realization of this objective. Questions

[2]See Perry Anderson, *Lineages of the Absolulist State,* London, 1984; M.N. Pearson, *Merchants and Rulers in Gujarat;* C.H. Bayley, *Indian Society and the Making of the British Empire;* Hun Islamoghlu (ed.) *The Ottoman Empire and the World Economy,* O.U.P. & M.S.H. 1987; Edward W. Said, *Orientalism,* New York, 1978; Burton Stein, *Peasant state and society in Medieval South India,* O.U.P., Delhi 1980; F. Perlin, 'State formation reconsidered, "*MAS* XIX, 2, 1985; Andre Wink, *Land and Sovereignty in India: Agrarian Society and Politics under the eighteenth century Maratha Swarajya,* Cambridge, 1986; David Washbrok: Recent Trends in the Historiography of Mughal India, (paper read at Conference on Political Economics of Ottoman, Safvid & Mughal Empires", Harvard.

regarding the nature and legitimate objectives of state power, and the basis of the moral authority of the state were also raised. Thus, the question of despotism bothered many medieval Muslim thinkers. Ziauddin Barani considered despotism to be basically un-Islarnic, and a characteristic of the Byzantine rulers Qaisars, i.e., the czars, and the Sassanid rulers *(Kisras)* of Iran. Barani was of the opinion that a prime cause of the autocracy of the Byzantine and Iranian rulers was the absence of proper religious check on the rulers. Barani was, of course, wrong because Christianity and Zorastrianism were well established in these kingdoms. Interestingly, Barani argues simultaneously that Iranian forms of sovereignty were necessary and inescapable in his times, and that a truly Islamic state (which he equates to a kind of primitive communism where everybody lived at the same rudimentary level) having existed only under the first four Caliphs. Implicitly accepting that the ulama were unable to provide a check on royal arbitrariness, Barani puts forward the concept of *azm-i-durust* or correct determination as the essence of royal policy, distinguishing it from despotism and tyranny. He says:

".... every resolve *(qasd)* of Kings should be 'correct determination' if its object is well-being, welfare, virtue, good reputation, or if it is a means of beneficial ends, provided of course, that the King's object is within the bounds of the possible."[3]

Barani's emphasis on fundamental objectives rather than forms in determining the nature of the state recalls the debate in the West making a distinction between despotism and absolutism, the former signifying the use of state power from above to effect social and economic reforms in the face of opposition from vested interests, whereas an absolutist state was basically a status quo state. Instead of examining the

[2]Ziauddin Barani: *Fatwa-i-Jahandari,* Eng tr. by Dr. Afsar begam as *Political Theory of the Delhi Sultanat;* Kitab Mahal, Allahabad, n.d (originally printed in *Medieval India Quarterly,* AMU, Vol. III, Nos. I & 2, 1957 (refs. are to the latter), p.30.

conditions under which the noble objectives set up by a ruler, as comprising *azm-i-durust,* could be implemented, Barani goes at a tangent and tries to derive/explain despotism and the arbitrary actions of despots on the basis of the contradictory nature of human beings.

Medieval thinkers had very definite ideas regarding the nature of the society it was the duty of the state to protect. Although the egalitarian quasi-communist tribal order prevailing under the first four Caliphs remained an ideal, the social order which had evolved since then and which was soon accepted as normative, was an urbanised society in which the traders and artisans played an important but subordinate role, with the country-side remaining largely nomadic or practicing pastoral nomadism,[4] The Arab, and later, the Turkish tribal elites were not prepared to share power with the rising urban elements, the merchants and artisans. Hence, an unstable social order evolved which was highly hierarchical in nature, with the nobly born tribal elites exercising virtual monopoly of power. In this situation, political opposition, including egalitarian sentiments, often appeared in the shape of sectarian movements. Fakhr-i-Mudabbir being one of the earliest political thinkers in Medieval India, made no bones in asserting the right of the nobly born Turks to monopolize state power and to ensure that the "low, mean and ignoble" people were not only denied a share in government, but were kept obedient and subservient. Thus, he says:

"Posts of *diwan, shagird* and *muharrir* should be given only to those who had been *ahl-i-qalam* (belonged to the educated sections), and whose ancestors had served rulers and amirs. Other (sections) should not be allowed to acquire knowledge of literature, mathematics and accounting *(siyaqat),* for such people are miserly, deceitful, commercial in their dealings, and display low qualities ... "[5]

[4]Fernand Braudel, *Grammaire des Civilisation* reprint, Paris, 1987, pp-96-7, 100.

[5]Fakhr-i-Mudabbir, *Adab-ul-Harb-was-Shujaat,* Ethe. 2767, f.49a.

All the positive values were termed "noble", and all the base qualities were dubbed commercial or ignoble. There was the further problem that in India the traders and the urban elements were large non-Muslims. Hence, Fakhr-i-Mudabbir goes on to say that the *na-asl* should not be given power over high born Muslims. "They disturb the high born people and lead the Kingdom to decline and fall. They become arrogant with a little gain, become excessively ambitious and show ingratitude in not being able to attain their ambitions, and join the enemies, and have no shame for their misdeeds."[6] These sentiments persisted, because as late as the 16th century, we find Tulsidas echoing the same sentiments.[7] Thus, the elites, Muslim or Hindu, had the same hierarchical outlook. The lower orders were not only to be denied a share in public affairs, but were considered a menace to social peace and tranquillity.

The question is: who were the *razils* or *kam-asl* in the medieval context? Not all traders were contemptible: in West Asia the leading trader of the town *(malik-ut-tujjar)* was almost a social equal of the nobles. This was the same in India during the early phase of urbanisation, as reflected in the *Panchatantra.* Barani gives his own definition of the mean and the ignoble, and tries to provide a philosophic basis for keeping them away from state power. He says that at the time of creation, some minds were inspired with the art of letters and writing, others with horsemanship, and yet others with weaving, stitch-craft and carpentry, hair-cutting and tanning. Men should practice only those arts, crafts and profession "for which men have been inspired (and) are practiced by them."[8]

Barani's philosophy and classification of people has a striking resemblance to the theory of caste in India. Barani

[6] *Ibid,* ff. 49a.-b.

[7] See Savitri Chandra Shobha, *Social Life and Concepts in Medieval Hindi Bhakti Poetry,* Delhi, 1983, pp. 86-100.

[8] Barani, *Fatawa,* p. 177.

goes on to ascribe to those who have adopted nobler professions, qualities of virtue—kindness, generosity, valour, good deeds, protection of other classes, recognition of rights, justice, equity, etc. On the other hand, the low born who practiced the baser arts and ignoble professions were capable only of vice—immodesty, falsehood, miserliness, misappropriation, ingratitude, injustice, shamelessness, etc. Conscious that not all low-born people were lacking in noble qualities, Barani makes his preference for noble birth clear by saying "Even if a man of base or low birth is adorned with a hundred merits, he will not be able to organise and administer the country according to expectations, or be worthy of leadership or political trust." Hence, it was desirable to select people of free, gentle and noble birth "even if this advantage happens to be vary meagre."[9]

Punishment, even despotism, became necessary because the mean were "plentiful and abundant." According to Tulsi, the mean and the ignoble preponderated over the noble-minded.[10] According to Barani, they had been "created unspeakable brutes", and he compares them to "animals and beasts of prey." Any failure to put down these elements would lead to a breakdown in which there would be "complete community of women and property."[11]

In such a situation, despotism was not only inescapable, but even desirable. As with so many political commentators, Barani, while condemning despotism, finds a social justification for it. The question, however, was: how to maintain the moral authority of the state or of the ruling class when it had such a narrow social base? Despotism alone was not an answer. Religion was an important factor but Islam hardly held any appeal for the large majority of the non-Muslim population. The role of *adl* or justice, therefore, became an extremely important factor. Ideally, justice

[9] *Ibid.* p. 175.

[10] Tulsi, *Dohavali* 348, quoted by Dr. Savitri Chandra *supra*.

[11] Barani, *Fatawa*, p. 32.

implied making no distinction between rich and poor, relation and stranger, noble and ignoble. Barani raises justice to a position almost higher than religion, for dispensing justice was for the ruler "greater than seventy years of devotion." However, justice also implied preservation of the existing social order in which profession were rigidly organised on a hereditary basis, i.e. on the basis of the original choice made by man.

The social structure postulated by Pakhr-i-Mudabbir and Barani was a rigid and unchanging one. However, during the 13th and 14th centuries, new social relations were developing in the country specially in areas under Sultanat rule. Towns and town life were expanding, as exemplified by the example of Delhi, "the biggest city in the Islamic east" according to Ibn Battutah. Other big cities in India included Daultabad, Patan, etc. The rise of new crafts based on the new technologies (spinning wheel, carder's bow, paper, later the "Persian wheel" etc.), and a new rural class which centralised in the its hands a larger proportion of the rural surplus than ever before were also important factor in this process.[12] These processes, and the type of administrative centralization carried out by the Sultans, including the institution of some of the finest metallic currency then available in the world, aided the process of the growth of a money economy in the country. Commenting on the new type of "money-minded" society which seemed to be developing, Barani caustically remarks:

"..... whenever plenty of profit is seen in regretting and selling at high prices, and not much profit in other professions, people discard their own professions by an instinct of nature. Soldiers take to agriculture; cultivators, seeing plenty of profit in it, take to trade; regrators owing to the influence of their own wealth, extend their hands to high

[12]Irfan Habib, Technological Changes and Society, 13th and 14th Centuries, Presidential Address, See II *Procs. Indian History* Congress 1969.

posts; shop-keepers try to become officers; men of noble birth become merchants; and transport merchants *(karwanis)* desire to become government officers *(amirs)* and commanders of the army."[13]

It would appear that for Barani, the main source of danger for the existing set up was trade, on account of the wealth of the merchants and their incipient ambition of becoming *amirs,* and secondly, on account of the attraction trade offered to nobles, especially the lower nobles. Elsewhere, Barani wants the state not to tax traders from neighbouring countries so that grain and cloth might become cheap.[14] Fakhr-i-Mudabbir emphasised the importance of safeguarding roads, and ensuring that the *sarais* were well established for the sake of the poor and the *karawanis* so that goods could be transported from place to place and be available to merchants.[15] Thus, the merchants were to be helped, but were to be kept under control. This was so both because of their wealth—always a source of trouble, and because most of the merchants were Hindus, and the soldiers and a large number of city folk Muslims.

Regarding the countryside, the picture presented by Barani is far from clear. The fear of soldiers becoming cultivators, and the (richer) cultivators becoming traders appears to be far from reality, at least as far as the 14th century was concerned. Nor can these sections be considered potential regrators of food grains. Anyhow, Alauddin Khalji's policy of curbing the village zamindars/rich cultivators was not pursued by his successors. Probably, it was considered counter-productive or unimplementable. Control over the *khuts* and *muqaddams,* and the *gumashtas* appointed for the collection of land-revenue was however, related also to the question of social justice or public welfare. Fakhr-i-Mudabbir enjoins the *amils* and *gumashtas* not to violate the *shara* in

[13]Barani, *Fatawa,* pp. 69, 54.
[14]*Ibid,* p. 84.
[15]*Adabul Harb* f. 47b.

collecting land-revenue when they went to their *vilayats* and posting *(aml)*. They were not to impose any cesses not sanctioned by the *shara* and not to reduce the people to such a state of abject poverty, as would make it difficult to collect *kharaj*.[16] Barani emphasises the liberal policy of Ghiyasuddin Tughlaq in this matter. He wanted that all the people, Hindus and Muslims, should be employed, whether in agriculture or in handicrafts and that they should not be worried by poverty or absence of means.[17]

Thus, despite a despotic political order, the benevolent aspect was not missing completely as far as the mass of the people, especially the ordinary peasants, were concerned. That is, as long as the peasants were submissive—a point emphasised repeatedly by both Fakhr-i-Mudabbir and Barani. As long as these sections continued to pay the taxes *(kharaj-jizya,* etc.) without remiss they were not to be persecuted but preserved.

There was a growing divergence between the concept of a narrow, oligarchic state favoured by the political thinkers of the time, and the growing reality. Non-Turkish elements, both Indian and non-Indian, could not be kept out of high offices of state for ever. This was manifest from the challenge posed to Balban by Imaduddin Raihan, who was an Indian Muslim. Even earlier, it was found that Nizam-ul-Mulk, the wazir of Iltutmish was, a *julaha* (weaver) by caste, who had concealed his low birth.[18]

The Khalji revolution opened the door of high office to non-Turkish elements, Afghan and Indian. However, Muhammad Tughlaq's experiment in choosing and appointing to high offices persons who were denounced by Barani as mean or ignoble, or *bazari* calls for comment. Apparently, these were mostly Muslims drawn from what might be called the lower castes (or OBC in modem parlance)—wine-distillers *(khammar),* barbers *(hajjam),* gardners *(baghban),*

[16]*Ibid.*

[17]Barani, *Tarikh-i-Firuz Shahi,* Bib. Ind., p. 438.

[18]Barani, *T.F.S.,* p. 39.

weavers *(julaha)* even singers *(gayak)*. The Hindus mentioned in this connection were only a few: Ratan who was an expert in accounting was placed in charge of Sind with his *iqta* in Siwistan; Kishan Bazaran Indiri who was given the charge of Awadh, and Karma, who gradually rose to the position of naib wazir. Their caste background is not known but apparently they did not belong to the Hindu landed upper classes. For the others, there is no suggestion that they were actually practising the professions, but that they were drawn from professions considered "ignoble".[19] This suggests that these were the sections which manned the lower rungs of the administration in an expanding, centralized state, their ambitions rising in course of time. The desire of people like Barani, apparently, was to confine them to the lower rungs of the administration. We shall see the rise of similar sections among the Hindus during Akbar's rule, and their entry into the higher rungs of administration. Todarmal, and Rai Rayan Patr Das were two such prime examples. Interestingly, the only Muslim favoured by Muhammad Tughlaq who had a trading background was Alaul Mulk Khurasani who had been qazi of Herat while he had a ship to trade. He was placed in charge of Lahari Bandar, then the principal port of Sind with the goods passing up and down the Indus. Muhammad Tughlaq had also promised to give Shihabuddin Gaznavi, who was the leader trader *(malik-ut-tajjar)* of Khambayat, the charge of Khambayat and a high office. But this could not fructify for he was looted on the way to Delhi. The Sultan gave him a large sum of money and three ships were obtained for him to return to Hurmuz.[20]

Apart from these, Muhammad Tughlaq also tried to in-

[19]Barani, *T.F.S.*, p. 505-6.

[20]Ibn Battutah, *Rehla*, H.A.R. Gibb, iii 672-74 .. He did not prosper there. According to Battutah "This is what happens to wealth generated in India. Few can take back money from them and even the few who do so are overtaken by some calamity".

duce foreigners (*aizza*)-Mongols, Uzbeks, Khurasanis etc. into the nobility.

Muhammad Tughlaq's effort at the horizontal and vertical expansion of the ruling class largely failed. A sizeable section among the *aizza* rose in rebellion or turned against Firuz Tughlaq while he was in Sind[21]. The inclusion of lower class Muslim converts into the nobility was resented by the established validity, Indian as well foreign. When Firuz Tughlaq ascended the throne, he retained some of the Mongol and Uzbek nobles such as Qabtagha Amir Mehmen and Amir Ahmad Iqbal. He ousted the "low-caste" Muslims inducted into the nobility by Muhammed Tughlaq. The only name of a "lower class" Muslim in a higher position mentioned under Firuz is that of Ikhtyaruddin Madho Hajjam (barbar or surgeon) who, we are told, had 13,000 horses in his stable at Bhatner, each costing 1,000 or 2,000 tankas[22] But it appears that he was a trader, rather than a noble.

The prejudice against the lower classes was an aristocratic prejudice shared by the Hindus and the Muslims. The Hindu caste system reinforced it, but such an attitude was anterior to the coming of the Turks to India, as is obvious from the remarks of Nizam-ul-Mulk, Fakhr-i-Mudabhir and Barani.

By the time Firuz ascended the throne, the racial arrogance of Turks and other immigrant Muslims had diminished to the extent that-a converted Tailang Brahman, Khan-i-Jahan, and after him, his son, could hold the post of wazir during most of his reign.

Much has been said about the relationship of the state and religion during the period which can hardly be taken

[21] A division arose among the Mongols. While in Sindh, Navaz Qurgun, son-in-law of Tarma-shirin, who had received favours for years from Muhammad Tuglaq, rebelled, and many Mongols joined him. But some of Mongol nobles remained loyal and were admitted to the special counselling groups of Firuz. (Barani, *T.F.S.* 553, 584-85, Afif *Tarikh-i-Firuz-Shahi*, 49-51.

[22] Barani, *T.F.S.* 554.

up in detail here. The question was really of the relationship of the state with organised religion on the one hand, and with popular religion based on the sufi and bhakti saints, on the other. Regarding the first, Barani's views on the subject are comprised in his concept of *jahandari.* Barani accepted that a truly Muslim state based on *din-dari* was not possible in India. In a state based on *jahandari,* while all deference was to be paid to *shara* and the Muslim theologians, the governance of the state depended on the secular ruler who could frame *zawabit* or state laws for the welfare of the state. As Professor M. Habib says "Barani leaves us in no doubt that in cases of conflict the state laws over-rode shariat.[23]

But the question is: did this theory safeguard the minimum religious rights of the Hindus? If Barani, who continuously gives vent to tirades against the Hindus whom the calls "the greatest enemies of Mustafa" is to be followed, it would appear that the position of the Hindus even in an Islamic state which was moderate, being based on *jahandari* or secular considerations, was uncertain, a lot depending upon the interpretation of *shara* and the interests of the state by the ruler. This is reinforced by the attitude of Firuz who used *shara* as a justification for charging *jizyah* as a separate tax distinct from *kharaj,* and refusing to exempt brahmans from it. He also destroyed some temples of old standing near Delhi on the ground that they were beguiling Muslims and were a source of immorality, with men and women congregating there in large numbers on special occasions.

While no individual rights were sancrosanct in an autocratic stage, that *shara* could restrain individual arbitrariness, and safeguard the sanctioned religious rights of the non-Muslims, is exemplified by the case of Sikandar Lodi who sought a *fatwa* from the qazis whether he could stop the practice of the Hindus congregating at Thaneswar for a ritual bath in the pool there. The qazis ruled that not only could temples not be destroyed, but that "old, well-estab-

[23]Inrotuction to *Fatawa,* p. 6

lished religious practices could also not be stopped."[24] The point here is that while acts of individual arbitrariness could not be put a stop to, the sanctioned religious rights of the Hindus were well known and recognised even by the ulama. We may consider this to be an integral part of the state based on *jahandari,* irrespective of Barani's own opinion in the matter.

The sufi saints, particularly the Chistiyas had, it is well known, advocated keeping aloof from the state which they considered evil. They acted, to some extent, as public tribunes, and provided moral succor to the weak, and an outlet for popular discontent. Within their means, they also provided a measure of popular relief. The rulers tried to utilize the popular esteem enjoyed by these saints for their own purposes. By a careful policy of according them honour and esteem, by extending indirect support through *futuh* (gifts), the Sultan and ruling elements were able to present the saints as friends and well wishers who had extended their benign patronage to them[25] even while keeping aloof.

A more critical attitude towards the state can be discerned with the growth of popular monotheistic movements, and popular sufism during the latter half of the 14th, and the 15th century. The popular monotheistic saints posed a conceptual challenge to the narrow, oligarchic state favoured by Fakhr-i-Mudabbir, Barani and others. These saints were themselves drawn from the lower order of society: Kabir was a weaver, Raidas a cobbler, Nanak came from a family of village accountants. All of them were non-brahmans, and were close to the people because many of them had passed their early lives under great hardships, including penury. There was a change in the attitude of the sufis too. From the late 14th century, many of them were drawn from the

[24]Nizamuddin Ahmad, *Tabaqat-i-Akbari,* Bib. Ind. Calcutta, p. 336.

[25]This point has been made by S. Nurul Hasan in his unpublished Oxford thesis, *"Chishti & Surhrawardi Silsilahs in N. India during the 13th and 14th Centuries."* (Seen with the permission, of the author).

ranks of the ordinary people and started composing works in the local languages—Hindi, Bengali, Punjabi, etc. It signified that there was in existence by this time a large community of lower caste Muslims who needed to be addressed not in Persian as before, but in their own languages.[26]

The most influential figures among the monotheistic saints were Kabir, Nanak, and later Dadu. The starting point of Kabir's religious thinking and preaching was his stout affirmation of the fundamental equality of man, irrespective of race, religion or wealth, i.e. his opposition to the existing hierarchy. Nanak who freely acknowledge his debt to Kabir, affirms the fundamental equality of man even more strongly. But unlike Kabir who nowhere alludes directly to the state, Nanak goes forward to postulate a state based on righteousness and. equality, the tone for which is to be set by a guru who combines in himself *miri* and *piri* spiritual and worldly power. Although the terms *piri* and *miri* were used by Nanak's successors, it has been argued that they were implicit in the teachings of Nanak.

It may be postulated that as a result of the disintegration of the Delhi sultanat, the erosion of the power and prestige of the Turkish elites, and the gradual dissemination of egalitarian concepts and beliefs by popular sufi and bhakti saints, the atmosphere would be more conducive to the emergence of a more open-minded state or states where the lower orders, especially the traders and artisans, would have greater space. The situation, of course, would vary from region to region. That there was great opportunity for such a state to emerge in the maritime states of Gujarat and Bengal or the Deccan than the rigidly hierarchical states of Rajasthan or the Gangetic Valley could also be visualized. Whether such developments occurred would need a closer study than has been carried out so far.

[20]See S.A.A Rizvi, *A History of Sufism in India:* Vol. II, Delhi, 1983, which gives a list of such works in Hindi, Punjabi Bengali.

III

It may be postulated that the integration of north India under the Surs, followed by the Mughal integration under Akbar, showed that the era of small states was over, and that the concept of a regional balance of power was unworkable. In fact, once the Lodis had been able to unify the Ganga Valley by defeating the Sharqis, the groundwork of such an integration had been laid. The Mughal integration also re-affirmed and re-established the power of feudal, hierarchical elites without closing the space for other social groups and elements. The position was a complex one, and in the writings of Abul Fazl we see strong support for a hierarchical state and society, side by side with egalitarian notions and precepts.

Abul Fazl's concept of state and sovereignty have to be seen in the context of his understanding of society, as also his religio-spiritual notions. Following the ancient Hindu traditions, as also influenced by thinkers such as Jalaluddin Dawwani, Abul Fazl classified human being into four categories: the first being the warriors, second the artificiers and merchants, third the learned, and fourth the husbandmen and labourers. By relegating the learned i.e. the religious classes (brahmans, ulama) to the third, not to the first category as in the Dharpiashastras, Abul Fazl tried to downgrade the high pretentions and self-opinionated ideas of these sections. He also based himself on the existing social reality. Interestingly, Dawwani had put the learned above the artificiers and merchants, but below the warriors.[27]

However, wishing to distance himself from the Hindu notions of birth, Abul Fazl emphasizes innate qualities as the basis of classes or categories of people. Thus, he ascribes to various sections qualities which he almost playfully identifies with fire, air, water and earth. Also, when he cites the ancient Greek tradition of classifying human being

[27]Jalaluddin Dawwani, *Akhlaq-i-Jalali.*

into three on the basis of their qualities: nobles, base and intermediate. These again, were sub-divided into nine categories[28] which we can ignore here. The noble included those who had pure intellect, sagacity capability of administration or of composition or eloquence, personal courage such as military duty. The base and intermediate sections included the various professions. Amongst these, the ignoble or base, comprised those who were opposed to common weal of mankind such as the hoarding of grain *(ihtekar),* those opposed to any virtue, such as buffonary; and trades such as a barber, a tanner, a rope-dance or a sweeper from which "the disposition is naturally averse from". Butchers and fishermen "who had no other profession but to take life" were also included in this category. They were relegated to separate quarters in the city, and were forbidden under threat of fine from associating with others. In terms of character, these sections were marked by "evil disposition and conduct" evidenced by traducing one's neighbour and disclosing his faults.[29]

The intermediate section comprised various callings and trades; some that are of necessity such as agriculture, and others which could be dispensed with such as dyeing and others, again, simple, such as carpentry, iron-rnongery, and the manufacturing of scales or knives. Elsewhere, the intermediate category of men were those characterized by good intentions and virtuous purposes, had a large tolerance of. views on account of amiableness of disposition, and who spoke charitably of all men.[30]

Abul Fazl's views about human beings, particularly the lower classes, called the base or the ignoble, reflected in large measure the prejudices of the contemporary upper classes. It was implied that the lower orders should not aspire for a share in state power, and that the task of

[28] *Ain,* Bib. Ind., i. 291.
[29] *Ain,* i, 291. ii, 237, 241.
[30] *Ain,* i 291, ii, 251.

administering the state should be the preserve of those belonging to noble families, and the upper castes.

Abul Fazl's social concepts influenced his concept of the state in several ways. On the one hand, prevalence of evil sections in society was a justification for royal despotism, for only a king who possessed the necessary qualities could control these sections. Secondly, it was necessary for a king endowed with *farr-i-izidi* to establish social stability not only by not permitting "the dust of sectarian strifs to arise", it was "obligatory" for him "to put each of these (sections) in its proper place, and by uniting (their) personal ability with due respect for others, to cause the world to flourish."[31] Thus, stability, even dignity implied the maintenance of one's due station in life. Akbar is quoted as saying that the *daroghas* should be watchful "to see that no one from covetousness abandons his own professions." Elsewhere, we are told that Akbar quoted with approval Shah Tahmasp's statement that "When a menial takes to learning he does so at the expense of his duties."[32]

Nevertheless, the concept of hierarchy was, to some extent, at variance with the concept of *sulh-i-kul,* that is, that the state should not discriminate between followers of different religions since all of them had some merits as well as points of demerits, As Abul Fazl says: "... the sages of every religion assembled at the court, and as every religion has some good in it, each received some praise. From a spirit of justice, the badness of any sect could not weave a veil over its merits. Second-the season of *sulh-i-kul* was honoured at the court of the Caliphate, and various tribes of mankind of various natures obtained spiritual and material success."[33]

[31] *Ain,* Blochman, i p. 4.

[32] *Ain,* iii 451. On the other hand, for absence of a sense of caste prejudice in Akbar, as exemplified by the case of Khidmat Rai Mukandi, a *chandal,* see *A.N.* iii p. 604.; I. Habib 'Akbar and Social Inequities', *Procs I.H.C.* L iii, 1993, pp. 300-10.

[33] *Akbar Nama,* Bib. Ind. p. 274.

A ruler endowed with *farr-i-izadi,* was according to Abul Fazl, imbued with a sense of justice, tempered by liberality and forgiveness. This is what Abul Fazl means when he says that the ruler "sits on the eminence of propriety. "It was, due apparently, to these factors that Abul Fazl nowhere uses the type of harsh language or advocates the type of measures against the lower orders suggested by Fakhr-i-Mudabbir or Barani. In fact, despite his strong belief in hierarchy, Abul Fazl was concerned with the need of absorbing into the king's service men of talent, irrespective it would seem, of their social background. Thus, he states that Akbar was moved by the spirit of the age for he "knows the value of the talent, honours people of various classes with appointments in the ranks of the army, and raises them from the position of a common soldier to the dignity of a grandee."[34] These views were reiterated by Akbar in the advice given by him to Prince Daniyal when he was sent to Allahabad in RY. 42/1597-98 "Judge nobility of caste and high birth from the personality (of the individual), and not goodness from ancestors, or greatness from (the nobility) of the seed."[35]

Abul Fazl's concept of a liberal, humanitarian and tolerant state, based on royal absolutism under a ruler of high endeavour endowed with the highest moral and spiritual qualities, and enjoying heaven's mandate, so that he was not dependent on any set of religious leaders for legitimization, was also underpinned by the Turko-Mughal tribal concept of complete and unflinching loyalty to the chose leader. To that extent it was strikingly different from the Afghan tribal tradition where the leader was only first among equals. According to the Mughal concept, which was patrimonial in nature, the officials or amirs serving the emperor were merely his *naukars* (servants)—a term frequently used for them. This gave full freedom to the ruler whom he chose to serve him.

[34] *Ain,* Blochman, i 264.
[35] *A.N.,* iii p. 722.

Although Abul Fazl tried to portray his concept of state and sovereignty in terms of old Iranian traditions, there can be little doubt that the type of secularist poly-religious state, based on a composite ruling class drawn from different ethnic and religious groups, hierarchical in nature yet open ended to some extent, and humane in its dealing with the masses, based on the concept of equal justice for all, irrespective of birth, religion or status, was an ideal which was far in advance of anything postulated or practised in Asia, or in Europe at that time. It is interesting to note that Abul Fazl nowhere uses the words *dar-ul-Islam* or *dar-ul-harb* to describe the polity of his times, because such distinctions had ceased to be meaningful, this being one of the justifications advanced by him for the abolition of jizyah, Abul Fazl was convinced, or would have us believe that Akbar's conquests were not based on a spirit of aggradisement, but was part of a larger plan to establish an all India polity based on justice and tolerance, in other words, a state which could be called a *dar-ul-sulh*.

Two questions arise: to what extent were the noble ideals expounded by Abul Fazl put into practice? Second, why was the type of poly-religious, tolerant, open-ended, secularist state instituted by Akbar unable to maintain itself after his demise, leading to demands for restoration of a more specifically Islamic state?

The first needs a detailed study which is hardly feasible with in the framework of this paper. However, it might be stated that while the traditions of religious toleration were strengthened under Akbar, with the abolition of jizyah and other discriminatory cesses, the concept of throwing career open to talent was followed in a limited manner. The rigid mould was loosened somewhat by favours being shown to a poor and indigent brahman like Birbal, or by Khatris such as Todar Mal and Rai Patr Das, and a large number of kayasthas drawn from the class of writers or class of educated people rising in the imperial service as junior administrators. Also, during the 17th century, we have examples of ordinary people rising in the Imperial services. Thus, Fath Khan who a *filban* (elephant driver) rose to the rank of 2000; Mihtar Khan Khasa Khel who began as a *darban* to the servants of the palace being appointed qiladar of fort Akbarabad and made a grandee with a mansab of 3000/3000. Likewise, the sons of Miyan Guda who was a *kalal* (wine-drawer) by caste, and began as a *darban* to the palace and of the enclosure of the *diwan-i-am-o-khas* and the *ghusal-khana,* rose in life and became amirs.[36] At the same time, the Mughals were keen to maintain the separate identify of the various ethnic sections comprising the Mughal nobility—the Mughals, the Shaikhs, the Afghans, the Rajputs, the Deccanis etc. Thus, towards the end of Aurangzeb's reign, Prince Azam dismissed from service a man who had obtained a mansab of 150 *zat* by pretending to be a Mughal but was a barber by caste. He was handed over to the kotwal for punishment so that "hereafter people of these castes *(aqwam)* should not show themselves as belonging to the ranks of the Mughals.[37]

Even the limited opportunities for persons drawn from the lower orders or the poor and the weak among the upper sections of Hindus and Muslims, to rise in the service of the state had a social and moral significance which should not be underestimated. It provided an opportunity for other sections in society also to aspire to exercise power: and authority, and to further broaden the social base of the ruling class. However, the 17th century saw growing contradictions between the basically hierarchical nature of the state and the strongly held prejudices of the ruling classes about the lower orders, on the one hand, and on the other, the growth and affluence of sections among the lower orders, such as the master-artisans, peasant proprietors *(khud-kasht)*

[36] *Zakhirat-ul-Khawanin,* Karachi, i pp. 218, 222, 246.

[37] *Akhbarat* d. 18 *Muh.* 49 R.Y. Aurangzeb/23 May 1704 (Reference kindly provided by Dr. I. Habib).

and a section of traders, both on account of the political consolidation of the state, and the opportunities for economic development. In consequence, in course of time, there was a growing atmosphere of discontentment and strife.

The maintenance and consolidation of the Akbarian model of the state, implied that:

(i) The social base of the Mughal state, and of the ruling classes, broaden continuously, with greater space to the lower orders;

(ii) that the ruling classes move towards acceptance of a truly secular ethos;

(iii) that the mass movement led by radical bhakti and popular sufi saints, upholding cultural plurality and toleration, are further strengthened, and

(iv) that there was a rapid enough economic growth to cope with increasing administrative and developmental costs, and to meet growing aspirations.

None of these conditions could be adequately fulfilled during the 17th century. Like any elite landed group, those who formed the ruling class had little desire to allow outside elements to enter it. This was as much applicable to the Rajputs as to the Mughals. The Rajput rajas were deeply wedded to the concept of hierarchy, and social privilege based on caste. There-is no evidence to suggest that they welcomed the induction into the nobility of the Marathas whom they did not consider as being socially their equal, or even accord them the status of kshatriyas, as is evident from Mirza Raja Jai Singh's comment to Aurangzeb about Shivaji that as a high born Rajputs he would not eat food touched by him, nor have matrimonial relations with him.[38] The allergy of the Rajputs to the Jats who were the resident cultivators *(khud-kashts)* in the area is well known, with the Rajputs rajas playing a leading role under Aurangzeb to suppress the Jats. The allergy of the Mughals, Irani and

[38] *Haft Anjuman*. Sarkar's collection, f. 139 a.

Turani nobles towards the Afghans and the Indian Muslims (Hindustanis) who were slowly entering the service, and gradually grew in numbers and importance towards the end of the century was one basis of the growing factionalism in the nobility during the latter half of the 17th century.

The attempt of the Mughal emperors of maintaining a balance between various ethnic and religious and regional groups in the nobility in order that they may not join hands against the ruler, benefitted the insiders, and, to a considerable extent, discouraged any effective broadening of the social base or ethnic composition of the Mughal ruling class and state.

At the popular level, the concepts of *wahdat-ul-wajud* and *advaita* mingled with sufism and bhakti, and set up a powerful stream of thought which influenced Jahangir and many others. Chishti and peripatetic sufi saints, as also nirguna bhakti saints, such as Dadu, Rajjab etc. carried their message of egalitarianism and social justice to the people. Also, they considered love and personal devotion to God more important than adherence to the scriptures of any religion. Dadu went the farthest in this field: he proclaimed that he had no faith in the scriptures, considered himself neither a Hindu nor a Musalman, but adhered to a non-sectarian *(nipakh)* path.[39] The teachings of the liberal sufis were, in essence, the same.

Both the Muslim theologians and brahmans stoutly opposed this essentially secular ideology. Chaitanya, Sur and Tulsi, the most popular traditional saints of north India, advocated devotion to a personal living God. While not communal in their approach, in practice, though not strictly in theory, they brought back all the ritual of idol-worship, and reaffirmed the position of the brahrnans as the leading functionaries of the new faith which developed. Also, these saints tried to re-interpret the scriptures, rather than

[39]Savitri Chandra, *Social Life and Concepts*, supra pp. 41-3.

treating them as irrelevant, as both Kabir and Dadu had maintained. The Muslim orthodox reaction gathered around Baqi Billah, Shaikh Ahmad Sirhindi and the Naqshbandi movement. It rejected the *wajudi* concept, emphasized the study of *shara* and reaffirmed the supremacy of Islam and the theologians. According to them, the Hindus were to be treated nor as equal partners, but as *zimmis* i.e. protected people, who were separate and subordinate. The Mughal ruling class at first tried to brush aside the orthodox opposition rather than countering it. Unable or unwilling to move forward from a limited concept of secularism based on equality, toleration and upholding of imperial interests to a more dynamic view of the world-based on science and rationalism, the Mughal ruling class carne under increasing pressure to compromise with the theologians.

The 17th century in India was a period of many divergent trends. The territorial unity of the country reached its climax under Aurangzeb towards the end of the century. Simultaneously, assertion of the principle of regional independence was raised or revived directly or indirectly, by a number of groups and sections (Marathas, Afghans, Sikhs, Jats etc.), coupled with re-assertion of religious particularism. At the cultural level, the Mughal court and ruling class espoused, by far and large, secular values, drawing freely upon the cultural traditions of Central Asia and Iran, as also the rich cultural traditions of India. The new Mughal ruling class which was drawn from peoples belonging to various ethnic and religious groups, tried to forge a new cultural ethos which is reflected in the buildings, music and painting, manners and customs and literature of the period. If culture is to be treated as a matter of communications, all these forms were important. The two most important literary medium of communication were Persian and Hindi. It is regrettable that the two are generally studied in isolation, although it is clear that during the 17th century, both increasingly catered to, and were patronised and supported by the same social set, viz. the Mughal nobility, including the service classes, including junior administrators (kayasth, khatris etc.), and traders who had gathered around it, as well as some of the autonomous rajas and their courtiers. That familiarity with Hindi bhakti poetry was widespread is testified to by *Fuad-ul-Fuad,* Abdul Wahid Bilgrami's *Haqaiq-i-Hindi,* and by Badayuni himself. Thus, much before the rise of Abdur Rahim Khan-Khanan, personages such as Shaikh Gadai who rose to the position of *sadr* wrote verses both in Persian and Hindi.[40] All these writings were obviously for the benefit of the new composite ruling class which was developing in the country. Akbar's massive translation programme followed in the 17th century by the efforts of Dara, led to the translation not only of religious works, but popular works such as the *Singhasana Battisi* the *Tota Maina* and *Panchatantra* which had been translated earlier. The *Mahabharata* and *Ramayana* also catered to this new class. It is, therefore, not surprising that in addition to Persian, the Mughals provided official patronage to Hindi.

The intellectual and cultural ethos of the Mughal ruling classes have yet to be fully studied, as distinct from the outlook of individual rulers. While the Hindu and the Muslim nobles apparently continued to draw their moral sustenance from their own religious beliefs and practices, common administrative experiences led to an area of shared praxis. It is significant that the ultra orthodox ideas of Shaikh Ahmad Sirhindi did not find many takers in the Mughal ruling class. Similarly, Aurangzeb's orthodox views and his pandering to the ulamas was not to be liking of many nobles.[41] It is, therefore, not surprising that his efforts to woo the clergy was not to the liking of many of his nobles, or to

[40]S.A.A. Rizvi, *Alakhbani.* Aligarh, 1971.

[41]Athar Ali, *The Mughal Nobility under Aurangzeb,* Asia, 1966, p. 200; S. Chandra 'Religious Policy of Aurangzeb during the Later Part of his Reign; *I.H.R.* XIII Nos. 1-2, 1986-87; also in *Mughal Religious Policies, the Rajputs and the Deccan,* Vikas, New Delhi, 1995 pp. 194-215.

some of his orthodox measures such as reimposition of *jizyah* and his attempt to curb the Rajput rajas. Significantly, these policies were reversed after his death by his favourites, Asad Khan and his son Zulfiqar Khan.[42]

Thus, while the secularist type of state, based on equal respect to all religions, did not find acceptance during the 17th century, Aurangzeb's efforts to revive a more orthodox (though still a moderate) type of Islamic state, proclaiming the supremacy of *shara* and of Islam, but not rejecting a composite ruling class, met with greater opposition than he had anticipated, and was finally rejected. What emerged and was maintained during the 18th century was a state based on the compromise evolved by Shah Jahan i.e. one in which the supremacy of Islam was affirmed, but no discriminatory cesses, such as the *jizyah,* levied on the non-Muslims, and a composite ruling class and a composite culture actively promoted. This, in affect may be considered the real legacy of the Mughals as far as the ideological aspect of the state was concerned.

Regarding the developmental problematic during the 17th century, a number of questions have been raised by scholars, both within and outside the country. It has been argued that the Mughal state as constituted could neither ensure continued economic development, nor social justice, and that the Mughal ruling class had neither any interest or incentive for economic development, nor even possessed an ideology of economic development, its outlook being shaped and nurtured by a religious ethos in which such considerations were, at best, superficial or irrelevant.

The philosophy that traditional religions in Asia or similar regions were allergic or inimical to economic development does not have many takers to-day, and need not detain us. Regarding a developmental ideology, an ideology oriented towards the development of agriculture, can be

[42]Satish Chandra, *Parties and Politics as the Mughal Court, 1707-40,* P.P.H, 2nd ed., pp. 74-75.

found as early as the *Arthasastra.* Formation of villages on new sites or old ruins by inducing immigration from neighbouring areas or from surplus population from within, granting remission of taxes for new settlements, advancing grains, cattle and money to farmers for cultivation, and maximising cultivation by confiscating land from those who did not cultivate, and give them to those who could do so on a basis of sharing were parts of this ideology.[43] As a feudal polity developed from the 7th century onwards, and the strength and resources of the state weakened, the implementation of such a developmental strategy devolved increasingly on the local rulers and feudal elements.

As we have seen, with the establishment of the Delhi sultanat, a strong centralised state gradually developed, and was prepared to playa larger role in agricultural expansion and improvement. Muhammed Tughlaq's policy of the state giving loans *(taqavi),* for resuming agricultural production interrupted bynatural or human agencies, introducing superior crops (sugarcane, oil seeds, cotton, indigo, etc.) in place of inferior crops, and of improving irrigation (bunds, *taqavi* for wells, introduction of a new *rehat* etc.) was carried forward by the Surs and the Mughals.

According to a *Jarman* issued by Akbar to the Governors, they were asked "to promote agriculture, and conciliate the *raiyat* (peasants) and take measures to distribute *taqavi,* so that the number of hamlets, villages, towns and cities should increase from year to year." That a certain concept of regional specialisation had developed is obvious from the instructions to the *amal-guzar* that he should be acquainted with the soil of his charge since the agricultural value of land varied in different districts and "certain soils are adapted to certain crops."[44]

This advice was repeated by successive Mughal rulers, and is found in Aurangzeb's instructions to Rasikdas Karori,

[43]Kautilya's *Arthasastra* tr. R. Shamasastry, 8th ed. 1967, 131, 161-63.
[44]*Ain*-Jarrett ii, p. 46.

but meant for all higher revenue officials. They are asked to "bring about an enlargement in the area cultivated and, while shifting from the inferior crops *(jins-i-adna)* to high grade crops *(jins-i-ala)*, not leave waste any cultivable land, so far as they can."[45]

It has been argued that this strategy largely failed, or did not yield adequate returns because of structural defects. According to Bernier, the jagirdars had no long term interest in the development of their jagirs since they were transferable.[46] Supporting Bernier, Irfan Habib argues that the heavy land tax, and the mode of its assessment, did not leave sufficient resources at the local level for investment in agriculture. He therefore postulates an agrarian crisis which was reflected in peasant uprisings, and was an important factor in the downfall of the empire.[47]

While attractive, such a paradigm does not explain adequately the complex reality. While the gross exploitation of the bulk of the cultivators, and of their living on the level of subsistence can hardly be denied, recent research shows the existence of a small section among the peasantry which had the means and physical resources to invest in the expansion and improvement of cultivation. These were the *khud-kashi* which were often based on agrarian caste groups, such as the Jats. The *khud-kasht* formed a privileged group which dominated the village community. They invested in, and were the biggest beneficiaries of the policy of promoting the production of superior *(jins-i-ala)* or cash crops. They perhaps, were responsible in the cultivation and rapid expansion of new crops, such as maize, potato, red chillis, tobacco etc. Evidence from eastern Rajasthan relating to the

[45]*Farman* to Rasikh Das Karori, Eng. tr. Shircen Moosvi, 'Aurangzeb' s *Farman* to Rasikdas on Problems of Revenue Administration', 1665, in *Medieval India I, Researches in the History of india,* cd. I Habib O.U.P. 1992, pp. 197, 206.

[46]F. Bernier, *Travels in Mughal India*, p. 227.

[47]I. Habib, *Te Agrarian System of Mughal India* (1556-1707), Asia, 1963, pp. 317-351.

last decades of the 17th and the early part of the 18th century shows that the richer sections in the villages were the main force behind this process, even when the Mughal empire had passed its peak.[48]

Thus, it would be wrong to consider the jagirdars as the agents primarily responsible for the implementation of the policy of agricultural expansion and improvement. Although the state did try to give them a direct stake in agricultural development by stipulating that the full *jama* of the jagir allotted to them was calculated on the basis of their bringing all cultivable land under the plough and improving cultivation, the bigger nobles, whose holding constituted a high proportion of the total jagir lands, were too busy in court politics, conducting military campaigns, and leading an urban life style of affluence to pay much attention to rural affairs. This, we are told, was compounded by an increasing tendency of rapid transfer of jagirs, a practice which was accentuated during the second half of the 17th century, and especially in some areas, such as the Deccan. While rapid transfers was certainly administratively harmful, two factors have to be taken into account. First, since the cultivators generally paid land-revenue through zamindars who were hereditary, they were not as much affected by the frequent transfer of jagirdars as would appear at first sight. Also, the notion of frequent transfers depends on the statements of Bernier and Bhimsen. Bernier was neither familiar with Mughal administrative practices, nor known to have spent any amount of time in the country side. As far as Bhimsen is concerned[49] his remarks can, at best, be applied to the Deccan where he served, and applicable more to the smaller mansabdars with whose conditions he was more familiar. Experience shows that any weakness in the working of

[48]S.N. Hasan, K.N. Hasan, & S.P. Gupta, 'The Pattern of Agriculture Production in the. Territories of Amber, c. 1650-1750' *Procs. I.H.C.* 1966, pp. 249-63.

[49]Bhimsen, *Nuskha-i-Dilkasha* ff. 139a-140b; Khafi Khan *Muntakub-ul-Lubab*, ii 396-97, 411-12.

the central government under the Mughals resulted in a tendency to resist transfers, not the other way round. We have many cases in the Deccan itself where important nobles held their jagirs for long periods.[50] However, at root of the malfunctioning of the jagir system in the Deccan was not frequency of transfer of jagirs, or of corruption, or even lack of jagirs *(be-jagiri)* of which Bhimsen and Khafi Khan complain. All these were real enough, but they compounded rather than create the factors responsible for the crisis. Aurangzeb's effort to establish in the Deccan a more intensive administration, based on the Mughal revenue system of the north, i.e. regular assessment (in place of auction or *ijara)*, separation of revenue collection from administrative and police duties i.e. the establishment of the faujdari system, regular inspection of the number of mounts and soldiers *(tabinan)* to be maintained by a jagirdar would have had long term developmental benefits. However, it required a long period of peace and stability which implied a political settlement with the Marathas, (to which Aurangzeb was allergic) which, in turn, would have helped to overcome the resistance by local zamindars and others.[50a] We may conclude that here in many other spheres, the basic problem facing the Mughals was their inability or refusal to see the new socio-political reality represented by sections such as the Marathas which we have argued, was based on growth. rather than on stagnation and decline.

In our present state of knowledge, frequent transfers of jagirdars can hardly be postulated as a prime factor in agricultural stagnation or decline. Bernier's objection is not so much to the frequency of transfer, as the practice of transfer. He argues that only a hereditary nobility could have a

[50]Thus, Jan Sipar Khan, and his son Rustam Dil Khan had jagiris in Hyderabad subah for long. (J.F. Richards, *Mughal Administration in Golconda*, Oxford, 1975, pp. 80-81).

[50a]*Ibid.* pp. 191-204. These are based largely on papers from the Inayat Jung Collection.

stake in agricultural development, and in curbing royal despotism. It may be doubted to what extent a hereditary nobility carried out the expansion and improvement of agriculture in Europe (with the exception of the English and the Dutch). Also, experience with the Rajput thakurs does not suggest that they were ever active agents of such a process in their territories.

Thus, we come back to our argument that the most important element in the expansion and improvement of cultivation during the 17th century were the peasant proprietors, or *khud-kashi.* In some areas, they were apparently aided by the intermediary zamindars.[51] Although in Mughal revenue parlance, the zamindars continued to be presented as enemies who were untrustworthy, and always needed to be watched or punished,[52] these remarks applied more to the bigger, autonomous or *peshkashi* zamindars. The intermediary zamindars whose territories were regularly assessed, became an integral part of the Mughal administrative system. At the time of the assessment, the rights and perquisites of the intermediary zamindars were also fixed, and became a part of the *jama.* This recognition of the role and perquistes of the zamindars, gave them a measure of legitimacy to demand and collect from the cultivators other cesses and perquisites *(jaruhat).*[53] Though officially banned, these continued to be collected often with the connivance or even support of the local officials. We still do not know what role in the agricultural development process the local officials, such as the *amal-guazars,* played. Anyway, it would

[51]S. Chandra, Role of the Local Community, the Zamindars and the State in providing inputs for the Growth and Exansion of Cultivation, *I.H.R.* III No.1, 1976 (reprinted in *Medieval India; Society, the Jagirdari Crisis and the Village,* Macmillan, New Delhi, 1982, pp. 166-183).

[52]Irfan Habib, *Agrarian System,* pp. 334-35.

[53]I. Habib, *Agrarian System,* pp. 144-46. For the rights and perequisities of zamindars (deshmukhs and patels) in Mahrashtra see V.T. Gune, *Judicial System of the Marathas;* A.R. Kulkarni, *Mahrashtra in the Age of Shivaji,* 1969, pp. 31-43.

appear that under conditions of political stability, the attention of the intermediary zamindars was turned more to agricultural development than to mutual feuding, though the latter aspect was a persistent element.[54]

The improvement and strengthening of. the position of the *khud-kashi* and the intermediary zamindars, and the reiteration of a more traditional view of religion as propounded by the saguna bhakti saints such as Chaitanya, Sur and Tulsi in preference to the more egalitarian minded nirguna saints may perhaps be interconnected. However, it would not be possible to take a definite view in the matter without more research on the subject. The stregthening of the position of the intermediary zamindars and the *khud-kashi* was also not without social tensions and conflict. As noted above, in some areas, such as the Agra-Mathura-Bharatpur region, it led to conflict between the ascendant Jat peasants proprietors, and the Rajput zamindars. In the Punjab, the Jat Sikhs came in clash with Hindu rajas. In both cases, it led to a conflict with the Mughal government which was not prepared to concede the rising aspirations of the lower caste peasant proprietors, and sided with the upper caste chiefs and Rajas.

The process of expansion and intensification of cultivation led to pressure on the tribal elements which were still widespread, and occupied extensive forest lands in different regions of the country. The tribal people themselves were at different stages of development; some were still at a hunting-food gathering stage, and remained largely external to the system. There were, however, many tribes which were still pastoralists, though some of them had become semi-sedentary or practiced transhumance. Some of them had been able to develop a monarchical form, and even to dominate large tracts which included settled agricultural communities. Such was the case, for example, of the Gonds

[54]See Andre Wink, *Land and Sovereignty,* loc. cit.

of Gondwana. The interculturists and their contribution in the growing commercialization of agriculture during the 17th century have been explored by some modern writers in the context of the Punjab, and Sind.[55]

More such studies are needed for providing us a better understanding this aspect of rural society. Even Abul Fazl attempted to make "social diversities appear in conformity with the 'system' that had evolved ... Even territories which may have been only marginally agricultural were, therefore, represented as areas which were properly measured, regularly assessed and in no way different from those regions of the empire that were indeed agriculturally developed."[56]

This had serious consequences for the tribesmen. The pastoral-nomadic tribal communities were rarely able to generate the regular agricultural surplus they were assessed for. This sometimes led to conflicts, and whole-sale massacre of the tribals. Thus, in Sind, we were told that between 1620 and 1622, a series of campaigns were carried out against the Samyas who were dispersed over a large tract of Sind around the river Indus, with large numbers killed or sold into slavery. The Bichotia Rajputs of Awadh with whom there was frequent conflict also had a tribal background, as also the Ujjainiyas of Bihar.

The Mughal pressure to sedenterise the pastoralist tribals has a long history. As has been shown elsewhere, the [at who were pastoralists, became settled agriculturists between the 11th and 16th centuries, retaining many of the social characterists of the tribals. The Ahirs and Gujars became partly agriculturists, retaining many of their pastoral characteristics.

It has been pointed out that the semi-sedentary tribals,

[55]Chetan Singh, 'Conformity and Conflicts' Tributes and he Agrarian System of Mughal India, *'IESHR*, XXV (3) 1988, pp. 319, 340; Sunita Zaidi, 'The Mughal State and Tribes in seventeenth century Sind, *'IESHR* XXVI (3), 1989, pp. 343-62. See also A.R. Khan, *Chieftains in the Mughal Empire during the Reign of Akbar*, Simla, 1979.

[56]*Ibid.*

practising subsistence farming, were not able to produce all the goods needed by them. This resulted in trade, or plunder by the tribals. The Juds and Janjuhas of the Salt Range in the Punjab, the Bhatis of the Lakhi Jungle were cases of the latter, while the Lohani Afghans emerged as tribal traders.

The Mughal state had the primary responsibility of protecting the settled peasants from the marauding raids of some tribals. The Kolis of Gujarat had a bad reputation in this respect. Some tribals, such as the Meenas of Rajasthan, and the Badrias of subah Allahabad emerged as robbers, possibly on account of the loss of their lands to the more aggressive Rajputs. In some cases, as in the case of the Afghans and the Khokhars, the Mughals gave small mansabs to the tribal chiefs in order to use tribal manpower for policing purposes.

In some cases, conflict with settled agricultural communities forced the tribals to develop their own state forms, generally after they had reached a certain stage of pastoral nomadism. Examples of this have been provided by the case of Ujjainiyas of Bihar and the Dimanas of Assam.[57]

The process had both social and cultural dimensions. According to Bhattacharjee, in Assam "... the Dimasa state formation process entered into a crucial phase under Brahmanical influence. The Brahman priests occupied important position in the court. Myths were created to establish divine origin of the ruler..." "The traditional Dimasa deity *Kachai Kati* was transformed into *Rana-chandi,* and the ruling clan and the aristocracy got *kshatriya* status in Hindu society... The dimanas took to plough cultivation in flat or valley lands, although in the hills they continued the primitive jhumming ..."[58]

[57]K.S. Singh "A Study in State Fromation among Tribal Communities" in R.S. Sharma and V. Jha (eds.), *Indian Society. Historical Probings,* Delhi, 1974.

[58]J.B. Bhattacharya, 'The Economic Content of the Medieval State Formation Process among the masses of North East India, '*Procs. I.H.C.* ii L (1987), pp. 222-23.

In some cases, where commercialization of agriculture meant greater intensification, and needed greater labour, the neighbouring tribals were drawn upon for surplus labour. The greatest local beneficiaries of this were, however, the local zamindars, and the richer section among the tribalsl cultivators.

Thus, continued agricultural expansion under Mughal administrative-political institutions, prepared the ground for the growth of trade and manufacture in the country. The growth of agricultural production was sufficient to cope with the needs of growing trade and manufacture in the country during the 17th century. The arrival of new foreign traders, especially the Dutch and the English, and the entry of larger quantities of bullion into the country was only one aspect of this growth. The large production of cash crops—cotton, indigo, tobacco, etc. also opened the rural economy more widely for the development of a market oriented money economy. Possibly: the growth of the power and influence of the *khud-kasht* and the intermediary zamindars was a factory in the increased exploitation of the *muzarian* (cultivators), and the landless. As was so often the case, economic development and the growing exploitation of the working sections, and what French historians called the "marginaux" ("marginals"), went hand in hand.

While examining the potential of capitalist growth in India, Irfan habib[59] noted that there had been a marked growth of the money economy, development and expansion of agriculture and of handicrafts, and growth of domestic and foreign trade, leading to a considerable growth of merchant capital. Disagreeing with Moreland about the backwardness of financial institutions in the country, Irfan Habib argues that "seventeenth century European merchants and factors make no serious criticism of the Indian credit system, and there

[59]Irfan Habib, 'Potentialities of Capitalist Development in the Economy of the Mughal India', *Enquiry* III No. 35 reprinted in *Essays in Indian History*, Tulika, New Delhi, 1995, pp. 180-232.

is little inclination to compare it unfavourably with the European, though most of its peculiarities or differences are noted."[60] However, he considers that India was a not in a position to develop capitalism which he identifies with industrial capitalism In which the owners of the means of production (handicrafts, land) are progressively reduced to the position of wage earners.

One may disagree with the manner of posing this question. It may be argued that the development of industrial capitalism in South England was a unique phenomenon which could hardly have been replicated anywhere else in the world at the time, just as the urban revolution of antiquity was a phenomenon unique to West Asia. But once such a development has taken place, the question of its replication elsewhere arises, again depending upon specific historical conditions. The question, therefore, is: could an industrial capitalist system have developed in India during the 18th-19th centuries, *once such a development had taken place in England and Holland?* In other words, had social conditions, including monetization of the economy, growth of financial institutions, growth of merchant capital and its growing control over artisans through the *dadni* system, advanced sufficiently in India during the 17th century to make such a *subsequent* development at all possible? It is not our purpose here to embark upon this contentious issue. Our main purpose has been to show that medieval Indian social, and Mughal politico-administrative institutions and state forms did not inhibit the growth of a market oriented money economy, and that, in fact, despite limitations, there was a fairly rapid process of the growth of merchant capital in India so that it even financed the trading operations of some of the foreign companies active in the Asia-Pacific trade of the times. In consequence, merchant capital in India though spread out over a much longer period as compared to the west, had by the end of the 17th

[60] *Ibid* p. 227.

century, reached a state of development not inferior to the west. In many ways as recent research shows, like their western counterparts, the Indian traders operated basically on a family net-work, that they were not peddlers, the leading merchants operating both as wholesale merchants, financiers, middle-men etc., leaving detailed operations, including transportation, to a different set of junior operatives. It was on this basis that the Indian merchants had not only extended their operations to South-East Asia, China, West Asia and to the East Coast of Africa, but from Iran and Turan in Central Asia upto. Moscow, and were poised during the 17th century, to enter Europe.[61] Noting the initiative and success, and the entrepreneurial skill of Indian traders, a modem economic historian remarks: "Analyses of world economic relations in the early modem era ought to study on the commonalities in the Eurasian firm rather than perpetuating outdated oriental and occidental stereotypes."[62]

Internally, while the ruling class was not prepared to intervene actively to promote trade and commerce abroad, unlike many of the West European states, it was solicitious of protecting trade and commerce within its areas of control, and actively participated in it. As we have noted elsewhere, a notable feature of the seventeenth century was "the growing commercial mindedness of the Mughal nobility." Members of the ruling family, including rulers, princes and queen-mothers, important nobles and officials, and even qazis participated in trade through the Indian traders or the foreign trading companies, or lent money to them.[63] Despite the remark of the English factor at Surat in 1614

[61]S. Gopal, "Indian Merchants in Central Asia, 16th and 17th Centuries" Presidential Address, See. II *Procs I.H.C,* 1992 pp. 1-21; Stephen F. Dale, *Indian Merchants, and Eurasian Trade 1600-1750,* O.U.P. 1994.

[62]Stephen Dale, *ibid,* p. 134.

[63]Satish Chandra, 'Some Aspects of the growth of a Money Economy in India, during the Seventeenth Century', *IESHR* Vol. III, No.4, 1966, pp. 321-31.

that "great and small are merchants"[64] the number of such nobles may be small, as Irfan Habib notes.[65] However, that does not give us an index of the actual amounts of money invested by the great and powerful in commercial activities or giving money on interest to the traders. That it was not insubstantial is evident from the 18th century when its drying up had an impact on the trade of the Coromondal.[66] The nobility in general was spendthrift and led a life of ostentation in preference to saving was not peculiar to India. Nevertheless, some nobles did accumulate large sums of money.[67] On the same account, the fact that apart from members of the royal family, important nobles, such as, Asaf Khan, Safi Khan, Mir Jumla, Shaista Khan, Wazir Khan Governor of Lahore, etc. were actively involved in trade was an index of an attitudinal change. It is significant that unlike the earlier period, there is no condemnation on the part of contemporary historians of the participation of the nobles in trade or giving out money on interest. An index of this new attitude is provided by Abul Fazl who had advised the nobles "to indulge a little in commercial speculation and engage in remunerative undertakings, reserving a portion in goods and wares, and somewhat invested in the speculation of others."[68]

That a capitalist ethic was slowly developing in the country is borne out by the writings of the nirguna saint, Rajjab, from Rajasthan, who considers laziness a sin, and ascribes

[64] *Letters Received*, ed., W. Foster, Vol. II, 1613-15, p. 246. Tavernier says (at Surat) "... it is the principal trade of the nobles of India to place their money on the vessels on speculation for Harmuz, Bassova, and Mucha, and even for Bantaw, Achin and Philippines." (Tavernier i p. 31)

[65] I. Habib, Potentialities of Capatilist Development *loc. cit.* p. 226.

[66] S. Arasaratnarn, *Maritime India in the Seventeenth Century*, O.U.P., 1994.

[67] To quote only two examples, Ali Mardan Khan (1645) left one crore in cash and goods *(Aine-i-Salik,* iii 246-8) and Hafiz M Amin R. of Ahmadabad (1683), 70 lacs rupees and 1,35,000 ashrafis *(Maasir-i-Alamgiri,* 226).

[68] *Ani*, Bib Ind. i 291 (Jarrette, ii 57-58).

poverty not to misdeeds of a previous life but to laziness. Laziness, he says, was more powerful than sex, and the biggest enemy, for it prevented a man from earning wealth which was important for both his body and mind. Poverty begotten by laziness led not only to loss of wealth, but of godliness, and such a man, who allowed his family to suffer from poverty, was not only shameless, but had no right even to repeat the name of Rama. Interestingly, a miser *(kripan, mahajan)* who is condemned for not sharing his wealth with others, has some redeeming features-he lived in great frugality, bore hardships, and resisted all temptations in order to earn wealth![69]

It would be interesting to study wether similar sentiments can be found in the literature of other commercially active states. However, this does not, mean that an industrial capitalist system was round the comer. Possibly, the very disintegration of the Mughal empire, signifying the breakdown of the rigid, bureaucratized Mughal state system in which power was wielded by a tightly controlled, feudal bureaucratic elite, might have served to clear the way for the emergence of more open-ended regional regimes during the 18th century in which local elites, rural and urban, and traders would have a larger say.[70]

Thus, despite a number of negative features, during the

[69]*Rajiabanani (Karipan ka Anga),* quoted by Mrs. Savitri Chandra, The Nirguna Bhakti Tradition in Rajasthan and Rajjab' (paper to the Second International Conference on Rajasthan Studies, Udaipur, 1991, *memeo.),* printed in *Medieval India and Hindu Bhakti Policy, A Socio Culture study,* New Delhi, 1996, p. 150.

[70]V. Pavolv in his *Historical Premises for Indian Transition to Capitalism* (Eng. tr. Moscow, 1979) considerably underestimates the level of commodity production and scale of merchant-capital in pre-colonial India, dubbing it as one of the "stagnant (rather, slowly evolving) societies", a "patriarchal subsistence economy" with "pockets of capitalism". For recent discussion, see Satish Chandra, *The 18th Century* in *India: Its Economy and the Role of the Marathas, the Jats, the Sikhs and the Afghans,* and *Supplement,* K.P. Bagchi, Calcutta, rev. ed. 1991; Barun De, Pro Address, *Procs. I.H.C* Darwar, 1989; idem Problems of the Study of

medieval period, the state formation showed considerable developments. Directly or indirectly it aided and promoted economic growth, social change and cultural integration. In the field of ideology a moderate Islamic state, which, according to Barani, was based on *jahandari* was sought to be developed into a de facto's secularist state under Akbar. In course of time, it settled down as a liberal Islamic state. We have called it the Mughal model, despite some unsuccessful attempts to revert to the earlier model of a moderate Islamic state based on regulated religious toleration. In the political sphere, the security of the country from foreign invasions was based on a flexible foreign policy to prevent the formation of a large bloc of countries inimical to India, and the adoption of a defence line based on the natural geographical features around the Kabul-Qandhar line, and the Hindukush. In the social sphere, the rise of the *kharaji* zamindars and the *khud-kasht* in the rural areas, and in the cities of merchants, and the class of junior administrators (kayasthas, khatris, Hindustanis) were significant developments. The role of these sections needs to be assessed in greater depth. In the economic sphere, the 17th century saw India advance towards completing the first stage of a market oriented capitalist economy. However, any possibilities of further development disappeared with the colonial take over and India's integration into the capitalist world economy as an under-developed adjunct.

Indian History: With special reference to Interpretation of the 18th Century, Centre for Socialist Studies, Calcutta, No. 116 *(mimeo);* CA. Bayley, *Indian Society and the Making of the British Empire,* Orient Longman; I. Wallerstein, *The Modern World System. I,* Academic Press, 1974; Burton Stein, Eighteenth Century in India: Another View, *Studies in History,* No.1, New Delhi, 1989.

INDEX